THE STANLEY MATTHEWS STORY

Stanley Matthews in action against Arsenal at Highbury.

The
Stanley Matthews
Story

STANLEY MATTHEWS

OLDBOURNE
LONDON

OLDBOURNE BOOK CO. LTD.,
121 Fleet Street, London E.C.4.

© *Oldbourne Book Co. Ltd.,* 1960

*Set in 12 on 13 pt. Bembo and printed in Great Britain by
Purnell and Sons, Ltd., Paulton (Somerset) and London*

CONTENTS

LIST OF ILLUSTRATIONS

CHAPTER I

LAST YEAR AT SCHOOL

I HAD just had my thirteenth birthday. I had just one more year to go to Wellington Road School before I entered the world to earn my living. What was I going to do? I knew what I wanted. I wanted to earn my living as a footballer and had never wanted to do anything else. But would my father agree? I knew he would want me to help him in his shop, or, if I didn't do that, he might let me go in the building trade. I'd rather be in the building trade than become a barber; at least it would keep me outside in the fresh air. When I got older, I thought, when I was eighteen, I might be able to get away from home and join some first-class football club. After all, my father had taken up boxing when he was young.

My thoughts always seemed to come back to football, football, football. I was, of course, frustrated; I felt frustrated, and I acted frustrated. When a boy in his 'teens is not at peace with his father, when he can see his mother trying to keep things on an even keel, because she loves both of them, the boy, because of his lack of years and experience, will always come out the loser in the end. And at the age of thirteen I broke down. After leaving my father one morning after an early-morning work-out, I entered my home, sat down at the table, took one look at the breakfast my mother put before me, got up from my chair, and ran into the kitchen. I had never been so sick in all my life; I felt as if my inside was falling out and great beads of sweat formed on my brow. I collapsed on the kitchen floor. My mother, who had followed me into the kitchen, helped me to my feet, and then upstairs to bed. Then she went downstairs and returned with a powder which I took with some water, then nature took over and I fell into a troubled sleep. It wasn't until I was better again

9

that I remembered that my mother hadn't spoken a word to me from start to finish. Meanwhile, just as I was dropping off to sleep, my mother had returned to the living-room and was taking my uneaten breakfast off the table, when the front door opened and my father walked in.

"Hello," he said. "Where's Stanley?" My mother put the plate back on the table; she said, "Stanley's sick and I have just put him to bed. Now sit down, Jack Matthews, and listen to me; there's something I want to tell you, and if I hadn't been soft I'd have told you a long time ago. I've had enough of this nonsense between you and Stanley, and it's got to stop, right away." My father sat down; this was a side to my mother he had never seen before. But mothers, of all creeds and colour, are the same the world over; once they are roused, and they see their children troubled about something they can't fight against, they become the toughest of the tough to deal with. My father was on the brink of finding that out. My mother sat down at the table and looked into the troubled face of my father. She said, "Ever since Stanley told you that he wasn't going to be a boxer there's been an undercurrent of trouble between you two, but now it's gone too far and it's got to stop, and I'm going to stop it." She paused, but my father said nothing.

"Haven't you got the sense to see that he wants to do one thing and you want him to do another?" she continued. "When he grows up he wants to earn his living as a footballer, and you can take it from me that from now on he's getting my support and encouragement. I want you to stop all this silly nonsense about boxing, and go upstairs when he wakes up and tell him you have changed your mind and are going to help him." My father still said nothing—he was speechless! "If you do that, Jack, you'll make him the happiest lad in Hanley, and all this worry that is making him ill will disappear." My father got up from his chair, took the teapot off the hob, walked back to the table, and poured himself a cup of tea. He lifted the cup and was just about to take a drink, but instead he put the cup back on the table. He said to my mother, "I can't do it. What if he does become a foot-baller? He'll be finished when he's thirty years old, and what's he going to do then for the rest of his life? Answer that one!

What's he going to do then, without a trade at his fingers?" My mother got up from her chair, crossed over to my father, put her arm around his shoulders and said, "Listen, Jack. Nobody ever tried to stop you from becoming a boxer, did they? Knowing you as I do, if they *had* tried you would have fought just like our Stanley. Now what would have happened if your father had wanted you to be a footballer instead of a boxer?" My father said, "I wouldn't have let them, not for all the tea in China." My mother smiled. "I know you wouldn't. You always have had a mind of your own, and you were always crazy about boxing. Well, your son is just like you, but it's football with him. Now can you see you are wrong?" My father walked round the room for a minute or so, then turned to my mother. "Forgive me," he said. "I've been wrong, you are right. I'll do as you say; but I shan't give him my full blessing unless he plays as an international before it's time to leave school on his fourteenth birthday." "That's fair enough," Mother said. "Now go upstairs and tell him when he wakes up. Then you'll find he will be fit and well again for tomorrow, after you have removed all the doubts and fears from his mind."

A few hours later I woke from a troubled sleep, to find my father sitting on the bed staring in my face. I turned my back on him. He very gently turned me round and said, "Listen, son. I've been giving this football idea of yours some thought, and I am now prepared to let you have a go . . . if you can make yourself good enough to become a schoolboy international before you leave school. Are you on?" I sat up in bed and looked at him: I couldn't believe it. "It's a bet," I said, because I couldn't think of anything else to say.

I was back in training next morning.

.   .   ..   .   .

If you have ever been packed in the middle of a crowd of people in an underground train at the peak hour when everybody is rushing to get home after a hard day's work; if you have ever felt the blood rush to your head as you fought your way out of the middle of the mass of people and experienced the sweetness of the moment when you draw the first breath of cool fresh air into your lungs, and the pleasant sensation of a load being lifted off your body, and the panic vanishing from your brain, at being free again—if you have experienced these things, you will have some idea how I felt when my father made his peace with me. I felt a new person. I felt as if I had just been reborn, and that I had never experienced any of those dreadful fears and oppressions that so got me down. I felt at peace with the world, and now that I had the blessing of my parents I felt that nothing could stop me from achieving my ambition to be a footballer, providing I worked hard enough and took the rough with the smooth.

Up to this moment I had never given a thought to ever being a schoolboy international. I had been absorbed in the task of making my feet the master of the football, making it obey every whim; and if it would not, then I would take the ball out in some open space and practise and practise until it did. Then I would work out something a little harder and master that. Apart from this I was content to play in the school team. I remember thinking that I must go all out to be picked for the international team, but what I didn't know was that I had already been watched by the selectors and had impressed them. What I also didn't know was that not every boy was getting up as early as me, and under my father's rigid training I was exceptionally fit. Walking to and from school each day, the football I played at school, my private practice and early-morning training were paying off; but being picked for my country as a schoolboy international was not in my mind when I was told by my schoolmaster to report to the headmaster's study after afternoon classes. What had I done wrong? My mind flew over my recent escapades with the other boys; but, apart from the usual rough-and-tumble and innocent fun all boys get into, I couldn't think of a thing. However, it was a timid Stanley Matthews who knocked on the headmaster's door and waited for him to say "Enter". He called out, and I opened the door gently and looked across the room. He said, "Oh, it's you, Matthews. Come here and stand before the desk." I did as I was told. There was a short silence, during which the headmaster eyed me keenly. My stomach began to rumble. Then he spoke. "Well, Matthews, let me congratulate you. You have been picked to play against Wales, at Bournemouth, in three weeks' time. What do you think about that, eh?"

I couldn't believe my ears, and, what was worse, his news made me do all sorts of peculiar things. I could feel my face twitching, my mouth went dry, and my whole body started to tremble. I felt terrible. I think the headmaster could see that he had broken the news a bit too suddenly; he said, "I'm sorry to have given you such a shock, Matthews. I had no idea it would upset you like this. Now, come along—haven't you anything to say?" I managed to get my mouth open at last, and in a hoarse whisper said, "Yes, sir. May I have a drink of water?" He looked at me in amazement, then said, "Help yourself. There's a glass near the tap."

Whilst I was drinking the water the truth dawned on me; it was really true, I was to play as a schoolboy international, the headmaster wouldn't pull my leg. I returned to the front of the table and said, "I'm sorry, sir. Your news took me by surprise; I had no idea——" The headmaster broke in with, "It's all right, Matthews; I can imagine how you feel. You'd better not break the news to your mother and father as abruptly as I did to you. To get back to facts, and as I said before, you are in the English team playing against Wales, at Bournemouth." He paused and looked at me. "And this might be another shock to you—you have been chosen to play at outside-right." My face fell and I said, "Outside-right, sir? That's not my usual position. Do you think it will suit me?" The headmaster got up from his chair and walked over to the window. With his back to me he said, "I think it will suit you, because I know you will do your best in any position." He turned and walked over to me, patted me on the head. "Now run along and tell your parents the good news."

I made for the door. Just as I was opening it he called, "Matthews." I turned and faced him. "Don't forget this is your big chance; play a good clean game. And don't forget also that you have the school at the back of you, so don't let us down." I looked at him very earnestly and said, "I'll not forget, sir. Thank you, sir, and good afternoon, sir."

I left the room, flew down the corridor, and in a few minutes I was in the familiar streets of my home-town, running as fast as my feet would carry me home. I seemed to be running on air. I arrived in record time, opened the door, then stood looking at the table set for tea, with my mother and father just in the middle of having theirs. My mother took one look at me, jumped up and ran towards me; she said, "Whatever is the matter?" In a dream I walked past her and stopped before my father and blurted out, "I'm playing for England against Wales at Bournemouth in three weeks, Dad, and I'm playing at outside-right. I can be a professional footballer when I grow up now, Dad, can't I? You promised—you said——" I stopped and gazed at him.

He got up from the table and put his arm round my shoulders. "You hear that, Mother? Our Stanley's going to be an international—he's made it. Well, I'll be——" When I escaped from their embraces we sat down to tea and talked and talked and talked. I'll never forget that tea. I went to bed early that night, but never slept much; but I don't think anyone could blame me for that.

The next week was one of the happiest of my life. My father and I were now great pals, and all the spare time he got away from his shop we spent together, my father watching me practise, giving good advice, watching what I ate, and making sure that I got to bed early, and, by the same rule, up at the crack of dawn the following morning. I should put on record now that my father never once said that I had played a good game. His favourite remark was, "Not so bad. I've seen you play better and I've seen you play worse." I defy anybody to get a swollen head on those sparse remarks. In any case, my father always made short shift of anyone who blew his own trumpet, so I can understand that he had made up his mind that he wasn't going to stand any nonsense from me. I feel very grateful for the way he steered me through the awkward years.

When I got into bed at night I would count how many more nights I had to go to bed before the international match—seven, six, five, four, three, two . . . At long last came the final night. Soon after tea I watched my mother pack my few things, and at the same time she gave me some advice on all sorts of things I must do when I was away from home. This was understandable, as it was the first time I had been away from home on my own.

When 11 years old the author played centre half for Wellington Road School, Hanley.

A. Wilkes & Son

His career with Stoke City commenced at the age of 15, when he became their office boy. Very soon he played for their reserve team.

A portrait of Stanley Matthews taken in 1938—the year of
his first request for a transfer from Stoke City.

I kept nodding my head in agreement with Mother, then I noticed my father looking at his watch. He got up and said, "Come on, son, it's bedtime; you have a big day tomorrow." I got up from the chair, said good-night to them both, and went upstairs. The time was 7.15 p.m. Yes, it was a bit early, but I got into bed. I couldn't sleep, it was terrible. I got out of bed, had a drink of water, got back and tossed and turned again, got out of bed again and shook the pillows, then did a few deep-breathing exercises at the open bedroom window before getting into bed once more. Actually the next day was not the day the match was to be played. In the morning I was to travel to London to join the team, and the match was to be played the day after. But as far as I was concerned this was my last night at home, so my first international experience started the next morning. I remember tossing and turning to find a comfortable position in my bed, but it was no use. A shaft of light came slowly through the bedroom door, which was opening. I gazed towards it, and my mother came in. She was holding something in her hand, and tiptoed to the bedside and looked down at me.

In the darkness of the bedroom she said, "Are you awake, Stanley?" I sat up rather quickly and said, "Yes, I'm awake, Mother. I can't get to sleep." "It's all the excitement," she said, "that's what is doing it. But we mustn't have you tired in the morning. Here you are—drink this slowly; it will make you sleep." I took the glass from her and sipped the contents while my mother sat on the side of the bed and talked to me in a soft, soothing voice. I remember her taking the glass very gently out of my hand and then I woke like a giant refreshed. It was the next morning. My father had excused me from early-morning exercises for this day, so I bounded downstairs and into the kitchen. My father was out training, Mother was busy getting the breakfast ready. I said, "Hello, Mother. Give me a shout when breakfast is ready, I'll be in the back practising." I picked up a small ball, and was still kicking it against the wall when my father returned and called me in to breakfast. That was a jolly meal. I felt like a king, and the world seemed to be mine.

At last it was time for me to catch the train. I said goodbye to Mother, and Father took me to the station. Hardly a word passed between us until he had put me inside a compartment. I lowered the window, and as the train started to pull out of the station I leaned out and said, "Goodbye, Dad." He looked up at me and said, "You're on your own now, son—good luck to you!" As the distance between us widened I kept waving my hand, and when I was nearly out of sight my father gave me his one and only wave. The last view I had of him was standing with his head slightly bent, blowing his nose hard in his handkerchief. All the way to London his last words kept running through my mind—"You're on your own now, son." The more I repeated them, the more confidence I seemed to gain. Yes, I was on my own. I stared down at my feet, and thought, *You are the two that I depend on in my future life in more ways than one.*

I could write a whole book about my arrival for the first time in London, how I met the rest of the team, and how, after spending the night in London, we arrived at Bournemouth in plenty of time for the start of the match, but those details must be imagined, and I come now to the moment I ran down the tunnel onto the field at Bournemouth. The first sensation I felt as I ran on to the field was the noise and cheering from spectators in the packed ground. I had never seen so many people. I took a swift look round, and the sight of all those people made me catch my breath. It was thrilling to run over the playing pitch itself. This was a real ground, and at that moment, on that Bournemouth ground, as I felt my boots sink in the soft turf as I ran round to get warmed up, I realized there couldn't be anything else in this life for me. I could have shouted with joy. I felt rather nervous until the referee blew his whistle to start the match, but as soon as the ball came out of the centre circle I felt fine, and I settled down to enjoy the game. It was this game that made me decide that the outside-right position was going to be mine for the rest of my footballing life. I felt comfortable in it, as if I had been born for it, and as I ran down the wing with the ball before sending it over towards the centre of the field, or sending in a short pass to an inside forward, I remember thinking, *This is the life.* But I didn't score in that match, although we won 4-1, but by all accounts I had a good game. I had stressed the fact to my parents that I didn't want them to watch the game;

but whilst I was playing I was sorry for asking them not to be there. When I was back in the dressing-room after the match, an official came in and told me someone wanted to see me outside the ground. He told me to finish dressing and collect my things.

My father said, "Let's have some tea, son, and then we'll go home." We did just that.

. . . . .

Complacent means self-satisfied; serenity means contented tranquillity. To be a complacent person in the working-class idiom means "He's nothing to worry about, the lucky so-and-so." In my belief, there is no such person in this world.

Life is so full of ups and downs that anyone who gets that complacent feeling is in danger of getting a swift kick in the pants from Fate if he persists in trying to get through life in that state of mind. I have only ever felt complacent once in my life, and that was in my last term at school. My international début had been a success—so much so that Tom Mather, the manager of Stoke City Football Club, started to be a regular customer at my father's shop. Instead of coming at regular intervals like most of the customers, he started to pop in nearly every day, and he would always turn the conversation to me and my future prospects as a footballer. However, my father would not be drawn on this subject, and all Mr. Mather got was, "It's a bit early yet, don't you think?" But Father didn't know what Mr. Mather knew, which was that several clubs in the Midlands were talking about me. At the time I wasn't very interested. For the first and last time in my life I had that complacent feeling. I was more than satisfied with my present life, and in my young mind I could see nothing but success in front of me. It would be silly of me not to state that I knew that important clubs had me pencilled in their books for *future* reference (at that time they couldn't do much with a thirteen-year-old boy). I got most of this information from my school chums, who said their mothers had told their fathers they had heard in such-and-such a shop from such-and-such a person that such-and-such a club was watching me. Believe me, in small shops in the North of England you can keep a nearly accurate check on almost everything, and besides I had seen Mr. Mather in my father's shop. I had only a few more weeks to go to school, but before I finally left I wanted to achieve one ambition. I wanted to be in the schoolboys' international team to meet Scotland at Hampden Park. I had read all about Hampden Park, Scotland, and the thought of finishing my school-days playing on that ground gave me a wonderful feeling. I was sure to be picked, so I threw myself into hard, relentless training to make sure I wouldn't let anybody down.

The day before the team was selected I was out very early, training with my father. As he had now finished with his boxing, he was spending all his spare time training me. On this particular morning he had me sprinting over short distances, and was timing me over the sprints. Then I would repeat the run with the football at my feet (this kind of training was to prove invaluable to me later in life). I was taking a breather at the end of one of the sprints when I said to my father, "They are picking the team to play Scotland tomorrow, Dad. Will you be coming up to watch me play?" My father looked at his watch and then at me. He said, "I'll let you know when I read the afternoon paper tomorrow"; then he paused, scratched his nose with a finger, and said, "You know, son, you've still a lot to learn about everything that goes on in this life—never take anything for granted, then you won't get hurt too much!" I gave him a puzzled look and said, "What do you mean, Dad?" He smiled and said, "You'll find out if you live long enough. Now come on, let's get started again—you'll get stiff."

On the way home I got my father to stop at a sports shop window, and pointed out the pair of football boots I was saving hard to buy. I said, "In another eight weeks I shall have enough money to buy them." My father nodded his head. "Yes, and I bet you'll look after them when you do get them; it's a lot better than getting something for nothing." We reached home and breakfast in silence.

The following afternoon at school was one of the longest in my life. I kept watching the schoolteacher, waiting for him to tell me that the headmaster wanted to see me after classes. I began to think perhaps the headmaster only told people the first time they were picked. At last we were dismissed. I dashed out of the school yard and ran home as fast as I could. I burst into the house. My father sat at the table reading the paper; he looked up at me and put the paper aside. My mother said, "I'm just off to do some shopping. Your tea's on the table, Stanley." She left the room. I stammered, "Well, Dad, am I in the team?" My father looked me straight in the eyes and said, "I'm sorry, son; you have not been picked." The world slipped from under my feet. I just stared in front of me, feeling tears smarting in my eyes, and only when I felt the warmth of them running down my face did I realize I was still alive. My father had gone out. I was alone.

I sat at the table and picked up the paper, read the team out aloud, then let the paper fall out of my hands. I put my elbows on the table and buried my face in my hands.

The next few minutes were very important ones in my life. At first I felt very bitter, but my father's training and upbringing slowly but surely brought things back into a proper perspective, and I believe today that when I raised my head and looked round the room a new Stanley Matthews was born. I have never been a complacent person since. My father came back into the room and looked hard at me. I smiled, and I saw a look of relief sweep across his face. He walked forward, put his arm round my shoulders, and said, "You'll be all right now, son; you take my word for it, you'll always be all right," and he never spoke truer words.

CHAPTER II

BECOMING A MAN

As I trotted down the long street, each side bordered by terraced cottage houses, I sensed there was something wrong. Then the small ball I had been kicking ran in the roadway from the flagged pavement. My intention, of course, was to prevent it doing this, but I had lost concentration. My mind had wandered from the ball to the street itself. I picked up the ball and put it in my pocket, then gazed around me.

The street was deserted. It should have been full of boys shouting to each other and playing games. And then I realised that it was Saturday morning, and they would all be on the spare ground just round the bottom corner of the street playing their usual Saturday-morning game of football. I ran down the street as fast as I could and turned the corner. It was anything but quiet round there. I took in the familiar scene at a glance. In front of me on a piece of ground without a blade of grass on it were at least twenty boys, yelling and shouting. "Give it to Tommy"— "Shoot"—"Send it to Jimmy on the wing"—"Get shot of it". The boy with the ball ignored all the advice and tried to bustle his way towards goal. Just as he was going to shoot, the ball was whipped off his toe by another boy, and it landed at my feet. I kicked it back on the field. "You're just in time, Stan. Come on our side, we're a man short. Put your jacket on their goals."

It didn't take me a second to take off my jacket and join in. The goals were made up of two piles of jackets; no wooden uprights or crossbars, just the sky above. There were no markings on the ground, and nobody wore any shorts or jerseys. You had to guess which side another boy was on—anyhow, it didn't take you long to memorize the various faces. There was no referee (which made the game all the more enjoyable), and the ball was a standard football in a very sorry state of health, by no means as round as it should be. There was no half-time, we just played on and on until our mothers came out to say it was dinner-time. Then, and only then, did we stop. But this particular game finished in a different manner. I had been playing for a long time, and each side was trying to get a winning goal, but I am sure nobody knew the correct score, when the ball came over to me on the wing. Amidst all the usual advice from the other players, I made my way towards the goalmouth; but seeing it packed with boys waiting for me I cut out again to the wing and they were after me like a pack of wolves. I waited until they were nearly on me, then lifted the ball over their heads towards the goal. One of our boys ran to it, trapped it as it hit the ground, drew his foot back for his shot, kicked at the ball, hit it at the same time as one of the other side kicked it—and there was a loud bang! We all walked forward and stood round the deflated piece of leather. It was a sorry sight.

There's nothing more disappointing to young boys than an unfinished game of football. I stopped at the corner of the next street and looked at the spare ground on which I had spent so many happy hours; it was the place to put into practice all the theories I worked out when I was thinking about football. However, as I looked at that miserable ground I thought *There would be plenty more Saturdays to play on it*, and with that in my mind I turned the corner and made my way to my father's barber's shop, where I was due to lend a hand at lathering the chins of his customers on the busy Saturday afternoon.

I would be fifteen in a few weeks' time, and since leaving school I had passed my time by helping Father in his shop and practising the art of ball-control. I knew I couldn't sign as a professional footballer for any club until I was seventeen, and that seemed to be ages off to me. Anyway, I was happy enough with things as they were. I was getting stronger and stronger, and faster off the mark. So I hadn't much to grumble about. As I walked along I glanced down at my shoes and stopped dead. They were cut and marked and they were my best pair. I'd forgotten about everything that morning. I found a piece of newspaper in the street, picked it up and tried to rub a few of the marks off, but

it wasn't very successful. After a while I gave up the struggle
and decided to face the music. If Father didn't notice them,
Mother would, so I was in a real mess. Shoes cost money, and
even at my age I knew that I couldn't afford to waste my parents'
money playing football in good shoes. I entered the shop and
made for the nearest chair, and stood behind it to hide my feet.
The shop was half full. My father looked at me and said, "There's
no need for you to stand behind that chair trying to hide your
shoes. I know you've been playing football in them—one of my
customers saw you. I'll have a word with you when we get
home. Now come on, give me a lift; I'm getting busy." And
busy we were. It was tea-time before we saw the last customer
out of the shop. My father took off his overall and said, "Don't
bother to sweep up. There's someone waiting to see us at home."

We left the shop and walked home at a brisk pace. Not a
word was said about the shoes. When we arrived home my
mother went to the teapot on the hob and brought it to the table,
and we sat down to tea. A knock came on the door. My father
shouted "Come in", and in walked Mr. Mather, the manager of
Stoke City. Father looked up from his plate and said to Mr.
Mather, "Tell him." Mr. Mather looked at me and said, "Stanley,
I have some good news for you. Your father has agreed to let
you come on the Stoke City staff on your fifteenth birthday, as
office boy; then you'll get all the football you want. What do
you say?" What did I say? I was speechless. This was the greatest
thing in my life, and I told Mr. Mather so. I told Father so, too.
"That's settled, then," he said in the middle of my excited thanks.

* * * * *

My fifteenth birthday came on a very cold day. It was a timid
Stanley Matthews who stood all alone gazing up at the sign which
read—*Stoke City Football Club.* I was outside the ground, and the
sign and the size of the building behind it filled me with awe. I
clutched at the small parcel I held under my arm, then I moved
towards the door, over which was written *Staff Entrance.* I
stopped again and looked back at the sign. It really was true—
when I walked through that door I would become part of the
Stoke City Football Club.

I looked around, but there was not a soul in sight. Very gingerly, I walked slowly forward, and when I was about ten yards from the door it began to open. A girl appeared in the opening. She looked at me and smiled, and I smiled back. We were about the same age. She said, "Hello. Is your name Stanley Matthews?" I nodded but didn't speak. "My name's Betty Vallance," she said. "My father's the trainer here." I nodded again. She gave me a puzzled look, which cleared when I said, "I'm pleased to meet you, Betty." She said, "You look very nervous, but really there's no need to be. You'll like it here; everybody's nice." She paused, and looked me over again. I said, "I have to report to Mr. Vallance." She said, "Yes, that's why I have come to meet you. I'll take you to him. He's on the field, putting some of the players through their paces. Come on, follow me." We passed through the door, and I closed it behind me and followed Betty down the passage. A feeling I can't attempt to describe came over me: I felt at peace with the world. This was going to be my second home. I had made my entrance. Now I needed only a warm welcome to make me feel at ease. I didn't get it. There is little sentiment in business if it wants to survive, and as I reached the playing pitch with Betty I saw her father on the touchline giving advice in no uncertain manner to some of the Stoke City players on the pitch. They didn't seem to mind; but to me, it being the first time I had been amongst professional footballers, it all sounded a bit hard and rough. It didn't take me long to find out that a club could not remain a first-class club unless it had rigid discipline.

Mr. Vallance noticed Betty and I; he stopped talking and walked towards us. He looked me over, then said, in a surprisingly kind and gentle voice, "So you're young Matthews." I said, "Yes, Mr. Vallance." He said, "Well, if you work hard and do everything you're told, you'll be very happy here. If you try to be one of the clever ones, you'll find we have a cure for that. Now go and clean the dressing-rooms out, then come back here to me." He walked away and I was dismissed.

Betty touched my arm and said, "Come along, Stanley. I'll show you where the dressing-rooms are." We left the field in silence. What a start to a football career, I thought. Sweeping out dressing-rooms! I knew that I would be expected to put the stamps on letters, run errands, and do all kinds of odd-jobs—but sweeping rooms out! What had that got to do with football? I used to sweep out my father's shop, but that was different.

Betty left me and I was in a miserable frame of mind when I walked through the door of the first dressing-room and saw the state of it. I sat down on one of the benches and cupped my chin in the palms of my hands. Then I saw the funny side of it. After all, if you want to learn a job properly you should start at the bottom, and I was certainly at the very bottom of this one. I got the brush and started in grim earnest, making that dressing-room look like a new pin. When I had finished I went to the second one and got to work on that, and before long the job was finished. I gazed round at my work, and felt a glow of pride that I had made a good job of my first task. Just as I was putting the brush back in the corner I heard footsteps coming down the corridor. It was Mr. Vallance. He looked round the room, nodded his head and said, "It looks as if you enjoyed doing that job. Did you?" I said, "I shall always try and do whatever you tell me, as well as I can." He walked into the room and said, "I think you'll be all right, son." He moved towards the door, then he turned. "How would you like to get changed into some football clothes and come down on the field with the rest of the boys. I'd like to try you out, to see if you can take orders on the field." I gave him a huge grin. "I'll be down in a minute, Mr. Vallance." I was running on the field in under five minutes, for the first time under starter's orders, and I loved every minute of that first morning. As I walked home at the end of the day I was the happiest boy in Hanley.

When I arrived home and entered the house my mother and father were at the table having tea. My face told them all they wanted to know. My mother put my tea before me on the table, and whilst eating it I told them all about my first day at Stoke City Football Club. They listened in silence, and at the end of my recital I could see that they were both relieved to hear that my heart and soul was in the new job. From that day on I worked harder than ever, and no matter what job I was given at the football ground I went out of my way to make a good job of it.

One day, out of habit, I looked at the notice-board on which the first team and the reserve team to play the following Saturday had been pinned, glanced over the well-known names and—with something of a shock—read my name amongst the reserves to play Burnley reserves at Stoke on the coming Saturday. It really was a shock as I was only fifteen and never thought I had a chance of making the reserve team until I was much older. *This will please my father*, I thought, and at the end of the day I hurried along to his shop to tell him. As I rushed off to catch him before he closed I met Betty Vallance. I told her the good news. She was delighted and told me she would be there to cheer me on. I smiled at her and said, "Thanks, Betty. I'll need it." When I entered my father's shop he looked surprised and said, "What are you doing here?" I said, "I want to walk home with you for tea. There's something I must tell you." I helped him to close up and ten minutes later we were walking side by side towards home. I told him the news. I could tell he was pleased, but all he said was, "You're a bit young, son, to play for the reserves. I hope they know what they are doing." I agreed with him and we walked on in silence for some time, then he said, "I think you'd better get some practice in sprinting with the ball at your feet. Never forget that once you've beaten a man he is chasing after you with no ball at *his* feet." Very early next morning we practised those fast sprints with the ball. Saturday came, and as I ran on to the field for the first time in the Stoke City colours I was given a great reception by all my school friends, who had turned up in force. I had a good game, all told. I made a lot of mistakes; but as I was so young, this was the game that drew the attention of the national press, and the publicity I got from it was enormous. Boylike, I couldn't get home quick enough to hear what my father thought. He was reading a paper when I got in the house, and looked at me over the top of it. He said, "Son, you'll play a lot better, and you'll play a lot worse." He paused, then went on, "Forget about the good things you did; remember the mistakes you made, study them, and correct them, then forget them completely. You'll never keep repeating them if you do that. Remember, a man who never makes a mistake never gets anywhere. Have you got that, son?" I nodded and said, "Yes, Father." "Well, sit down and have your tea," he said, and together we discussed the rest of the game.

During the remainder of that season the management gave me another try-out with the reserves, and I did much better. My sixteenth birthday came just before the season ended. During the previous summer months I never relaxed, and except for seeing Betty now and again I led rather a lonely life, as I had no real friends. I couldn't expect anyone to be always playing football in their spare time. Somehow I never got tired of it, but my friends did. During the next season it was no surprise to anyone that I became a more or less regular member of the reserve team. Even then the management didn't overdo it; but I played in twenty-two matches, and, in the words of Mr. Vallance, the trainer, I came on "like a house on fire".

I was now playing against professional footballers although I was still too young to join their ranks. I was playing with more confidence, and it was at this time that I finally solved one of my last problems. It was this: a wing forward with the ball at his feet has more or less got to beat the left-back of the opposing side to make headway. By now I could almost gamble I would, but I couldn't be *sure* of it. This worried me so much that I spent many sleepless nights trying to solve it. When I was on the field one day playing for the reserves it came to me. I decided that instead of letting the back come to me, I would go to him. He couldn't know what I intended to do. When I was right up to him I would cause him to think, by the body swerve I had cultivated, I was going one way, then when I saw his body sway in that direction I would move the other way and ought to get clear away. The ball came out to me on the wing; I drew a deep breath, looked at the full-back, and ran towards him. He looked flabbergasted. I ran up close to him, swayed; he went the same way. I moved off the way I had intended and had a clear run in front of me. It worked like a dream and I tried the move several times during the match, and got away with it every time. I left the field at the end of the match a very happy boy. It wasn't until I read the Sunday papers that I realized what the sporting world thought of my playing abilities. This sort of talk could make a young boy swollen-headed. My father also read the

Sunday papers, and he explained certain things to me in no uncertain manner. He said that overpraise and excessive flattery could ruin a young boy quicker than almost anything else. He told me that adulation was slow poison to anyone. However, as I now know, sportswriters must have something to write about, and to them I was good copy; they continued to lavish their praises. I was getting on towards my seventeenth birthday, and I hesitate to think how I would have reacted but for the level-headed attitude of my father.

•   •   •   •   •   •

The way time passes has always struck me as being odd. To the very old it passes all too quickly; to the very young it seems to drag along so very slowly. Is it because youth, being on the threshold of life, has so many unfulfilled dreams to look forward to? If it is so, that would account for why, three months before my seventeenth birthday, I felt that the day itself would never arrive. I wanted to sign that form which would make me a professional footballer. Each passing day felt like a week, each week a year. I seemed to be passing my time just waiting, waiting, waiting for that day. At the same time, there was great excitement going on in my home, and in my father's shop.

Although I had been on the Stoke City Football Club's ground staff since my fifteenth birthday, it didn't follow that I had to sign for them as a professional on my seventeenth birthday—that was up to my father and myself. I had been perfectly happy with Stoke, and thanks to Mr. Vallance, who had helped me with my training in my spare time, I had matured tremendously, and more than one first-class club wanted my signature on my seventeenth birthday. My father was now a busy man, managers from various clubs were always on his doorstep. Mr. Mather, manager of Stoke City, was also a very busy man. He was never away from my father's side for very long. It seemed that my name was beginning to mean something in the football world, and the national press were also beginning to take notice of me and predict a great future for me. I was a youngster of promise. My father was right in keeping the various managers away from me, because I could easily have fallen a victim to the tongue of any glib manager that came along. I knew that things were being sorted out for me, and I was not surprised when my mother told me, on the eve of my birthday, that Father wanted to have a talk with me. When my father came home that night my mother very discreetly mentioned she was going out for an hour to see a friend.

As soon as we were alone my father crossed the room and sat down in a chair by the fire. He said, "Look, son; as you know, I've been seeing a lot of people in the football world about you signing for them. The time has now arrived for you to be brought into it, so I can hear your point of view." He then explained who the clubs were and what they could offer me in the way of accommodation if I joined them, and all the other points that would crop up should I sign. I listened in silence. He closed with, "And of course there is Stoke City. I've kept them to the last. Mr. Mather is worried; he thinks he is going to lose you. Now, what club would you like to sign for?"

I started to speak, but my father put up his hand and said, "Think it over, son. I'm going out for ten minutes. You can tell me what you think when I'm back." He then left the room. As I sat there alone, I went over everything my father had told me. I picked up a pencil off the table and started to doodle on the margin of a newspaper. And then my mind cleared—just like that! I put the pencil down and when my father came back I said, "I would like to sign for Stoke City. I know that I will be happy there." He walked over to me and said, "You really mean that?" I said, "Yes, Father, I really mean it." Dad said, "Well, Stoke City it is. I'll slip round and tell Mr. Mather." He smiled. "I shan't have much trouble in finding him."

My future was taking shape. I was later surprised to find that the decision I had taken made so much news. I could understand the local papers taking it up, but what I couldn't understand was the spread it got in the national newspapers. Now that my choice of club had been finally settled I felt much more at home when I was at the Stoke City ground, and I really began to enjoy myself; it wasn't work to me, and I was getting paid for it. That was the best part of it—being paid for something you loved to do! The day I signed the contract with Stoke I slipped out quietly after the business—leaving my father to settle the details. "May I have your autograph?" somebody said. It was a girl's voice. I turned quickly, and standing a few feet away was Betty Vallance. I gave her a huge grin and she said, "Congratulations, Stanley. I hope you will do well, and may all your dreams come true. I know you'll be happy with us." I just stared at her, and finally said, "Thanks, Betty. I know you mean it." She said, "Of course I mean it. You deserve to get on."

I walked home thinking of Betty.

    ·   ·   ·   ·   ·

I grew from a boy to a man within a few weeks of my seventeenth birthday. It didn't take me long to find out that as soon as I had put my signature on the contract that made me a full-blown professional footballer I had entered a jungle. I was being paid £5 a week for my services during the season and £3 a week in the summer months. In the early 1930's that was big money for a boy of seventeen to be earning. Remember also that all the other Stoke players were getting the same money, and although they were my team-mates they didn't want anybody pushing them out of the first team.

Football as a living means the survival of the fittest, and each first-team player always has in the back of his mind the fear that a sudden loss of form might relegate him to the reserves. If he doesn't regain his form within a short period, it may mean the loss of his livelihood. It is a grim thought, but it is there in this game of football, and always will be. So all of you who watch football —never fall for the saying "he wasn't trying an inch" when watching a first-team match. It just isn't true. Every first-team player gives the game all he's got because he *has* to—it's his bread ticket. It didn't take me long to find this out, and also that in choosing football as a career I had chosen a tough way of earning a living. I soon found out that the men I played against had scant respect for the reputation of anyone. They went into a tackle to get the ball, and to a youth of seventeen, playing against experienced men up to twice his age, making the grade in big-time football can at times be a nerve-racking experience. The ink on the contract I had signed had hardly dried when, passing the notice-board, I glanced at the list containing the names of the players for the following Saturday's matches. My face fell—I wasn't on the reserve list. I glanced at the first-team sheet, and to my amazement saw that I had been picked to play away against Bury.

Stoke in that season were in the Second Division. I hurried home and told my parents of my good fortune. My father listened in silence. When I had simmered down he said, "Look, son, let's put first things first." I knew what was coming and said, "Well, aren't you glad I'm playing for the first team?" He said, "Certainly I'm glad, and I know you'll do your best; but at the moment I want to get your money sorted out for you." My face fell. "I don't know what you mean." My father walked over to the table in the living-room and sat down. Looking up at me, he said, "Listen, son. I have been talking things over with your mother, and at the moment I'm not worried about your football. What I want to get on a sound basis for you is your money matters." He handed me ten one-pound notes. "I want you to take this to the savings bank and open an account in your own name. Every week in future you will put in half your weekly wage and give the other half to your mother to help run the house. I shall want to see your savings book every week to make sure you have done it. Now get off to the bank." I took the money and made for the door. I looked back at him. "But Dad, what am I going to do for pocket-money?" He smiled and said, "Do like you always have—earn it. You get a bonus for winning, don't you? Make sure you win at Bury next Saturday and you'll have a pound note all to yourself. If you lose—well, you'll have to lather a few faces for me in the shop. I'll see you get a shilling or two." He looked at me hard, then said, "I'm not going to let you waste any money, so get that in your head. Now be off with you."

I left the house and walked to the savings bank and placed my ten one-pound notes on the counter. They disappeared from view and I was handed a book. I walked home in a disgruntled mood. "And I'm playing for the first team," I kept muttering. When I reached home I handed my father the book. He opened it, looked inside and handed it back to me. He then did a rare thing—he called me by my Christian name. He said, "Stanley, now, for the first time in your life, you've got some money of your own. Look after it, son, and it will look after you in times to come. See that you get a few noughts after that first one. You'll keep out of mischief doing that. I don't think you'll regret doing what I have made you do today." He got up from the table and walked to the door; without turning round he said, "I hope you win at Bury on Saturday. A pound is a lot of money." I sat down at the table and looked at the door he had closed behind him. "And I'm in the first team," I said aloud. I thought my father was unreasonably hard, but it didn't take me many years to find out how right he was.

I had opened my first banking account with my signing-on fee. When I ran on the Bury ground with the rest of the Stoke team to play in my first big match I was thrilled. The whistle blew and the battle was on. I soon discovered that this football was different from any I had played before, and I remember thinking I would have to pull my socks up if I wanted to keep in this class. However, I toiled away, learning from my mistakes; then suddenly Walter Bussy, our inside-right, centred on the eighteen-yard line. Maloney, our outside-left, cut into the centre. The Bury goalkeeper came out, but instead of catching the ball he attempted to head it away. Maloney nipped round him and scored. It's the only time I have seen a goalkeeper attempting to save a shot with his head. We won and my pocket-money was safe. I returned home in high spirits. I didn't play for the first team again for the rest of that season, so I couldn't have had a good game. But I had gone on that field a youth and come off a man.

CHAPTER III

INTERNATIONAL ONE

IT WAS a warm, sunny afternoon in June 1932. I was sitting with my head cupped in the palms of my hands looking at the still water of a small pond in the country not far from my home. The 1931–32 football season had finished some time back. I thought things over as I gazed at the water that fine afternoon.

In February I had become a professional footballer for Stoke City and played in one first-team match at Bury. What was going to happen to me in the 1932–33 season? If I was to get a regular place in the first team I would have to improve a lot. What could I do? I loved playing football, I lived for it. Why, even now, whilst most of the other players were taking a well-earned rest before the start of the 1932–33 season, here was I still at it, trying to figure out a method of play that would keep me in the first team. It didn't occur to me then that only experience of playing more games with the first team would help. I was still only seventeen, although I now knew what it was like to play against older, stronger and more experienced players. As things turned out, I am glad I did not realise I needed experience. As I sat there weighing up the credit and debit side of my playing I decided that I would devote all the summer to making myself as fit and as fast as possible for the coming season.

Yes, that was it, and I would also bring my body swerve, which even now was paying off well, to perfection. Furthermore, I would see whether I could cover the ground even quicker than I did now, with the ball at my feet. I was completely carried away with my thoughts and I jumped nearly a foot in the air there was a loud plop and the smooth water on the pond into ever-widening circles. I looked round hastily, and standing behind me, with a smile on her face, was Betty

Vallance. I got to my feet. I didn't know then that I was looking at my future wife, and mother of my two children. "Why, Betty," I said, "what are you doing here?" She held out the No. 6 iron she had selected from her golf clubs to practise with. "I was just knocking a few old golf balls around in the field at the back of you when I saw you deep in thought, so I thought I'd knock one in the pond to bring you back to life." I took the club out of her hand and said, "Well, you succeeded in doing that. You know, Betty, I've never played golf. What sort of a game is it?" She grinned all over her face. "It's harder than football to learn. You ought to try it. As a matter of fact, my father wants you to go to Scotland with him for a week or two this summer on a golfing holiday; he is keen to teach you the game." I shook my head and walked back to the edge of the pond. Betty followed me, and we sat down side by side. I said, "I'm afraid that's impossible, Betty. I'm staying where I am this summer. I'm going to practise and practise until I feel right for the 1932–33 season."

"You know what they say about all work and no play," said Betty. I thought about that: "I certainly want to learn to play golf," I said. I learned something else which was to stand me in good stead in the future—how to relax when it was required.

I continued to work hard at my football, but I also relaxed with Betty, who began to teach me golf. She was a very good player and a good teacher. The summer passed very quickly, and the time arrived for me to report for the start of the 1932–33 season. I began this season in the right frame of mind, and it wasn't long before I was in the first team. I wasn't played in every match, and this method produced big dividends. My playing abilities on the field came on by leaps and bounds, and by the end of the season I had played in sixteen first-team games, and, as Stoke won the Second Division Championship that season, I also got a Second Division Championship medal. I also reached my eighteenth birthday. So, as the 1932–33 season came to a close, I had much to be thankful for, and I was certainly in a more settled frame of mind than I had been at the close of the previous season. I had matured and now felt at ease in any first-game match, and my playing was catching the eye of the national press again. They predicted an international cap for me in the coming season. I spent part of the 1933 summer with Jimmy Vallance on a golfing holiday at Girvan in Ayrshire, Scotland. Betty joined us, and I had a very enjoyable break.

I reported for training for the start of the 1933–34 season, and this time I would be in the real big time, the First Division, with a regular place in the first team. That's how it turned out, and deep inside me I knew that at last everything I had worked so hard for had at last come true. I knew that I had "arrived", and, all being well, I had a future worth all the sweat and tears I had ever put into my past work. In this season, just before my nineteenth birthday, the newspapers got to work. It led to the English selectors giving me a place in "The Rest" against England in the international trial at Sunderland. My partner in that trial was "Raich" Carter, then of Sunderland. Even though I was so young, I knew that Carter was an ideal partner for me, and I thought I had a good game. This was my biggest break so far, and it showed that I was on the brink of the England team. Try as I would, I couldn't fight off my nervous excitement until I knew the names of the England team for the match against Scotland. I had learned from my earlier experiences never to anticipate anything, and when at last the team was made public, and I saw that Carter had been picked, but Sammy Crooks had been selected on the wing, I took it calmly. I was very disappointed, but I reasoned that the selectors had thought that I wasn't ready for a big international match, and they were the best judges.

I was pleased with myself with regard to the way I could now accept these decisions. So my nineteenth birthday came and so did the end of the 1933–34 season. It was June, and coming in for breakfast one morning after my usual practice I saw that certain expression on my mother's face. When my mother meant to give me some advice that certain "look" was always there. I said, "Good morning, Mother. What's for breakfast?" She put my plate down on the table and sat down and watched me eat. When I had finished she said, "How much do you think of Betty, ?" I said, in surprise, "Why, what do you mean?" She er head in a sad manner. "Do you love her?" I got up table and walked about the room. "What did you say,

Mother?" She said, "Look, Stanley, it's time you settled down. You spend too much time on your own. Practise, practise, practise. There are other things in life besides football, you know." I said, "What's that got to do with Betty?" Mother stood up and took hold of my arm. She said, "I'll tell you what it has got to do with Betty. She was round here last night waiting for you to take her to the pictures. You forgot all about it, with your football on your mind. She loves you, Stanley, but you are going to lose her." I made for the door. "I'll slip round to their house and say how sorry I am." My mother said, "She left an hour ago to join her father in Scotland." For once in my life I forgot all about football.

I could only think of Betty, my mind was in a whirl. Then suddenly I knew my mother was right. I did love her. What a sensational feeling that is when you find out for the first time you love a girl enough to ask her to marry you. I made a dash for the stairs. My mother called out, "Where are you going?" I turned and said, "To pack a bag. You are right, I do love her. I'm going right up to Scotland to ask her to marry me, and shan't leave Scotland until she does so." My mother said, "Don't bother about packing a bag, son, I've already done it; it's behind the door." I gave her a hug, picked up the bag, and I caught up with Betty in Scotland. We were married in the clubhouse of the Bonnyton Golf Club near Glasgow.

. . . . .

I kissed my new bride, looked proudly around our trim new house, then walked down the street in the direction of the Stoke City Football ground to report for the beginning of the 1934–35 season.

I was happy and contented, married life suited me, and although I was only nineteen I felt that I was at last completely settled. The season started well and I was in great form. My first break came early in September. I was chosen to play for the Football League against the Irish League at Belfast. We won 6–1, and I scored a goal. The newspapers got busy about my getting a place in the England side against Wales in the coming international match at Cardiff on the 29th September. I didn't worry, I had read all this before. But when I was sitting in my father's shop a few days later one of his customers came rushing in; he gasped, "Jack, your Stan's in the England team." My father caught hold of him by his coat lapel and said, "You wouldn't be kidding now, would you?" The man opened his mouth to say something but I never heard what he replied. I was out of the shop like a flash and ran all the way to the bottom of the street, to where the newsboy stood selling his papers. Before I reached him I could read the big black headline—*Matthews chosen for England.*

I went hot, then cold. I put my hand in my pocket and pulled out half a crown. I tossed it to the boy, snatched a paper from him, and read the names of the England team. It was true—it was true! The newsboy offered me my change, but I told him to keep it. I ruffled his hair with my hand, then dashed back to Father's shop.

I thrust the paper into my father's hand. I watched his face as he read the names in the team; it had an expression I had never seen there before. He gave me the paper and said, "Well, son, you've made it. Good luck to you."

You could almost hear the silence in the shop. I said, "Thanks, Dad. I think I'll get off and tell Mother and Betty." I ran out of the shop, and as I left the doorway the storm broke behind me, everyone started to talk at once. I bet my father had quite a session that afternoon. I ran all the way to my mother's house, which was on the way to my own. She had already heard the news. Then she pushed me off to Betty. I slowed down to a quick walk when I came near to my house. I entered the house and I heard Betty humming a tune to herself in the kitchen. I called out to her. She came to the kitchen door, a puzzled look on her face. "What's the matter, Stan? I thought you were at your father's shop." I threw the paper on the table and said, "Read that, Betty." She picked up the paper and read. Her face registered so many emotions that I lost count. It was a pleasure to watch it.

I had reached the height of my ambitions, to play for my country. We went out that night to celebrate.

When I turned out next morning I found I had become a celebrity overnight. All Stoke was talking about me, and whilst on my way to the ground for training I was stopped by several people, who congratulated me on being picked for England. The morning papers also gave me a big splash. It is no use trying to deny that you don't feel good when things are going your way. The day of the international match got nearer and nearer, and I must confess that I began to get a little nervous, but I tried always to push my feelings away.

The match was getting near to its finish. Not a goal had been scored by England or Wales. The packed ground at Ninian Park, Cardiff, was yelling its head off, the world seemed to have gone mad, and Ninian Park was my world that day. Attack after attack by the England forwards came to nothing against the strong Welsh defence, and all the Welsh attacks folded up in front of the England goalmouth. Excitement grew as the minutes ticked by, and with only one minute left for play I took the ball from my own goalmouth. I beat one man, then another, and cut out towards the wing, with the Welsh team after me. I cut in towards goal, but there wasn't an English forward in sight, so I made for goal with the ball at my feet. Darting this way, then that way, I beat another man, and then I saw I had only the goal-keeper in front of me. I tricked him out of his goal, swerved past him, and put the ball in the back of the net. Before the goalie could pick the ball out the final whistle went.

We had won. I had scored the winning goal. My colleagues carried me off the field shoulder high. When I returned to Stoke the following day thousands of people packed the streets. I rode in an open carriage with the Lord Mayor to the foot of the town-hall steps, and at the top the Lord Mayor thanked me on behalf of Stoke and England. The police could hold the crowds back no longer, they rushed up the steps towards me. I shouted to them to keep back, but they took no notice; I began to struggle, fighting for breath, then everything went black. . . . I heard Betty's voice and saw a sudden glare of light. I looked around me. I was in bed. Sweat was pouring from me. Betty was stroking my face. She said, "Stan, wake up; you've been dream-ing again." I gave a sigh of relief; I was safe at home, it had been another dream. I got out of bed and had a drink of water.

Yes, I had a few dreams like that before my first international.

But at last the great day arrived, and this time it was no dream. I was in the England dressing-room, already changed; none of the other England players had started to get ready. The dressing-room door opened slowly and a face appeared around the side. It was Roy John, the goalkeeper for Wales that day. His eyes moved round the room until he saw me sitting there all ready for the game. He could see that I was feeling just a bit nervous. He came over to me and said, "Don't be scared, Stan; these internationals improve as they go on. You don't want to come off at the finish." I shall never forget that visit from Roy. He made me feel at ease and helped me to get over the dragging, nervous wait before I took the field in my biggest game so far. Gestures like his make you believe that there are a lot more good men in this world than bad ones. Roy soon had to go. "Well, I'll have to go now, Stan. Keep your chin up; you'll do all right. By the way, what about exchanging jerseys after the game?" I readily agreed.

This visit by Roy John was the tonic I needed, and I took the field with the England side in a much better frame of mind than I should have done otherwise.

When the whistle went to start the game I felt fine and played quite normally. We beat Wales that day without very much trouble. How different from the dreams I had had!

In the first half, Freddie Tilson, the Manchester City player, who was at centre-forward, scored two goals, and his team mate, Eric Brook, who was playing at outside-left, scored another. We walked onto the field after the interval feeling very confident. A minute after half-time Westwood, of Bolton Wanderers, playing at inside-left, sent me a pass which gave me the chance of a life-time. I trapped the ball and, without wasting any time, cut in towards goal and crashed the ball past Roy John into the back of the net. I had scored in my first international. It wasn't a dream —it was a stone-cold fact. I was too elated to spare a thought for my friend Roy John, and it was not until I was in the dressing-room at the end of the game and Roy walked over to me that I felt sorry I had to score against him. With a dead-pan face he threw his Welsh jersey at me. "Here you are, Stan," he growled. "Next time I open my big mouth and waste sympathy on the likes of you, just shut me up." He smiled, and I threw him my English jersey. We did a little jig together. Yes, Roy is a great fellow; I shall always think well of him.

I got off the train at Stoke Station the following day, to be met by my wife Betty and my mother and father. The look in their eyes was wonderful. They had listened to the game on the radio, and my mother said that when I scored Betty was almost sick with excitement. As we walked home together towards Hanley I knew that I was the happiest man in the world. Here I was, not twenty years old, with the world at my feet, married to a charming girl, and with the best parents any man could have walking by my side.

We sat down to tea and talked about the match. I could see that my father was looking at me all the time. After tea, he said, "You know, son, at one time I never thought you would make it, you looked so thin as a boy; but you have, and I can only say that, from now on, you deserve everything you want from football, you have worked hard enough for it." From my father, this was praise indeed!

CHAPTER IV

INTERNATIONAL TWO

THE hands on the clock at the side of my bed pointed to 7 a.m. I got up and went to the bedroom window. I opened it wide and took seven deep breaths, with a very short interval between each one. As I inhaled the crisp, cold October air a feeling of well-being seeped through the whole of my body and the cobwebs of sleep were swept from my brain.

I gently closed the window and looked towards Betty, whom I had left in bed. She stirred slightly and seemed to wake up; in a sleepy voice she said, "Is that you, Stanley?" I said, "Yes, Betty. See you at breakfast." She snuggled back underneath the bedclothes, and I made my way to the bathroom. Shortly afterwards I left the house to begin my early-morning training.

This was more or less the routine I followed every morning when I was at home, and I looked forward to it. It never got stale, because it was my *life*; and having more or less done early-morning training under the watchful eye of my father from being a small boy, it had become a habit.

I finished my final sprint, and at a very brisk walking pace turned towards home, and breakfast. It was a lovely October morning not long after my first international match. I entered the house just as Betty was putting the finishing touches to the breakfast table. She smiled at me and said, "You're dead on time —8.15 a.m." I nodded and made for the table. I was so hungry I couldn't speak.

At last, having had my fill, I picked up the morning paper and started to scan the pages. Betty, in the act of clearing the dishes off the table, paused and said, "Don't they pick the Football League XI to play against the Scottish League at Stamford Bridge today, Stanley?" I said, "They do, Betty. The team will be in the evening papers."

I helped Betty to wash the dishes. As I handed her the towel I had been drying the dishes with she said, "I do hope you get selected." I took her in my arms and kissed her. "Well," I said, "I shall have to get moving or I'll be late at the ground for training!"

As I walked along the familiar roads on my way to the football ground, I kept thinking about the team being picked by the selectors that day. If I was lucky enough to be picked it would do me a world of good, because it would show that the selectors were satisfied with my play in the international match against Wales. Well, I would soon see what they thought, the team would be in the evening papers. All the same, as I walked along I felt a glow of anticipation creep through me.

When I reached the ground everything was soon forgotten in the bustle of training with the other men. Jimmy Vallance was a good trainer, and he kept us at it during training hours. Being his son-in-law made me no better off than anyone else, which is as it should be, but I enjoyed my work so much I didn't need to ask favours.

The morning's training came to an end and along with the other players I returned to the dressing-room and changed into outdoor clothes. One by one my team-mates left until I was there alone. I sat on the bench staring at the wall in front of me. I had arranged to meet Betty at my mother's for tea that afternoon; I would pick up my father at his shop and walk home with him. In the meantime I was going to have a light snack at a nearby café and return to the ground in the afternoon to try and improve a weakness I had in my play. But as I sat there staring at the wall I knew I couldn't feel settled in my mind until I had seen the evening paper.

I left the dressing-room and made for the café. I didn't stay very long before making my way back to the ground. I changed back into training clothes and soon I was engrossed in my private practice and forgot everything. Only when I noticed it was getting dark did I glance at my watch, and when I saw the time I had to run like a hare to the dressing-room, change in record time, then run all the way to my father's shop.

He was alone, with his clothes on ready to leave. "You're late, son," he said. "I'd given you up. Have you seen the paper?" I shook my head. "No, Dad," I said. "I was so late finishing training I ran all the way here; besides, I want to hear the news from you."

He smiled at me. "You know, son, you're a funny one. I've told you before not to expect too much." I cut in, "Does that mean I haven't been selected?" I sat down on a chair dejected and looked at my father; then I smiled and said, "Do you know, Dad, I *must* be a funny one. I've been in torment all day, and now I know the result I don't feel bad at all—only relieved. Anyhow, better luck next time."

"What are you talking about, son? You're in. Here—read the paper." I took the paper from him and read the team out aloud. Yes, there I was: Stanley Matthews. I dropped the paper and jumped to my feet. "Come on, Dad, let's get home and tell Betty and Mother." My father said, "They know already, but let's get going."

We left the shop and walked towards my father's house. I felt elated. My father sensed this sudden change in me, and as we turned the corner of the next block of houses he said, "You know, son, I suppose, by the same rule, sometimes you can expect too little."

I stopped in that dark street and looked at him. "Do you mean," I asked, "that you should always hope for the best?" He took me by the arm and we walked along in silence until we reached the house, then he said, "I mean, son, train your mind to take the rough with the smooth, both on and off the field; never give up, and never lose confidence in yourself."

We knocked on the door and Mother and Betty opened it together. What expressions they had on their faces! "Oh, Stanley," Betty said, "I am *so* happy." I mumbled something back; I couldn't speak clearly. I shall never forget that day.

When I read the morning paper next day after breakfast I saw that I had hit the headlines again. The football critics and sports writers had written about me in glowing terms, and predicted that if I played as well as I did against Wales it should be a mere formality for me to be picked for the next international against Italy at Highbury on November 14th. I didn't pay too much attention to this talk, however, as I was too intent on doing a good job of work against the Scottish League at Stamford Bridge.

When I was walking through the town during the following days I was stopped by countless people who, after congratulating me, would begin to talk about my inclusion in the England team to play against Italy as if it were a foregone conclusion. I didn't pass any comment, but I soon traced the reason for all this talk. The newspapers were tipping players for this match even before the Stamford Bridge match had been played. The reason was that at this time—1935—Fascism was flourishing both in Germany and Italy, and Mussolini, trying to boost the morale of the Italian people, thought that if Italy could beat England at football in London it would be a triumph of the first order for Fascism. Furthermore Mussolini had promised his footballers handsome bonuses if England were beaten, and the news had certainly got around that the Italians meant to win, almost at any price. As Mussolini was moving from greater power to still greater power, this news was played up by our press.

So I played at Stamford Bridge in a very important match, but all the football interest centred on the Italy v. England match a week or so after. We beat the Scottish League 2–1, but nobody seemed very interested in the result. The newspapers were more concerned the next day with the selection of the England-Italy team, and on the day the selectors met to pick the team, tension in the football world was terrific. To get a little peace from being stopped so often in the streets I decided to go along to my father's shop after my morning training and wait there until the news came through. The news finally reached us that I had been selected to play at outside-right against the Italians at Highbury.

I took my father's advice and left the shop to go home and rest, and walked at a brisk pace through the dark streets towards home. As I passed other people in the streets I could hear my name being mentioned in passing snatches of conversation, so it was quite evident that in hundreds of Hanley homes my inclusion in the international team would be freely discussed.

I reached home and Betty was delighted at the news, and to celebrate the occasion we decided to go to the cinema after tea. We both enjoyed the film. It was when I was walking to the ground for training the following morning that I realized that although my family and myself were taking my inclusion in the England team far more calmly than we had done just over a month ago when I had been selected for the first time, the people of Hanley had gone in the reverse direction—they were making a big song and dance about my inclusion in the England team to meet the Italians.

Every few yards I was stopped by people, sometimes by two or three at the same time, and at the rate of progress I was making towards the ground I knew that if I didn't do something about it it would be tea-time before I got there. So my new-found fame caused me to do a thing I had never done before. After getting away from the people who last stopped me I made a bee-line for the bus-stop and jumped on a bus that was just leaving. It was the first time I had ridden to work in my life, and if my father had caught sight of me sitting on that bus . . . well, I'll pull the curtain down on what he would have said.

Even on the bus I came in for more congratulations, and although I tried to hide it from my fellow-passengers I am sure they could tell by my nervous gestures as I prepared to get off the bus near the ground that their very sincere good wishes had greatly moved me.

As I neared the ground I was mobbed by a gang of youthful football fans, who thrust all kinds of books and papers at me to sign. I just gave up, got in the middle of them, and had the time of my life. After all, these were the people who paid my wages, and I was and always have been their servant. After a time one of the staff came out of the players' entrance and asked the fans if they would mind if I did some training for the big match. This gentle irony worked and I made my way towards the players' entrance, turned in the doorway, waved to them, then closed the door. As I walked towards the dressing-rooms everything seemed quiet and still. From that day on, if I wanted to get anywhere in a hurry, I had to go by a different route; but I did that only if there was no other way out. I love meeting the football fans.

As the day of the international match came nearer the tension mounted. The sports writers had a field day. In the first place there were five Arsenal men in the team first chosen; then, when Cooper and Tilson dropped out through injury, George Male and Ted Drake of Arsenal came in. This made a club record for an international match—seven Arsenal players out of the total eleven. This was news, and the press played it up big.

I said goodbye to Betty and a host of other friends who saw me on the London train at Stoke Station, settled myself down in a corner seat, pulled a book out of my pocket and started to read. Before very long I began to doze and then fell fast asleep. The train was on the outskirts of London before I woke up. This was a good sign that I was relaxed; I smiled when I thought of the state I was in only a few weeks ago, on my way to my first international match in Wales.

However, when I was sitting in the England dressing-room at Highbury, an hour before the kick-off, I could feel the butterflies coming back to fly round and round my stomach. I got up from the bench and mixed with the other players. I found this eased my tension, and as I listened to them, making no effort to join in the conversation, except by a casual remark or so, the butterflies slowly but surely flew away.

We took the field, and as I ran out with the rest of the team from the entrance of the tunnel and heard the roar of 50,000 spectators inside the ground I suddenly felt calm and relaxed. The teams were—ENGLAND: Moss (Arsenal); Male (Arsenal), Hapgood (Arsenal); Britton (Everton), Barker (Derby County), Copping (Arsenal); Matthews (Stoke City), Bowden (Arsenal), Drake (Arsenal), Bastin (Arsenal), Brook (Manchester City). ITALY: Ceresoli (Ambrosiana); Monzeglio (Bologna), Allemandi (Ambrosiana); Ferraris (Lazio), Monti (Juventus), Bertolini (Juventus); Guaita (Rome), Serantoni (Ambrosiana), Meazza (Ambrosiana), Ferrari (Juventus), Onsi (Juventus). Eddie Hapgood was the England captain, and after he tossed the coin and handed it back to the referee he shook hands once more with Monti, the Italians' captain. We ran across the field and took up our respective positions; as I passed Ted Drake, our centre-forward, I wished him the best of luck. I knew how he must be feeling; it was his first international.

I watched the referee from my wing position; he was looking at his watch, a silence had fallen over the ground, everything was calm and peaceful. The whistle blew, the game started, and the Italians, right from the start, tore into us like a pack of hungry wolves. It didn't take me many seconds to realise that this was going to be a rough game, and before the first minute had gone by we were awarded a penalty. Eric Brook, a deadly shot, took the kick, which to me looked a certain winner, but Ceresoli, the Italian goalkeeper, made the most fantastic dive across the goal and beat down the ball. After this the Italians went mad; they showed no mercy at all in the tackle or in anything else.

I could sense serious trouble brewing if this kind of play was kept up. Already the 50,000 crowd, who had paid good money to see a game of football, were giving vent to their feelings in no uncertain manner because they were witnessing a brawl, and they could see that the English players were disgusted. It was to get much worse, very much worse.

Ten minutes of playing time had passed when suddenly I received the ball at my feet and cut off down the wing. Looking round, I saw Allemandi, Italy's left-back, racing towards me. I knew by this time what to expect if I got within his clutches, and so—much to his surprise—I ran fast *towards* him. He was puzzled, and as he came in to tackle me I got him to go the wrong way. Before he could recover I was yards past him. This drew three Italian defenders out of position, and as they came at me I crossed a spinning centre towards the far side of the goal, and there, unmarked, was Eric Brook. Ceresoli never saw the ball which shot, off his head, into the back of the net. Within a few minutes of this goal one of our players had his legs kicked from under him outside the penalty area.

Eric Brook, our outside-left, who had just headed in the goal off my centre, was entrusted with the kick. Although the free-kick was taken a few yards outside the penalty area, Brook scored a lovely goal. He cracked the ball into the back of the net with such force that Ceresoli, the Italian goalkeeper, never even saw it coming; for a second or so he looked dumbfounded, then he turned in disgust, picked the ball up from the back of the net, and booted it towards the centre of the field.

I thought this goal would calm down the Italians, by showing them that rough play doesn't pay good dividends. I was sadly wrong, they played rougher than ever. The spectators howled their disapproval at the Italians, but it made no difference. Then what I feared might happen did happen.

Within minutes of Brook scoring our second goal, Eddie Hapgood, our captain, in trying to stem an Italian attack on our goal, was struck a savage blow in the face by one of the Italian forwards. He fell like a log to the ground. The next few minutes were nightmarish. Tempers on both sides flared up as Hapgood lay on the ground receiving attention from our trainer, and I felt very distressed indeed. I abhor scenes like this on a football field, and when it was discovered Hapgood had a broken nose and had to be carried off the field I felt quite sick and disgusted.

This incident rattled most of our players and it was fortunate for England that we had two tough nuts, in Eric Brook and Wilf Copping, playing with us. They gave the Italians a rough time, without resorting to foul tactics, by using the real honest English shoulder-charge. This made them marked men, and Brook had to receive attention, but carried on playing with his shoulder strapped up, while Wilf Copping finished up covered with bruises; but they did their duty for England that day, in that infamous match. Shortly after Hapgood had left the field, Monti, Italy's captain and centre-half, came off worse in a tackle and fell to the ground. He had to leave the field with a splintered bone in his foot.

When the game restarted, after Monti left the playing pitch, we could scarcely hold the Italians; then, when it seemed that at last they must break through the badly battered English defence and score, Ted Drake, our centre-forward, broke away and scored a magnificent goal in his first international match. As soon as play was resumed he got the full Italian treatment, and just before half-time he was carried off the field. I watched young Ted being carried in the direction of the dressing-room with tears in my eyes. At last the whistle went for half-time, and I walked off the field with the rest of the dejected English team for a well-earned breather. The half-time score read—England 3, Italy 0.

The language and comments used and made by the English

players in our dressing-room during the interval made my hair stand on end. I was still only a youth and some way off my twenty-first birthday, and I was relieved to see the tempers calm down when our team manager came into the room and told us that under no circumstances must we copy the play of the Italians. We were to go out, he said, and play like every English team had been taught to play. I felt relieved when I saw the effect these instructions had on our players, because if we had gone out and played the Italians at their own game it would have been a blood-bath.

The crowd roared as we took the field for the second half, and the roar doubled itself when they saw that Eddie Hapgood was returning with us. Before the referee blew his whistle to start the second half I glanced up at the stand to the spot where Signor Grandi, the Italian Ambassador, and the late Prince Arthur of Connaught sat side by side watching the match, and I wondered what they were thinking about this shocking affair. The whistle blew, and my mind came back to the game.

Right from the start we were on the run; the Italians evidently had had a "pep" talk in the interval and they fought like tigers to get a goal. Soon our defence crumbled, and Manzza, Italy's centre-forward, in an inspired few minutes, cracked two goals in quick succession past Frank Moss, our goalkeeper. The battle was now on in earnest, no quarter was asked for or given; it looked as if Italy might save the game, or perhaps win it.

The excitement was terrific, and the spectators sensed that England's sporting good name was at stake. Our players sensed it too, and Brook, Copping, Moss in goal, Hapgood and Male worked like heroes and saved the day for England. It was a marvel how they forced their tired and badly bruised bodies to obey their minds. They did, however, and at long last the final whistle blew. I sighed with relief. It had been a bad match for me. I couldn't do a thing right after the first quarter of an hour; I was suffering from nerves and the shock of being in such a ruthless match as this. It was the roughest I have ever taken part in. There is no excuse for rough games—never; and as far as I am concerned, my style of play never comes off best in this type of match.

I arrived back at Stoke to find Betty waiting for me at the station. I assured her that I was fit and well, then we went along to my mother's house and a home-cooked meal. Whilst I was sitting round the table with Betty and my parents I told them all I could about the match. My father said it sounded more like a political meeting than a football match, and he added that it was incidents such as this, with all the hatred they left in their wake, which could, if not curbed at the onset, lead to war.

How right he was. I have never been interested in politics, and at that time I really didn't know what a Fascist was supposed to be. But I did think that if they were anything like the players in the Italian team I wanted no part of them. This international game upset me more than I first realised and it took me quite a time to get back to my normal game.

The selectors dropped me for the next international and the following one, and indeed all internationals played in the 1934–35 season.

My twentieth birthday came and went and gradually I got back to my normal game, and as I left the field with the rest of the Stoke City players after the last game of the season I had forgotten the effect that the England-Italy international match had had on my game; but I never forgot the experience. I spent a happy summer relaxing, and as the start of the 1935–36 season came in sight I was looking forward to reporting to the ground for training.

CHAPTER V

MY APPRENTICESHIP ENDS

THERE was a happy atmosphere in our dressing-room at the Stoke City ground on the first day of the 1935–36 season. All the players reported for training, and whilst we changed into our training gear we swopped stories as to how we had spent our summer recess and there was the usual leg-pulling and wisecracks from the wits. The season was under way. It was good to get back once more amongst my team-mates, and when I left the ground at the end of the first day's training I was very happy and relaxed. The glaring light of publicity had for the moment been turned off me, I had not played in the international teams, and my name didn't appear in the sports pages of the national newspapers as much as it had in the past. For this I was thankful, I felt I wanted to get myself sorted out.

At this time I was very keen on practising the dribble. Dribbling had always come natural to me, but to bring it to the perfection I wanted I used to knock stakes in the ground and weave my way through them, imagining that each stake was a player. I practised for hours at this exercise, and when I found that I could go at speed, weaving my way through these stakes in all directions without touching any of them, I felt that I had improved my dribbling abilities considerably. Future matches proved me right, so this was another *must* for my private training. Another thing that my past playing experience had taught me was that a winger who had only one body-swerve to get past an opponent tasted success only for a time and once his opponent realised what was happening he very soon had the edge on the winger. I had been blessed with a two-way body-swerve, which made it difficult for my opponent to know which way I would finally go, and it was at this stage of my career that I decided to make this two-way swerve as good as possible. I worked really hard on the dribble and the body-swerve, and much to my delight, in the opening matches of the season with Stoke City, my concentration on what were really two natural gifts paid off. The supporters of my club roared their delight and approval when I put them into practice in a home game.

I was fast becoming a favourite with the crowds, but also becoming very unpopular with my opposing full-back. After each game I would check through my play, make notes of any weakness, then do my utmost to rid myself of it in my private practice. I was really enjoying my work, and, although I didn't know it then, the experience gained by playing regularly in a First Division team was to result in my rapid development into a strong, matured, although young, footballer. Betty was well pleased with me, and we were both enjoying life to the full.

One very cold November evening I walked into my home just in time for tea. There was a lovely fire burning in the grate, and Betty had just finished laying the table. Everything looked nice and cosy. Betty said, "You're just in time, Stanley. Sit at the table right away." I sat down and enjoyed the meal Betty set before me, then I made my way to my favourite chair near the fire and picked up the paper. I then remembered that the selectors were that day picking the England team to meet Germany at Tottenham on Wednesday, December 4th, 1935. I had not been selected for the past twelve months and I hadn't given the match much thought, as I knew that Geldard, Crooks, Worrall and Birkett were all ahead of me on the list of outside-rights. I also knew that if I had been selected Betty would have told me as soon as I had entered the house. So I was not surprised to read that Ralph Birkett the Middlesbrough right-winger, had been chosen as England's outside-right. After scanning the rest of the news I put the paper down, picked up a book, and settled myself more comfortably in my chair for an enjoyable evening by the fireside. Betty settled down in the chair opposite me. After a good half-hour of reading I put down my book and said to Betty, "You know, dear, I have a feeling deep inside that within the next year or so I shall be more or less the consistent choice for the outside-right position in the England team. If I keep on eating those wonderful cooked meals of yours they——" I ducked to miss the cushion she flung at me. "It's a good job I know you as I do," she said. "Consistent choice indeed!" We both laughed and settled back once more in our chairs. Time, however, proved that there is many a true word spoken in jest.

My big surprise came on Saturday, 30th November, the last day in the month. I noticed that the sports writers were giving their views and opinions on the chances of the England team beating Germany in the coming international on the following Wednesday, December 4th, at Tottenham. In fact they were playing it up quite big. Hitler at this time was raising propaganda in Germany. The Nazis in Berlin were in fact in the early stages of their effort to conquer the world, so I was very much surprised to find that no mention was made that this match might turn out to be a free-for-all—like the Italian match was just over twelve months ago. I scanned the papers again, but there was no mention of it at all. Yet a win for Germany would do the Nazis a power of good. Well, I thought I could be wrong, but why should I worry? I wasn't going to run onto the field with the England team next Wednesday. Then, tucked away at the bottom of a sports column, I saw my name. The writer said that after seeing me playing with Stoke City in our previous Saturday's match he was greatly impressed with my game, as I seemed to have matured into a really fast, tricky wing forward; if I kept this form, he predicted it wouldn't be long before I was knocking on the door of the England selectors' room. I felt good on reading this; it is gratifying to know someone is taking an interest in you.

That same afternoon as I ran out onto the field with the Stoke players, hundreds of other team players were doing the same. By the end of all the games played some would have had good games, some bad games, and some would have injuries that would keep them off the field for weeks. This happens every week, but this particular Saturday was different. Ralph Birkett ran onto the field with the Middlesbrough team, and he was the unluckiest man in football that day; he came off the field injured and had to be withdrawn from the England team. It must have been heartbreaking for him, but the risk is always there. I was, of course, unaware of his injury until I arrived back home and found that the selectors had chosen me to replace Birkett. My mind flew back to the news I had read about myself in the newspaper that same day. Apparently the selectors had also been watching, and this incident taught me a lesson I never forgot. *Every footballer has every chance to play for his country if he will always give his best at all times whenever he is on a football field, and behave himself when he is off it.* You get a place in football on merit only, there are no favourites. Sometimes, through injury, a player who is on top of his form can lose his place for a very long time, and sometimes for good, in an international team. If the substitute brought in by the selectors impresses them by a good display he may get a second chance, and still another until the original choice never gets back. This was the position now. I had every chance to prove myself, and although I felt sorry for Birkett I was determined to try to hold the wing position down for myself.

I was a very busy young man over the week-end. Reporters were on the phone after me all the time. The newspapers turned the spotlight on until I did not know whether I was coming or going. The shock of being told three days before the match to play for one's country was enough to upset older players than me, but as I left the house to catch the London train I felt calm enough. I said good-bye to Betty on the station platform and settled down in a corner seat and pulled out a book, just as I had over twelve months ago on my way to the Italy match. This time, however, I didn't go to sleep; I couldn't even concentrate on the book, my mind was jumping about all over the place. I couldn't find the cause of all this unless it was delayed shock, due to the last-minute selection.

I was very weary when I reached Euston Station, London. But I went to bed very early that night and slept like a top, which goes to show what funny beings we humans are. I woke up in the morning feeling fit and well, without a care in the world.

I felt quite at home in the dressing-room before the match at Tottenham. I still felt the "butterflies", but not as badly as last time, and as I ran through the tunnel onto the field I felt wonderful. I glanced quickly round the packed ground. Instinct made me do this as I knew that my father was somewhere in that 40,000 crowd; he had borrowed an old car to drive down from Hanley to see me play. Of course I never saw him, but it was good to know he was there. The teams lined up, the referee blew his whistle and the game started. Unlike the Italians, the Germans played a good clean game. I was rather surprised, but, as it was, I felt pleased.

The game had been in progress only a few minutes when I took the ball on the wing about the midway mark. Quickly getting it under control, I sped off down the wing. I saw Muenzenberg, Germany's left full-back, moving towards me and ran forward full of confidence, taking the ball right up to him. He took it away from me. I couldn't believe my own eyes. I asked myself, how did he do it? A few minutes later I tried again, but this time I didn't go so close to him; I tried the body-swerve. I half fooled him, but didn't get away with it—he again took the ball away. This stopped me dead. I remember thinking, *You've been kidding yourself, my boy. This back is far too quick and too experienced for you.*

Muenzenberg was a revelation to me; never in my short career had I come up against anyone in his class. His positioning was superb. He tackled easily, and, to my dismay, was yards faster than I was. It was said after the match that he was at the peak of his form that afternoon and couldn't put a foot wrong. So far as I was concerned, he was the complete footballer and a master of defence. In trying to escape the attentions of Muenzenberg I moved over to the centre of the field, and in next to no time I found myself yards inside the Germany penalty area, completely unmarked, with the ball at my feet. I was certain I could score. I saw the wide-open goal gaping at me. I picked my spot at the back of the net and took a great kick at the ball. I kicked the turf. The ball travelled about five yards. It was quickly cleared away by a thankful German defence. It was the first time in my life I really heard a crowd of 40,000 groan like one man. For seconds I stood rooted to the spot. I couldn't believe what I had done, or rather failed to do. I, the young man who was always striving for perfection, had committed the cardinal sin of all ball games, which is to take your eyes off the ball. I thought I must be dreaming. I forced myself to lift my head and trot off back towards the wing, and when I heard some of the comments of the crowd on that miskick my confidence went. I was destroyed. I might as well have left the field and returned to the dressing-room after that. The longer the game went on the worse I got, and at last, when the final whistle went, I returned to the dressing-room with a heavy heart. I knew that the result of the game was England 3, Germany 0, but of the game itself I remembered very little.

Despite the sympathy of my fellow players, I felt so ashamed of my performance that I crept away, as soon as I could manage to do so, and made my way to the station to get the train home. When I reached the station my mouth was so dry and my throat so parched that I slipped into one of the refreshment-rooms for a cup of tea. I stood close to the counter sipping my tea and began to feel much better as the hot liquid quenched my thirst, then I glanced at my watch and saw that I had only about ten minutes before the train left. I finished off my tea in a final gulp and made my way to the platform. I was lucky enough to find an empty compartment near to the front of the train. I got in and made myself comfortable. With a great hiss of escaping steam from the engine, the train slowly pulled out of the station and I was on my way home. As I sat gazing at the steaming window I tried to keep my mind a blank, but it was no use. If the things that happened to me in this match had taken place in an ordinary league match it would have been bad enough, but in an international match, and one that I wanted to make good in—well . . . A cold shiver ran down my spine. And then I thought of my father. He had been at the match—what would he be thinking, what would he say when he got home? The next thing I remember was a porter shouting the name of my station. I jumped quickly to my feet, gathered my things together, and walked slowly in the direction of my home. As I walked along I thought of Betty and my mother waiting for me there, and my father who would be still on his way back from London.

It was a very unhappy young footballer who walked through the streets of Hanley that night. I stopped outside my house, took a deep breath, put my key in the lock, turned it, opened the door, walked in and saw Betty and my mother sitting near to the fire.

It all looked so cosy and warm. They both jumped up when they saw me. I turned round and closed the door, shutting out the cold December night. The best way I can think of to sum up this match and my part in it is simply to say that Ralph Birkett was selected for the next international.

.   .   .   .   .   .

"Matthews Fails in International"—"Matthews Misses A Great Chance". I gazed dismally at the headlines in the newspapers the day after the international. I agreed with what they said.

Betty said, "Isn't it time you were off?" I glanced at the clock on the mantelpiece, tossed the papers on one side, said goodbye to Betty and left the house. I walked at a brisk rate to the ground, taking my number-two route.

When I entered the dressing-room the conversation between the players stopped for a split second. Everybody looked in my direction and there was an awkward silence. I quickly overcame it. "Sorry to let you down, lads. Now you won't want my autograph." It broke the tension. Somebody laughed, and in a few minutes everything was back to normal. I was home again. We finished the morning training and left the ground.

I had a light snack, after which I returned to the ground. I had something important to do. I took three or four balls out to the turf and put them near to the spot from which I had missed the open goal. I hit those balls into the back of the net every time. I lined them up again and booted them in again and again. I felt better after that practice, it got something out of my system. Then I took a ball and ran round the ground with it at my feet. I was about to gather up the balls and call it a day when I had a sudden urge to try the shooting practice once more. I lined up the balls, then kicked them in quick succession into the back of the net. I felt much better.

It was getting dark, so I gathered up the balls and went back to the dressing-room. In the gathering gloom I thought I could see someone standing near the tunnel entrance. I called out. A voice answered back, "It's only me, son."

It was my father. I walked quickly towards him. I hadn't seen him since the day before the international. As I got closer I suddenly felt awkward and shy. He was there and saw the match. I felt I had let him down. I said, "Hallo, Dad. What are you doing here?"

My father reached out and took two of the footballs from me; then he said, "Betty called and asked your mother and me round to tea, so I told them to go along and I would come along here and pick you up and walk home with you."

I said, "How did you know I was here?"

He replied, "Because I know what you are going through at the moment."

We walked in silence towards the dressing-room. When we reached the passage leading to the room my father said, "I'll wait for you outside."

I nodded, then went down the corridor to change. A few minutes later I joined my father, and off we went together. After walking a few yards I said, "Well, what did you think of my performance yesterday?" My father didn't answer right away; at last he said, "Look, son, I'm not worried about what you did yesterday; I'm more worried about what you are likely to do the day after tomorrow, Saturday, when you play your next match with Stoke City. I wish I had the command of words to tell you just what I want to tell you, but I'll do my best to straighten you out if you want me to. It's up to you now, son. What do you say?"

I was a little puzzled by my father's attitude; but, knowing deep down inside of me that he had only my interests at heart, I said, "Right, Father. What's on your mind that will help me?"

We walked along in the dusk, and when we passed under a street lamp I stole a look at my father's face; it was thoughtful. "The way I look at it, son, is like this. To learn a trade you must serve an apprenticeship. In the building trade, or engineering, or any other trade you care to mention, a youth must start when he is fourteen and serve until he is twenty-one. During those years he makes all kinds of mistakes, but the craftsman he is working with puts him right until he reaches the age of twenty-one. Then he's on his own, his apprenticeship is over. Any mistakes he makes after that may get him the sack. In your job things are slightly different, there are no basic rules, and the situations you meet differ in every match. You don't work under anybody, you're on your own all the time, but you get your experience by watching the other players on the field, learning all the time by watching their mistakes and their good play.

"In a few weeks' time you'll be twenty-one and your apprenticeship will end, but before it does there is one more thing you must learn, and that is—never try and correct a physical mistake by a physical effort without first getting your mental outlook right. When you missed that open goal yesterday it didn't alter you in the physical sense at all. It did, however, destroy your mental outlook, and that's where you came unstuck. Your mental outlook was suffering before that because the German left full-back had you worried; never before had you played against anyone half so good.

"You let him sense that you knew he was master, and that was fatal. You should have thought things out and tried other methods, but not for one instant should you ever have admitted that he was better than you, because if you do that you lose your confidence. If you ever meet this situation again, don't give up, try this and that, and try, try, try all through the match, keep your mental outlook right, never admit defeat, and with your playing capabilities you will one day reach the top—and, what's more important, stay there."

My father paused, then went on, "You see, son, I have never told you this before, but I know that you have it in you to be one of the greatest footballers this country has ever seen. But if I had let you run on to the field next Saturday afternoon in the state of mind you were in when I met you at the ground this afternoon you might have ruined yourself for life.

"Forget about what the papers say, and what people are saying about you at the present moment. Remember crowds are very fickle but they love a winning team, and a footballer that plays the game and gives them what they have paid to see—pure football. In the future you'll make many more mistakes, but don't let them upset you—learn from them, but keep your mental outlook undisturbed; you'll also have some fine successes—learn from them too, by keeping your head. If you do this the crowds will love you. Now go out on Saturday and play your normal game, and never again lose confidence in yourself."

We were nearly home. I looked at my father and said, "Thank you, Dad—thank you very much." I took my door key from my pocket, opened the door, and we both entered.

When I ran with the rest of Stoke City's players on to the ground the following Saturday afternoon my father's advice came back to me in full force. I could feel the change in the attitude of the crowd towards me. Furthermore, the first time I received the ball and made off down the wing the opposing full-back came at me full of confidence. Evidently he had seen me play last Wednesday or had been reading the papers. I glanced quickly at his face as he got near to me; it looked a bit too confident for me. He lunged at the ball but never saw it or me; I was past him and had centred the ball goalwards before he had picked himself off the floor. By half-time the look on his face was a very worried one indeed.

As I ran off the field to take the half-time breather I glanced at the spot where my father was watching the match. I grinned at him. His face was one big smile; it was a tonic to me. I pulled every trick out of my football bag in the second half, and the crowd loved it. My father had indeed given me the answer, and it was the finishing touch I needed. It was my father's final lesson to me.

The sports writers in the Sunday papers that weekend were worried men, they couldn't just make me out; it was funny to read the write-ups of the match, they couldn't fathom the change in me.

On February 1st I celebrated my twenty-first birthday. We had a very nice informal party, with my family and friends, and I attained my majority in a very happy frame of mind. The 1935–36 season drew to a close, and although I was now playing very well I never got anywhere near to catching the England team.

We played the last game of the season, in which I had played one international match, which, thanks to my father, had taught me so much, and Betty and I packed our bags for our motoring holiday, and football also had a holiday all over the country. As

Betty and I were leaving the town we called to see my parents; after staying for about an hour we said goodbye and got into the car.

They stood in the doorway. I started the engine and was just about to move off when my father shouted, "Don't forget, son, your apprenticeship is at an end; you'll start next season as a master."

Betty and I smiled and waved to them. I let in the clutch, and in a few minutes we were leaving the town and a well-earned, carefree holiday was under way.

CHAPTER VI

MY FIGHT BACK TO THE TOP

THE 1936–37 season was a month old. I had made a good start and had settled down to my usual winter training routine. I didn't spare myself. When relaxing in the evening in my home I had taken to reading all the books I could find dealing with the art of football. In those days I was scoring a lot of goals for my team, and I was so keen to make good at Stoke that I got the impression that the more goals I scored the more pleased would the club be, and the spectators. I had developed a habit, on getting the ball, of cutting in towards goal and taking a shot—with fairly good results. Then I decided to alter my style. The books that I had been reading and a study of my own past games brought me to the conclusion that a winger would be better employed making scoring openings for the centre-forward and inside men instead of trying to do the scoring himself. The more I thought about this matter the more convinced I became that I was right. Having made up my mind, I altered my style immediately— with the season barely a month old. I had previously always been marked by the full back, and I thought that this change would give me more freedom and I could collect balls from deep in my own half.

As we went further into the playing season my altered style paid big dividends. The other forwards began to score more goals, and after watching the goals steadily increase I knew in my heart that I had found the style of football to play for the rest of my football life. I have never altered it. This new style enabled me to add several new approaches down the wing, and the forwards could take up their positions in the goalmouth and wait for my centre. One of my favourite moves was to take the ball as near to the deadline as possible, then trick the full-back and centre the ball; from this position it was impossible for any of our forward line to be off-side, and when the ball reached the goalmouth it was always exciting for me to witness the hectic scrambles to get the ball into the net—and to keep the ball out. This change of style brought my critics screaming round my head. They said that when I took the ball to within a few feet of the goal-line I was wasting time and allowing the defence to cover up. They didn't say that it also allowed my forwards to get set for the pass, that I couldn't send an off-side pass from this position, and, most important of all, that I always had about three defenders around me, trying to get the ball. They were therefore not in the goalmouth when the ball went over, and that is why the goals came so easily. My critics were wrong. I dribbled to get on top of the defence, hoping to shake the confidence of my opponents, and once I had the opposition in two minds the path was clear to make endless openings for my colleagues. Others said I didn't get "stuck in". If to earn a living at football I had to trip a man, kick his ankle, use my elbow to get the ball, I would never have made it a career.

Be that as it may, I was rapidly making a bigger name for myself. I was getting results; and the bigger the results, the more I practised. Then, human nature being what it is, the tide turned, and the sports writers said it was time I was back in the England team. I didn't take much notice of that because England was blessed with a number of very good outside-rights, and I knew that the selectors' confidence in me had not been restored. My twenty-second birthday came and went, and one day in April I read in the paper that I had been chosen to play for England against Scotland at Hampden Park, Scotland, on the 17th April, 1937. My father-in-law, Jimmy Vallance (who was a Scot) said, "Congratulations, Stanley. But when you get there watch out for that Hampden roar; it's worth two goals start any day."

The next day Stoke was in an uproar, because, apart from my being chosen to play for England at outside-right, two of my colleagues had also been chosen in the forward line. Freddie Steele, our centre-forward, was picked to play at centre-forward for England, and also our outside-left, Joe Johnson, was selected for the outside-left position in the England team. Three Stoke forwards in the England forward line! It was enough to make any town proud. The newsmen got busy, and the days that followed were very hectic indeed. There was a young brilliant Scot playing left full-back for Preston North End; his name was Andrew Beattie. He had been selected to play in the left full-back position in the Scottish team at Hampden Park. This was Beattie's début in a Hampden game and I was opposing him for the first time. He was destined to play for his country for many years. As far as I was concerned, he was the player I had to overcome; and, judging by his record, I would have my work cut out to do so. Therefore I knew that in this vital game I would not be playing against a pushover. I was determined to get the better of him, and in the days prior to the match I weighed Andrew Beattie up from all angles and laid my plans. In doing this I suddenly realized how much my mental outlook had changed since my last international. I wasn't in the least bit worried but prepared myself for the coming tussle with Beattie, knowing that he would pull out everything he had to stop me getting past him. The newspapers, of course, made the most of this coming struggle, but when they phoned me for my opinion I just said "No comment" and went ahead with my training.

After breakfast on the day of the match the England team gathered in a private room in their Scottish hotel and were briefed for the match. We were told to swing the ball from wing to wing and to make a gap down the middle for Freddie Steele, our centre-forward. When we reached the ground and entered our dressing-room I looked round at the faces of the various players. I could see that some of them were feeling the strain; my pre-match feeling this time was to get on the field as soon as possible. I had a touch of "butterflies" in the stomach, but I didn't feel as nervous as I had before. The teams that day were— SCOTLAND: Dawson (Rangers); Anderson (Hearts), Beattie (Preston North End); Massie (Aston Villa), Simpson (Rangers), Brown (Rangers); Delaney (Celtic), Walker (Hearts), O'Donnell, F. (Preston North End), McPhail (Rangers), Duncan (Derby County). ENGLAND: Woodley (Chelsea); Male (Arsenal), Barkas (Manchester City); Britton (Everton), Young (Huddersfield Town), Bray (Manchester City); Matthews (Stoke City),

Carter (Sunderland), Steele (Stoke City), Starling (Aston Villa), Johnson (Stoke City).

We received the call to take to the field. I ran towards the tunnel with the rest of the players. When I walked on to the Hampden turf for the first time in my life, I took one look around the ground and stopped dead in my tracks. The noise from the crowd was terrific, but the people! There were 149,407 people in that ground that day, the biggest crowd I had ever seen in my life. For a moment it unnerved me, and I felt like turning round and running off the field again. What a sight, and what a sensation it gave you. However, as I took part in the kick-around before the match started I regained my composure, and when we lined up in our playing position waiting for the starting whistle I looked down-field at Andrew Beattie. Then the whistle went and I heard the Hampden roar for the first time. It sounded like a tearing hurricane, and I felt as if I was going to be suddenly picked up off the playing pitch and flung into its roaring jaws. Then, from the left wing, I received a sweeping pass from Starling; the ball landed at my feet, I brought it under control, and made off down the wing. I saw Beattie on his way out to meet me. As if by magic the roar ceased, indeed there was an uncanny silence. Was it because the crowd sensed that in a few seconds they would know the answer to all those newspaper articles— *Could Beattie master Matthews?* I remember my brain going icy cold; it ticked over almost without my help as the distance between Beattie and myself lessened. Beattie came at me, but I couldn't see his face; my eyes were on the ball and then on his feet. I quickly feinted to the left; he went the same way, and before he could regain his balance I vanished from his sight to his right and centred the ball towards the goal. There was a mad scramble in the goalmouth, and Dawson, the Scottish goalkeeper, emerged holding the ball, which he thankfully booted upfield. I trotted back upfield feeling fine. I had won the first tussle, and for the rest of the afternoon Beattie could only chase my shadow.

The game continued to sway from one end of the field to the other, both sides playing good clean football, then five minutes before half-time our after-breakfast briefing paid off. The Scottish defence were having a hard time dealing with our wing-

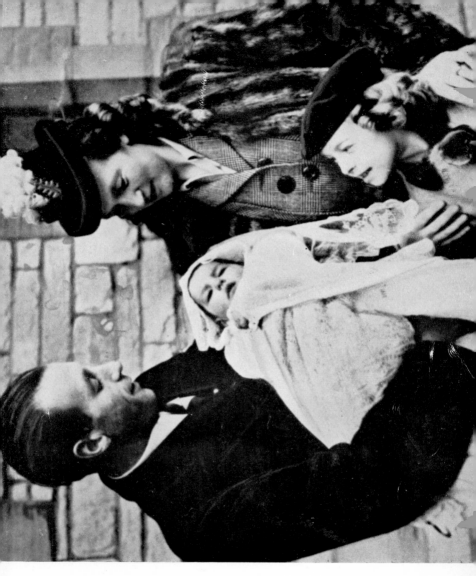

Stanley Matthews holds his baby son after the christening ceremony. With him is his wife Betty and their daughter, Jean. (March 1946.)

Arthur Hallas

The Lord Mayor of Stoke-on-Trent, Mr. Percy Williams, presenting the illuminated address in recognition of the author's forty-four appearances for England, in the Town Hall on the 29th March, 1946.

Daily Express

to-wing passes, and as they left the middle to chase Starling he slipped the ball to Joe Johnson, who immediately passed to Freddie Steele, unmarked in the centre. Steele banged the ball into the back of the net, and we walked off the field at half-time a very happy set of men. The England team had played exceptionally well in this first half. George Male, the England captain, and Alf Young were light-hearted during the interval; indeed we all felt very pleased with ourselves, and thought we had the Scots well weighed up. We took to the field for the second half full of confidence. We had, however, underestimated the fighting spirit of Scotland; but the biggest mistake we made was in underestimating the Hampden roar. If ever a match was won and lost by the roar it was this game. As soon as we started the second half that roar started and never stopped until the end of the game. Believe me, a roar from 149,407 people is some noise indeed. You could say that it injected itself into the veins of those Scottish players and within minutes they were playing like supermen. The game had only been on two minutes when Tommy Walker, the Scottish inside-right, seized on a pass from the wing, cut in towards goal and slipped the ball to O'Donnell, who scored a lovely goal. The roar gained in volume after this goal, and I am afraid that it shook the confidence of some of our players. When, twelve minutes from time, Bob McPhail beat our goalie, Vic Woodley, from fifteen yards out the game was as good as over. I tried with everything I had to get the ball into the goalmouth; and although the England team made a last desperate rally, we finally had to admit defeat when, three minutes from the end, McPhail headed a third goal, to make the score Scotland 3, England 1. We left the field a well-beaten side.

Yet we had outplayed the Scots in the first half. Even the Scottish journalists considered England to be a little unlucky, and some declared it was the best England eleven seen at Hampden Park for years. I knew that I had done my best and was satisfied with my play; the rest of the team also had nothing to feel ashamed about. Collectively we thought the Hampden roar had beaten us. I returned home a happy man; I had fought my way back, and the English papers next day had nothing but praise for the England team.

c

CHAPTER VII

I ASK FOR A TRANSFER

Two or three weeks after the Hampden international match the
season came to an end. It was holiday time again, and I spent
most of the summer with Betty playing golf. Betty had always
been a good golfer, and under her watchful eye I had played
myself down to a moderate handicap. I found that the walking
that was entailed in the game and the fresh air on the country
courses agreed with me, so I was feeling pretty fit when the time
came for me to report for the opening of the 1937–38 season. I
made a good start with the Stoke City team, and the England
selectors must have thought that I was in good form because they
selected me to play in the England team against Wales at Middlesbrough on November 17th, 1937. England won 2–1. I was
selected again to play for England against Czechoslovakia at
Tottenham on December 1st, 1937. England won that game
5–4. Then I was selected to play against Scotland at Wembley
on April 9th, 1938. Scotland won 1–0.

I had nothing to grumble at with three international caps in one
season. The season had hardly started before I realized that I had
become a real football celebrity. I started to get terrific publicity
in the national papers, and this brought in its wake requests for
my photograph from fans in all parts of the British Isles. Betty
had to give me a helping hand to deal with this mail, and the
photographs and stationery and stamps made me dig deep into
my not-too-well-lined pockets. Film and stage celebrities have
fantastic salaries, but a footballer's weekly wage in those days
was about equivalent to what a star of the stage or films spent on
one good meal. So I soon found out that now, although I was
where I always wanted to be, I could hardly afford to stay there.
Another aspect was that I almost lost my private life. People

always seemed to be ringing me up or calling round at the house—the poor old teapot never got a chance to cool off! I also found out that I couldn't speak my mind as freely as before. I had to be so careful, or else I got this—"As I was saying I bumped into Stan the other day, and he said that . . ." And you all know how words can take on a different meaning when repeated. Yes, it didn't take me long to find out the price of fame; but Betty and I sorted it out between us, and in time it ceased to worry us. We found that being at all times natural and normal was most of the answer, and the rest was just plain tact. In these early days of fame I ran into a heap of trouble which was not of my making. Around the latter part of November a rumour quickly spread around the city that bad feeling had developed between myself and one or two of the players. This was quite untrue; we were a very happy team. I was pulled up time and time again by people who should have known better, to ask me if it was true. I am by nature a peace-loving man, I don't like trouble of any kind, and I would be the last man in the world to cause trouble in my own camp. After a time the rumour seemed to simmer down, but it left a nasty taste in my mouth.

Early in January I began to feel restless and disgruntled; perhaps it was the rumour about the team, perhaps every young man gets this feeling at some time or other. I do know, however, that on February 8th, just a week after my twenty-third birthday, on my way to the ground for training I suddenly made up my mind to ask for a transfer and start a new life with some other club in a different part of the country. Without a word to anyone, I approached the directors the same day, thinking my request would be granted without difficulty. How wrong I was; and if I could have seen into the future, wild horses wouldn't have dragged me before the directors to ask for my release. It was the first and last time I have ever asked for a transfer. Mr. Booth and his board invited me to meet them and discuss the reasons for my request. I did so. I told them that I was not happy at Stoke, that I was browned-off and wanted a change of atmosphere, adding very firmly that my request had nothing to do with the rumour in the city that there was bad blood between me and some of my colleagues in the Stoke team. After a full hour's discussion the board, much to my surprise, refused to accept my request until I had given the matter more careful consideration. I left the board-room and made my way home. I told Betty of my decision to leave Stoke. She was upset, but she didn't try to force me to change my mind. She said it was my own affair, and what I did would be all right with her.

The next morning my transfer request was in all the news-papers, and I couldn't move in the streets on my way to the ground without getting involved in arguments that didn't always concern me. When I arrived at the ground I asked for leave of absence, which the directors granted me for a few days. I hurried back home. Betty gave me a surprised look and ex-claimed, "Whatever's the matter, Stanley?" I hurriedly explained the situation. Her face cleared. I said, "Look, Betty. I think we had better get away from Stoke for a day or so until this thing dies down." She nodded and said, "Yes, I think that's a very good idea. Where shall we go?" I said, "What about Blackpool? It's a town we have never visited, and nobody knows me there, so we should get some peace. Get some things packed whilst I get the car fixed up." An hour later we were leaving our house; but before we left the town I decided to call on my father and mother and let them know what was happening. My mother welcomed us, and I said, "Is Father in?" Mother said, "Yes. He should be down at the shop, but he's just getting ready to go to your house to see Betty and ask her what you are playing at." My heart sank.

As we entered the living-room my father was just finishing putting on his tie. He looked relieved to see me and said, "Thank goodness you've come round. Now what's all this fuss about, son?" I explained fully to my parents what the position between the club and myself was. There was silence for a few seconds, then my mother said, "Sit down for a minute. I'll go and make a pot of tea." Betty followed her into the kitchen. My father walked over to the fireplace and stood with his back to the fire. He said, "Well, I hope you know what you are doing, son. I am sure they will never let you go." I said, "I don't see why not, Father. I haven't got a grudge against the club, and they haven't anything against me. I feel it will be a good thing for me to have a change." My father walked over to the table and sat down, then he said, "Look, son. I know how you feel, and I'm with you all the way. You are twenty-three years old, so you are old enough to make your own mind up about your future life—*but don't you realize what value you are to your club?* You are one of the biggest footballing names in the country, so try to think what you must be worth in extra gate money alone to Stoke City. You are a star attraction. They won't let you go for all the tea in China, and I can't say I blame them." "I can't see it like that, Father. It's a free country, and I am entitled to play where I like, providing everything is on the level." My father said, "Don't get me wrong, son. I'm not trying to give you advice; I'm looking at the matter from a layman's point of view—and you can take it from me the people of Stoke and Hanley will have something to say, just you mark my words. You see, son, you are not your own boss, you belong to the people now. If I packed my bags and left Hanley to-morrow, nobody would bother; but you will walk out into a packet of trouble. But you'll sort it out, and sort it out in the right way, so I'm not worried about it. You'd better get off to Blackpool before the storm breaks."

Half an hour later Betty and I left the house, and I pointed the nose of the car in the direction of Blackpool. I was a worried man; my father had upset me with his talk of trouble. We arrived in Blackpool early that evening and booked in at a modest hotel. After we had settled in and enjoyed a good meal Betty and I had a stroll along the famous promenade. As it was my first visit to this world-famous seaside resort I was very interested in exploring. I found that the air was wholesome and clean. Furthermore, as we walked around the town unnoticed by passers-by we both felt much better and more relaxed. As we passed the famous Tower I stopped and spent several minutes gazing up at it, with a feeling of awe; it looked so big, and powerful, and commanding, yet at the same time it had a friendly look, as if inviting you to step inside, to view the wonderful things it had to offer you. If it had not been out of season, I am sure I would have gone in; instead we retraced our steps back to the hotel.

At breakfast the next morning my troubles started with a vengeance. The daily newspapers had my name plastered all over the front page. It seemed that the Stoke paper, *The Evening Sentinel*, had headlined that I was not happy at Stoke. Within a few hours of the paper reaching the streets seven leading industrialists of the town had got together and decided to call a public protest meeting in the King's Hall on the following Monday. Also they had bills printed which read "STANLEY MATTHEWS MUST NOT GO!" and had them posted on hoardings all over Stoke and Hanley. I read the news with a sinking heart. Soon after breakfast the phone started to ring. Reporters from London were after me—my Blackpool trip was doomed to failure. The phone never stopped ringing, and I had thought it would be peaceful in Blackpool! By now all Blackpool knew I was in their town. Anyway, Betty and I left the phone ringing and got out in the fresh air, but when we arrived back at the hotel for lunch it started all over again. One message decided what I must do. It was a message stating that Mr. Booth, the Stoke City chairman, wished to see me in private as soon as possible. I turned to Betty and said, "Let's get packed and get home, and get this settled as soon as possible." We did just that. As soon as it was possible I had a private talk with Mr. Booth. I was sure that the directors had changed their minds and that Mr. Booth would tell me I could go on transfer. Instead it was the other way round, and as the conversation progressed between Mr. Booth and myself I could see that there wasn't a chance of my being released. I stuck out for a transfer, so in the end we parted with no progress having been made.

The days that followed were very hectic. Football reporters from London phoned day and night. Some of them made special journeys from London to see me, and Tom Mather, the manager of Newcastle United (who was manager of Stoke when I joined them at seventeen), travelled overnight to Stoke with a blank cheque in his pocket. He was accompanied by Mr. A. G. Stableforth, a director, who was prepared to pay whatever price Stoke might place on my head. It was also rumoured that Everton, Bolton Wanderers, Derby County, Leicester City and Manchester City were interested in obtaining my signature. But the one thing that did touch me was the wonderful support given me by the people of Stoke and Hanley. I knew that I had many friends in the city and town, but I never knew how much they really thought of me and to what lengths they would go to show their appreciation of me. Advertisements were put in the local press, drawing attention to the coming meeting on Monday, and thousands of handbills were given out. The wording on the handbills read:

STANLEY MATTHEWS MUST NOT GO
Public Meeting of Stoke City Supporters
KING'S HALL, STOKE
Monday Next—7.30 p.m.
TO URGE THE RETENTION OF STANLEY MATTHEWS

As the day of the meeting drew near, some of the industrialists claimed that the controversy was undermining output in the potteries, and the sooner it was settled the better, otherwise the life of the city would be disrupted. I was amazed to see what a transfer request could do to people. On the night of the meeting three thousand Stoke City fans attended, and more than a thousand, who could not get inside the hall, paraded the street demanding I should not leave Stoke. I just couldn't believe my own eyes, but it was true, I saw the parade. It was decided at this meeting, presided over by Mr. Ashley Myott, chairman of the Wages and Conditions Committee of the British Manufacturers' Federation, that a deputation should meet the Stoke directors and myself at separate meetings. This was carried out. On February 15th, 1938, the directors announced they had declined to accept my request, which meant I would have to finish the season out. However, I had by this time had more than enough, and, swayed by the warmth of my own townsfolk and the manner in which they had taken my interests to heart, the difficulties between the directors and myself were overcome and I agreed to stay, which I did for a further nine happy years.

I walked home very slowly after I had made my mind up to stay with Stoke. Betty and my mother and father were there. I said, "Well, it's all settled: I'm staying. And I'll never ask for a transfer again. I wouldn't go through that lot again for a million pounds." I meant every word of it. I saw the three faces that I loved more than anything else in the world take on a new appearance. It was then I realized how much they had been troubled and worried on my account. I sat down on the nearest chair, and turning to my mother I said, "What about making one of your special brews of tea, Mother? I could do with a cup." My mother and Betty both laughed and made for the kitchen. I looked at my father and said, "Never again, Dad. Never again." I slept as sound as a log that night, and woke in the morning like a giant refreshed; it felt good to be alive again. As I made my way to the ground to train I saw smiling faces everywhere. It made me feel good to be at peace with them.

．　　　．　　　．　　　．　　　．

Not long after the international match against Scotland at Wembley, when Scotland beat us 1–0, the team to tour the Continent was announced. I didn't try to cover up my joy and delight on hearing that I had been selected. I had never been out of my native land before, so it was thrilling to think that I was to have an opportunity to see other countries and their people, whilst getting paid for doing so. Betty was delighted with my good fortune, and we spent some happy hours together, getting my things packed up for the big adventure. At last the time arrived for me to join the team. Betty came to the station to see me off, and as the time for the train's arrival drew very near a silence grew between us. This would be the first time we had been parted for any length of time since our marriage. Whilst we were thinking our own thoughts the train drew in and then we both began to talk at the same time—now the time had come to part there seemed so much to tell each other. After saying good-bye to Betty and promising to write at regular intervals I boarded the train, and as it steamed slowly out of the station I leaned out of the carriage window and waved. My first trip to the Continent had started.

The time was, of course, only a few months before the Munich crisis, Hitler was making regular speeches to the German people, and the whole of Europe was in a state of fear. Mussolini was giving his partner in crime his whole support. The small countries were being insulted and bullied, and the word "Sudetenland" was on the tip of every tongue in the world as the dictators of Germany and Italy, with ice in their hearts, planned the downfall of Czechoslovakia. Our first match was in Berlin on the 14th of May, when England would meet the best footballers Germany could produce, who at this very moment were training hard in the Black Forest. The England players on their way to meet them had only just finished a hard football season in Britain. As the train rattled along the down-line to Euston Station I had two dominant thoughts in my mind. The first was the Tottenham football ground nearly three years ago when I had first played against the Germans, and my bad performance there. The second was a German left full-back by the name of Muenzenberg. I was looking forward to meeting him. I found myself licking my lips in anticipation of our second meeting.

We arrived in Berlin two days before the match was due to be played and were given a sober welcome. I was fascinated with my new surroundings and enjoyed every minute of it, everything was so different. At the first opportunity I went off on a sightseeing tour with Bert Sproston, who played at that time for Leeds United. Bert and I went into a small café for a cup of tea, and I was just sipping mine when all the other diners made a rush for the door. I looked at Bert and said, "I expect some big cheese is passing." Bert said, "Yes, it must be someone of importance, judging by the rumpus." We continued with our tea-drinking. A tall German who was standing near the door must have overheard us; he turned to us smiling, and in perfect English said softly, "You underestimate the importance of the occasion. Our beloved Führer has just passed by." He spoke as if he were talking about God. Before I left Germany I was fully convinced that the whole of the German people thought Hitler *was* a god. At the same time I must say now that throughout my stay in Germany I didn't meet one German who showed any hostile feelings towards me or towards the rest of the England players. In fact everybody we came in contact with seemed to go out of their way to be nice to us.

As the match drew near, it became quite clear to us that the Nazis wanted to win this match more than anything else in the world. The England team realized also that there was more at stake than just a game of football. In this match, as never before, we would be playing for England. We met the German team on the eve of the match. They looked like a bunch of bronzed Greek statues. The best food and the finest physical culture experts in Germany had done a good job in the Black Forest. Every one of the German players appeared to be in first-class condition. The German footballers and the Nazi officials laughed a lot that night. By comparison, the England players were very quiet, and we must have looked pretty well washed up as we stood amongst the Germans. Perhaps that was why they laughed so much. I spent most of my time looking at Muenzenberg, who had blotted me out in the match on the Spurs' ground three years before, and thought he looked a little older; but I was three years older myself. As I looked at him I made a silent vow that, come what may, he wouldn't repeat his success in the game the next day; somehow I would be the master this time. Before I went to bed that night I posted a letter to Betty telling her of my hopes for the match. I felt better when I had done this and I got into bed to enjoy a good night's sleep.

We arrived at the huge Olympic Stadium in Berlin and found it packed with 110,000 Germans. It is one of the finest arenas in which I have ever played, and the turf—well, it was all a footballer could wish for. Our dressing-room was situated at the top of a huge stand and it took us several minutes to get to our room; we had to climb up hundreds of steps to reach it, and I do mean hundreds. However, we treated the climb up and down—six times in all—as a great joke, thus upsetting any plan the Germans may have had for upsetting us. Laughing together like a bunch of schoolboys, we started to change into our football gear. It was then, and then only, that we got rattled for the very first time. Just before the kick-off an F.A. official came into our room to wish us luck. He also gave us an instruction that wiped all the smiles off our faces, and indeed it made us drop everything and gather round him in alarm and dismay. He said, "It has been decided that both teams will line up in front of the distinguished visitors' box. When our national anthem is played the German team will salute; so in order to get the crowd friendly towards you we want you to give the Nazi salute during the playing of the German national anthem." For a few seconds we stood round the official and just looked at him, then bedlam broke loose. As I glanced at the tense faces of the England team, all talking and shouting at the same time, my thoughts flew back home to Stoke and Hanley. What would my family and townsfolk say if they saw a photograph of me giving the Nazi salute? My mind went numb. I glanced round the room again and a deep sense of fear entered my heart. I thought, *This is the end of the match—before it has begun.* I could see that the thought of saluting Hitler and his thugs didn't appeal to the rest of the boys any more than it did to me, and they were in many cases telling the official so in no uncertain language. When the first stages of our anger had died down the F.A. official spoke again. He said that the F.A. was in close touch with Sir Nevile Henderson, the then British Ambassador to Berlin, and that in many ways we ourselves were ambassadors for England that day. He also pointed out that the international situation was so sensitive at this time that it needed only a spark to set Europe alight. Furthermore, he said that when the British athletic team had given the "eyes right" salute at the Olympic Games in Berlin, in 1936, many Germans took it as a deliberate snub. Then panic set in when it was discovered there was only a few minutes left before we were due to take to the field. What should we do? At the last moment I am glad to say that traditional British common sense came to our rescue, and we all promised to conform to the F.A. directive.

When, a few minutes later, we followed our captain, Hapgood, on to the field the Germans gave us a good welcome, but the roar that greeted the Germans as they took the field made our welcome sound like breeze in summer-time. As we lined up for the national anthems the crowd grew silent, and it was then I heard, along with the rest of the English team, a few pipy voices from behind the goal call out "Let 'em have it, England!" It came from a small band of Englishmen on holiday in Germany. If any of them should at any time read this book, I want them to know that those few words of encouragement did wonders for the

English team; they also did a good deed for England that day. As the anthems were being played my eyes took in the sight before me. It was most impressive. Goebbels, Hess and Göring, who were sitting in the distinguished visitors' box, must have enjoyed the scene. The huge stadium was dotted with thousands of blazing-red swastikas and a meagre half a dozen Union Jacks. We lined up for the kick-off, and I can safely say that the one thought in all the England players' hearts was to win this game.

I knew by all the talk I had heard whilst in Germany that my growing reputation as a winger had reached German football circles, and I knew also that they still didn't think I was a match for their left full-back Muenzenberg. When the ball came out to me on the wing I knew the testing time had arrived. I got the ball under control and made off down the wing. Glancing up, I saw Muenzenberg coming towards me with the same look on his face that he had worn three years ago. It was in fact a replica of that moment. Everything was quiet, the crowd seemed to sense that this was a moment worth seeing. As I raced forward with the ball at my feet I could almost feel the good wishes the rest of the England players were sending me. I arrived within a few feet of Muenzenberg. He ran at me. I disappeared from his view with the ball still at my feet. It wasn't until I had centred the ball goalwards that I realized that I had beaten him more easily than I had dared to anticipate; then I realized that he had slowed up in the last three years, or perhaps I had got faster. After a few more tussles I found that I was his master, and you can't blame me for feeling jubilant. He caused me no worry for the rest of the match. The rest of the England team were also in fine form, and we gave the Germans something to think about in the interval, with the score standing at England 4, Germany 2. Cliff Bastin, Jackie Robinson, Frankie Broome and I each scored a goal in the first half. I had again found myself with the ball at my feet and the open goal gaping at me as I had done in the last match against Germany; but this time I made no mistake—I booted that ball well and truly into the back of the net. In the second half we continued to give the Nazis a football lesson, and after further goals from Robinson and Goulden, and the Germans replying with one, we ran out easy winners, the final score being England 6, Germany 3.

The one memory I shall always treasure of this day is of a tall, distinguished-looking gentleman stepping into the England dressing-room after the game. "Well played," he said heartily. It was the late Sir Nevile Henderson.

CHAPTER VIII

MY THEORY ON TRAINING RECEIVES A JOLT

PERHAPS it all started in Berlin when Alf Young, the England centre-half, dug his teeth too deeply into the chicken he was eating; the teeth came in contact with a hidden bone and as they were not those which he had been born with they cracked in two. The rest of the team were merciless in the manner they teased Alf Young to make him open his mouth so that he would reveal the absence of his dentures, and I was the worst offender in this respect. Alf's home club was Huddersfield Town, and he was a very likeable chap but very self-conscious. Therefore he did all he could to avoid laughing at us, or with us, but of course he wasn't always successful. Whenever he laughed there was an uproar from his team-mates and poor Alf would dash off to hide himself until things got quiet again.

After our Berlin triumph we had before us a thirteen-hour train journey to Zurich, Switzerland, where we were due to play the Swiss national team at the Hardsturm Stadium on the 21st of May.

The F.A. party had all settled themselves comfortably in the train, which was now on its way to the Swiss border. Then Alf Young sat down next to me, and as I glanced up at him from the book I was reading he gave me a sweet smile. It was a lovely smile. He had his dentures back in his mouth again. He said, "You know, Stan, you're a lucky man. You'll have the time of your life in the match against Switzerland." He paused and looked at me as if he expected me to make a comment. Knowing Alf as I did, I merely nodded and turned my eyes back to my book. Alf, unabashed, went on, "The left full-back in the Swiss team is a dance-band leader called Lehmann; he and his band play till four o'clock in the morning in a night-club in Zurich. They'll have to carry him off the field after he's been chasing you round for half an hour." I dropped my book in my lap and looked at Alf with astonishment. I said, "You're kidding." Alf got on his feet, patted me on the shoulder, and said, "It's on the level, Stan. You'll soon find out for yourself." He walked away with a grin all over his face.

When Alf Young had disappeared from view a babble of conversation broke out amongst the other members of the England team who were in my compartment. I listened to them with both my ears wide open. They seemed to think we were on to a good thing in the coming match. It came out that England had only played Switzerland once before, at Berne in 1933, and had had an easy 4–0 win. This present England team was playing very well indeed and it shouldn't be hard to beat this Swiss team, especially if what Alf Young said was true. But *was* it true? I didn't like this talk, it was overconfident, and football is a funny game. You must be confident, but being overconfident is as bad as being underconfident.

We arrived at Zurich and sorted ourselves out at our hotel. I couldn't get outside quickly enough to see with my own eyes the breathtaking beauty of this lovely country. They had just had thirty hours of continuous rain before we arrived, but everywhere still looked like an enchanting fairyland to me. I was very loth to leave it all when summoned to the hotel for a meal.

In the papers the following morning the Swiss football writers, without exception, said that after the heavy rain the ground would suit the English as the turf was just like it was in England in the winter season. Furthermore, not only the press but the Swiss football fans themselves openly forecast that the England team would win easily.

I was now beginning to agree with them. It was true that the Swiss left full-back was a bandleader. It was true that he was called Lehmann. It was true that he stayed up every night until the early hours of the following morning playing in a night-club. I sought out Alf Young and told him how sorry I was for not believing him when he first told me. On the other hand, I couldn't credit that a man who stayed up half the night could ever make himself fit enough to be selected for an international team. At that stage of my life, after the way I had been brought up on a strict diet of "early to bed, early to rise", I couldn't understand anyone wanting to play football if he worked all through the night. I was looking forward more than ever to running on to the field at the Hardsturm Stadium and meeting this superman in the flesh.

I had finished my private early-morning training and was about to enter the hotel and go to my room to get changed for breakfast. Stopping at the entrance, I looked around me. It was very quiet at that early hour. The scene before me—the towering mountains capped with snow, the quaint cottages dotted here and there, and the peacefulness of it all—made me take in my breath more sharply. I couldn't for the life of me believe at that moment that the world was in a turmoil and on the brink of war.

Hanley looked or seemed so far away. What a lucky young man I was, getting all this for free, and enjoying my work at the same time—and being paid for it! I thought of Betty and wished she was here to enjoy this with me. Suddenly I felt very hungry and I turned into the hotel to get some breakfast. I felt all tuned up. In fact I doubt if at any time in my life I had felt fitter. It is a grand thing to feel like that. Then as I ran up the stairs to my room I suddenly thought about the bandleader—how would he be feeling? A glance at my watch told me that he wouldn't have finished work by more than three hours.

It was the day of the match. As I was doing full justice to a well-cooked breakfast I noticed that the prevailing talk amongst the English party breakfasting near me was very light-hearted. I thought what a difference it was from the morning of the match in Berlin a short while ago. Then the breakfast conversation had been forced and taut; in fact everybody had been on edge until we had knocked the German team for six. Here, however, everybody seemed relaxed, and the match we had to play that day might have been a friendly. After breakfast I settled in a corner and read the papers. They all said England would win easily. They also said that a big crowd was expected and that the weather should be ideal for the game.

In the England dressing-room before the match the players were in a jovial mood. I remember thinking at the time that I had never seen an international team take the field in such a light-hearted manner. The excited Swiss crowd gave us an unexpected welcome as they saw us run out on to the springy turf. It did our hearts good to hear the roar they set up; it equalled the roar they gave the Swiss team when they appeared. We lined up for the kick-off, and it was then that I saw bandleader Lehmann. I thought he looked a pleasant enough chap.

Glancing towards the centre of the field, I saw there was no ball on the centre spot. Then we heard the drone of an aeroplane over the excited shouting of the Swiss spectators. A plane came in low over the ground, and the pilot dropped the ball spot on the field. This was a novel way to start a match. The referee blew on his whistle, the game was on, and how that crowd roared!

We started off in grand style but couldn't get the ball into the net. Then I received the ball and made off down the wing. I looked up and saw that I was going to have to pass Lehmann for the first time. I passed him quite easily. For the first twenty minutes or so I was able to trot round Lehmann as I liked. *This will be a rout*, I thought; *it will even put the Berlin score in the shade.*

The England team were playing with the utmost confidence, and each player must have been thinking that it was only a matter of time before the goals started to mount up. Suddenly a change came over the game. We had been playing almost half an hour without scoring a goal; then, dead on the half-hour, Aeby, the Swiss outside-left, came out of nowhere and headed a goal.

The terrific roar the Swiss spectators set up had to be heard to be believed, but before the echo of that roar came back from the mountains and died away Jackie Robinson (Sheffield Wednesday) was brought down in the penalty area. The England team sighed with relief when Cliff Bastin (Arsenal) scored from the spot-kick and levelled the score to 1–1. Then the fiery enthusiasts in the red shirts of Switzerland really got to work. They tore into us like a pack of wolves who had been without food for two or three weeks.

Lehmann, instead of going to sleep as I had been led to expect, came to life and quickly got my measure. He had been thinking things out. For one thing, he suddenly developed the staying power of a Marathon runner. Secondly, he was running about the field like quicksilver. Thirdly, he never let me get the ball at all; he seemed to anticipate all the passes that came my way, and bounded up and whipped the ball away from my toes before I could get a touch of it. He was still galloping about the field like a racehorse at half-time. I could only stare at him; it was unbelievable.

In the England dressing-room at half-time everybody was much quieter; they were thankful to ease their limbs and get their breath back. I walked over to Alf Young and said, "If that chap really stays up to four o'clock in the morning, I suggest we recommend similar training methods for the England team. He's killing me."

Alf Young smiled, but that was all—he had more than his hands full watching Bickel, Switzerland's elusive centre-forward.

We took to the field for the second half in a much quieter mood. We realized that we would have to go all out to win this match. When the match re-started we tore into the Swiss team with everything we had, but the red shirts stood firm and sent attack after attack back upfield. We were now up against it. I could do nothing against Lehmann. Not only did he look after me, he also found time to sprint to the other side of the field to lend a hand to Minelli at right-back. Talk about falling for the leader of the band! I have treated bandleaders with great respect since that match. Disaster hit us twenty minutes from the end. Alf Young bent forward to meet a centre from the right wing with his chest; the ball bounced a yard in front of him, rose awkwardly on the treacherous surface, and struck his arm. There were excited shouts of "penalty" from the Swiss players and crowd. Cheering broke out when the long-legged and cycle-breeched German referee, Dr. Bauwens, pointed to the spot. Dismay swept through the England team when Abegglen, the inside-left and veteran of the side, took the kick and placed it out of Woodley's reach.

Try as we would after this penalty, we could do nothing against this Swiss side; they played like demons, never letting up for a second, and when, at last, the final whistle went we had to admit something we had strived hard to avoid—defeat.

Although the awarding of the penalty by Dr. Bauwens caused a tremendous controversy for weeks afterwards, it would not be fair to deny the Swiss a victory hard fought for and thoroughly deserved.

It is a match I shall always remember, in more ways than one. It gave me great pleasure to shake Lehmann by the hand at the close of the game, but I am afraid I had to turn down his invitation to hear his band. I should think, however, it must have been a most excellent one, with a leader as dynamic as he in front of it. If I had accepted his invitation and sat up in a night-club until 4 a.m. it would have put me out of my stride for months.

I felt sorry when the time arrived for us to leave Switzerland. The people were kind and friendly and most generous. We were due in Paris to play France on the 26th of May.

On the journey to Paris I found the ever-changing scenery absorbing and full of interest, and although it was quite a long journey the time never dragged. Our party, however, was in a much quieter mood. The defeat at the hands of the Swiss had shaken us all up, and we knew that the French team was supposed to be a much stronger side than the Swiss one. As soon as we entered Paris the atmosphere of this world-famous city got me. The city has a special something of its own. It didn't take me long to get out and about, and I saw with my own eyes all the famous sights that I had only read about until then. I wrote Betty a long letter on my impressions. I liked Paris very much.

Of the match itself there is little I can write about. We prepared for it without frills and fuss and regained most of our lost prestige by running out comfortable winners, with the score England 4, France 2. This game brought the tour to a close.

With the tour at an end I suddenly felt homesick. I felt I couldn't get home quickly enough. Whilst I had work to do I never thought about anything else except to write home, but as soon as the work was completed and all tied up, my one thought was to get home, which I suppose is only natural. I was soon on the home train at Euston Station in London. It wouldn't be long now. It didn't take long really; but to me, looking at my watch every five minutes, it seemed every bit as long as the longest continental train journey I had ever taken.

At long last we drew into Stoke Station and I was looking out of the window. I spotted Betty and my mother and father waiting for me on the platform. I shouted to them. They came running towards my compartment. We talked all the way home. Later, when we were alone, I said to Betty once more, "I wish you could have been with me instead of being here where nothing ever happens. You would have enjoyed it." Betty smiled, then she said, "Oh, I wouldn't say that, Stanley. Something wonderful has happened whilst you have been away." I looked at her with bewilderment in my face. "What do you mean by that, Betty?" She smiled and said, "I'm going to have a baby."

CHAPTER IX

AT HOME AND HAMPDEN PARK

THE world was full of trouble during the summer of 1938. Hitler was leading everybody up the garden path. The greatest politicians in the world were trying to make sense of it all, but to no avail. So by the end of July that year war-talk was on everyone's lips.

Under those circumstances it may seem odd that I was feeling happy. It was a lovely summer, the weather was perfect. Betty and I were contented, looking forward to the birth of our baby at the end of the year.

Somehow I just couldn't believe there would be a war, and after Mr. Chamberlain's return from Munich with the little piece of white paper that he and Hitler had signed tucked away in his pocket, I said to myself, "There, what did I tell you." Indeed, after the return of Mr. Chamberlain the people of Britain seemed to change overnight. Spirits rose, war-talk ceased, and the average man found his main interest was the start of the 1938–39 football season. The crisis was over.

The season started during the war scare, but only a few weeks had gone by before things settled down. I was happy with the Stoke City team by the time the public's interest returned to their most popular winter sport.

I had played in all the international matches in the 1937–38 season, and now I was looking forward to being selected (if thought worthy of that honour) for the England team to meet Ireland, at Old Trafford, Manchester, on November 16th, in the current season. But I was selected to play for the Football League against the Scottish League at Wolverhampton just a week before the international match against Ireland was due to be played.

I played in the Football League match at Wolverhampton, and my partner at inside-right was Willie Hall of Tottenham Hotspur. I had a good game because the ball ran for me all through the game, and I was able to get centre after centre goalwards with good effect. Willie Hall and myself said good-bye after the game and I returned to Stoke thinking what a grand footballer and what a nice chap Willie was.

I returned to the house after my early-morning training next day, had breakfast, then picked up the papers to read what the writers had to say about the previous day's game. I was just sipping some tea when I turned to the first sports page. What I saw there made me swallow the tea too hastily and I had a coughing bout. Betty flew in from the kitchen and slapped me on the back. She said in alarm, "Whatever is the matter?" I managed to stop coughing, and with a look of utter disgust on my face I tossed the paper to Betty, at the same time saying, "Read that out loud, Betty." She looked at the heading in large type, then read it out loud—"Matthews starves Hall out of England team." Her mouth remained open for a second, then she turned to me and said, "What do they mean, Stanley?" I got up from my chair and walked over to the window; I felt sick. It was raining outside. I stood still, watching the raindrops hit against the windowpane, gather together, and run down the window. Betty was talking to me from behind but I couldn't make out what she was saying. Why do papers print things that are not true? Why did anyone accuse me of starving a player on purpose? Betty gave me a cup of tea. "Here," she said, "drink this, then tell me all about it." I took the tea-cup and sat down. "This is terrible, Betty. They are accusing me of ignoring Willie Hall in yesterday's match. In view of the coming international match in Manchester next week, it looks as if I was trying to spoil his chances of being selected for the England team. It's not true! Why, after the match Willie and I left the best of friends. Besides, nothing was said in the dressing-room after the match. You see, each game is different. Sometimes the ball runs one way and sometimes the other, and you play your game accordingly. I wonder what Willie Hall is thinking at this moment?" Betty told me not to worry, but at the same time I could see that the news had upset her as well. Willie had always been a good friend; he would be the last man I would starve out of a game.

I looked at my watch: I should have been on my way to the ground over ten minutes ago. I hurried out of the house.

When I arrived at the ground my team mates took the matter up with me, and, to make it worse, all the papers more or less said the same thing—I had starved Willie Hall in yesterday's game. It was with much misery that I got through that day.

The day for the selection of the England team for the match against Ireland came, and I waited for the news just as eagerly as I had done in the past when I was a youth; then I heard that Willie Hall had been selected as my partner again in the international match at Manchester. A great weight fell from my shoulders, I could have shouted out with relief and joy. Most of all, I made up my mind that, come what may, Willie would not be neglected this time if I could help it. If Willie had not been selected I dread to think what the result would have been; the papers would most certainly have made a big issue out of it. I hadn't starved him out of the England team, he had now been selected. I walked home to tea a happy man once more.

I met Willie Hall again when I joined the England team. We didn't discuss the incident, but I discovered later that Willie was as surprised as I at the press allegations, and he certainly didn't bear me any ill-feeling. In fact he suggested that we should be room-mates on the eve of our date with Ireland. This put a definite end to any remaining rumours.

When Willie and I retired to our room to get a good night's sleep on the eve of the match we chatted together, but at no time did we mention the subject of my starving him out of the match at Wolverhampton. Nor—and this is very important in view of what happened the very next day—did we discuss any tactics on how to beat the Ireland defence. We just chatted about things in general, then, when we were settled in our respective beds, turned off the lights and said good-night. I fell asleep almost at once.

I was awake early next morning. I got up and did my breathing exercises, then left the hotel for a sharp walk. When I returned I joined Willie for breakfast.

In the England dressing-room before the match everything and everybody was under control; we left the tunnel and ran on to the field to the roar of the packed stadium. The whistle blew and the match was on. I knew in my mind that all eyes would be on Hall and Matthews, to see what would happen in this match. We soon put all doubts to rest. Willie Hall never put a foot wrong all the afternoon, he was magnificent.

The understanding he developed with me was uncanny. He knew when to run on the outside, when to slip forward, and when to stand still. This time I couldn't blame anyone for saying we had stayed up half the night plotting our moves, because it looked as if we had done just that. I also could do nothing wrong. The ball ran for me all through the match. The passes I received were always just right and at the right speed.

I felt sorry for Billy Cook, the Irish and Everton left-back. He was a very dapper man and a great full-back. Willie Hall and I drove him to distraction that afternoon. He did everything he knew to stop us but failed. I can understand how he must have felt. That afternoon Willie, besides claiming an England scoring record with five goals, must have also registered the fastest hat-trick in international football. He scored three goals in three and a half minutes.

It was a great comfort to me, in view of the criticism levelled against me the previous week, to know that I had supplied four of the passes that went towards Hall's goals. Yes, this was Willie Hall's day of triumph, his finest international; and indeed, although I must regard it as my finest international as well as Willie's, I like to think about it as my happiest. My happiest because Willie and I, together, proved to all football fans that there never had been trouble between us.

About halfway through the second half of this match I was taking the ball past Billy Cook once more. As I passed him, with the ball still at my feet, he called out, "Stan, if you bring that ball near me once more I'll wring your neck, so help me I will." I nearly ruined my centre laughing at the tone of voice he had used. Ten minutes from the end we were six goals up. Ireland hadn't scored.

The crowd stood up and yelled their heads off every time

Willie or I received the ball. They kept yelling for just one more goal. By the way the spectators acted you would have thought that both teams were striving for the winning goal. I was feeling sorry for the Irish team, they seemed demoralized and at a standstill.

Then, just seven minutes from time, I got a pass inside my own half. I suddenly made up my mind to have a shot at goal. I weaved my way down the field through the tired Irish players, passing one, then another, and still another. When I reached the penalty area there was Billy Cook in front of me. Still as game as ever, he came at me in a do-or-die effort, but I eluded him, ran on and slipped the ball into the net through a small space between the far post and Twomey, the Irish and Leeds United goalkeeper.

The scene that followed is difficult to describe. As I turned to run back up the field I saw hats being flung up into the air, hundreds of them; and the noise—well, I think the only way I can describe that is to say that if I had been asleep near a runway and suddenly a jet plane started up, the effect would have been the same. It frightened me.

When the game ended, with the score England 7, Ireland 0, we all shook hands and made for the tunnel. The England team stood back to let Willie take the honours, and what a cheer he got as he ran from the field. Imagine the shock I received when I reached the tunnel entrance to find the volume of cheering gathering force. It struck me as odd that although this was Hall's greatest triumph I should get so much of the cheering. I can only put it down to the fact that I scored the last goal, and that was still fresh in their minds.

Willie Hall had tears in his eyes in the England dressing-room when we all gathered round him and congratulated him on his performance. His style of play was so unassuming—just like Willie himself—that his greatness was not always appreciated. He was one of the best partners, if not the best, I ever had. A grand man both on and off the field. He was, however, not the luckiest of men, for eight years later, in 1946, he lost his right foot as a result of thrombosis, and later had to undergo a further amputation on his left leg. This was a tough blow, and being so disturbed in my mind by his misfortune I went to see him. When we met he was leaning on crutches with some difficulty. I asked him how he was getting on. He replied, "Fine, Stan. Only trouble is that whenever I see a stone or a brick in the street I go to kick it, and find myself doing a thing I never used to do—kicking over the top of the ball." Willie laughed uproariously as he said it.

Although I felt a pang for the great little Spur, I also felt very proud to have played with him in his finest hour. It did me good to see him and taught me a lesson. If I ever begin worrying over trifles I think of Willie; his shining example of how a man should act in his finest and darkest hour soon puts me to shame. Willie Hall is a man I shall always admire.

After the match the team split up and we all went our various ways. I sat in the train on my way back to Stoke and read the papers. What a different version from the week before. What they wrote about Hall and myself and the way we had cut the Irish defence to ribbons still makes me blush, but at the same time I wouldn't be human if I denied that it gave me a great deal of pleasure.

When I turned out next morning to go to the Stoke City ground I was stopped by people all the way. I knew how to deal with this situation by now—I left the house in good time. If the people of Stoke wanted to stop and talk to me—well, they were entitled to do so. They paid my wages every week, and I felt just as pleased with them as they with me.

On the 22nd October England played Wales at Cardiff and lost 4–2. On the 26th October, just four days later, England played the Rest of Europe at Highbury, London. England won 3–0. On the 9th November England played Norway at Newcastle. England won 4–0. I played in all three matches.

The next international wasn't until 15th April, 1939, when England played Scotland at Hampden Park. So that meant that the England team had a five-month breathing space.

After the Norway match in Newcastle I started to devote more and more of my spare time to Betty, as we expected our baby to arrive towards the end of December. We got all sorts of things ready, and decided if it was a boy we would call him Stanley;

if a girl, Jean. Betty went to hospital on the last day of the year and I sat at home waiting for news. New Year's Eve came, and I sat listening to the people outside letting in the New Year. I fell asleep. I nearly fell over myself trying to reach the telephone when it rang. A voice said, "It's a girl. Both are doing well." I thanked God with all my heart. It was New Year's Day, 1939.

* * * * * *

I was alone at home, and as I sat in front of the glowing fire my thoughts went back to a few hours ago, when I had held in my arms for the first time my newly-born daughter Jean, just six hours old. I had not wanted to leave my wife and daughter; nevertheless I felt I was the happiest and luckiest man in the world. I gave a sigh of contentment and stretched out my legs towards the fire. The door-bell rang.

I got up from the chair, switching on the lights as I went to the door. My mother and father stood on the doorstep. Before many minutes had passed we were sitting before the fire, talking about Betty and the baby.

It did not seem very long before Betty and the baby were home and I was celebrating my twenty-fourth birthday on the 1st of February. The baby—Jean—was just one month old. My household routine was very different now, but I never got tired of nursing and playing with Jean. The grandparents fussed around the baby, and our house could no longer be termed a quiet one, but we were all so happy and peaceful.

By early April the end of one more season was in sight, and on the 15th England were due to play Scotland at Hampden Park in the last international match of the season. The team was announced and I was selected for the outside-right position.

As England hadn't had a win at Hampden since 1927, the England selectors were keen to break down the Hampden roar in this match, and the newspapers took up this line—about England this time defeating the Hampden roar. As this turned out to be an important match, I will give the teams for that day— SCOTLAND: Dawson (Rangers); Carabine (Third Lanark), Cummings (Aston Villa); Shankly (Preston N.E.), Baxter (Middlesbrough), McNab (West Bromwich Albion); McSpadyen (Partick

Thistle), Walker (Hearts), Dougal (Preston N.E.), Venters (Rangers), Milne (Middlesbrough). ENGLAND: Woodley (Chelsea); Morris (Wolves), Hapgood (Arsenal); Willingham (Huddersfield Town), Cullis (Wolves), Mercer (Everton); Matthews (Stoke City), Hall, G. W. (Spurs), Lawton (Everton), Goulden (West Ham), Beasley (Huddersfield Town).

On the day of the match I arrived at Hampden with the rest of the England team in a blinding rainstorm. To make it worse, the wind was howling and screaming at the same time, and I remember thinking that the ground wouldn't be half full. I was wrong. The ground was packed. The Scots love their football, and I realised then that nothing short of an earthquake would keep them away from an England v. Scotland match.

I got another surprise whilst changing in the England dressing-room just before the match was due to start. The dressing-room door opened and in walked the chairman of the F.A., Mr. Brook Hirst. All the England players stopped what they were doing and turned to look at him. He said, "Well, boys, I haven't come to tell you how to play, but I offer these words of advice. Man for man you are as good as, if not better than, your opponents, but you will be handicapped to-day by the spirit and fire of a Scottish crowd. Everyone out there will be doing his bit to help Scotland win, but I believe you boys can win for England. So go out there and never mind about that Hampden roar."

He finished talking, glanced keenly around the room, and left us. We stared at each other and nobody made any comment, but as I stole glances at the various faces around me I could see that Mr. Brook Hirst had left his mark.

We ran out of the tunnel on to the field, and before we had reached the centre of the playing area we were all drenched to the skin, and the ground beneath our feet was like a glue-pot. What a day for an international match—but what an international match it turned out to be!

As I glanced round the stands just before the kick-off I saw the Duke and Duchess of Gloucester sitting facing the rainstorm; they saw the game through.

The whistle blew and the game was on. We found ourselves playing into a very strong wind that blew the rain in our faces with such force that at times it blinded us; nevertheless the England team played with great determination and we more than held our own in the first twenty minutes, then a "gift" goal put Scotland one up. One of our defenders passed the ball back to Woodley in goal. The mud, however, slowed up the ball, and before Woodley could reach it the Scottish centre-forward Dougal, who did not seem to be in a scoring position, nipped in smartly and banged the ball into the back of the net. The goal started the Hampden roar. The bagpipes screeched loudly, the wind howled louder than ever, and the rain pelted down. We England players looked at each other in dismay, while the Scottish team danced back to take up their playing positions to the music of the bagpipes.

I remember thinking, as I looked round at this fantastic setting, that if anyone tried to describe this scene in a book the readers would think that the author had indeed dug deep into his imagination. However, the game restarted, but the conditions put pure football right out of the game.

The best both teams could do was to keep the ball in the air; to try and pass along the ground was out of the question, besides being dangerous. Also to say that one man had a good game and another a bad one would be just plain silly. No player could be judged good or bad on a day like this. As we walked off the field at half-time with the score 1–0 for Scotland it was my opinion that the team with the most stamina would come off best.

The scene in the England dressing-room at half-time was pretty grim. As we took off our sodden, mud-stained football gear to change into clean outfits there was a deep silence. It was as if the team were saving every scrap of breath to do battle in the second half.

When the time came for us to ease our weary limbs off the benches and take the field once more, I thought: *Now it's the Scots' turn to play with the wind in their faces.* You can imagine my surprise when I walked through the tunnel on to the field to find that the wind had dropped and the rain was coming down in a gentle shower. What a break it was for Scotland!

The second half started, and immediately we tore into the

Scots. This seemed to take them off guard. In the first few minutes only the mudlarking of that wonderful Scottish goalkeeper Jerry Dawson, of Glasgow Rangers, kept us out. Shot after shot was saved at point-blank range, and as he saved the crowd roared. The England team never let up, and after about twenty minutes' play the Scots began to show signs of cracking. The rain and wind had returned. It rained harder than ever and the wind blew harder than ever, but it couldn't blow away the Hampden roar and it couldn't drown the bagpipes.

The Scottish spectators sensed that their team were tiring, so they gave the roar all they had. It worked. The Scots revived and held us at bay. Twenty minutes from the end England were still one goal down, and the Scots were getting perky again; they could smell victory. It was then that our captain, Eddie Hapgood, the England left full-back, got the whip out. And it was then, for the first time in my life, that I fully realized how inspiring was the leadership of men like Eddie Hapgood. Such men can move mountains if they have made up their minds to do so, such is the faith they have in themselves to overthrow and overcome anything that steps in their path, however great the odds.

It was obvious to me and the rest of the team that our captain had made up his mind that this was one game we were not going to lose. He urged us on again and again, until at last Pat Beasley, our left-winger, found himself in a shooting position near the Scottish goalmouth. In a flash he cracked the ball past Dawson with his left foot, and it hit the back of the net like a rocket. We were on level terms. This was the tonic we wanted. Eddie Hapgood still wasn't satisfied—he wanted the winner; so we toiled and sweated in that quagmire under the scathing tongue of our captain.

The rain pelted down on our weary bodies and mingled with the sweat on our brows, but the Scots held out, the roar rang out, and the bagpipes never stopped their wailing. It wanted just ninety seconds' playing time to finish the match, and I saw the referee glance at his watch. It looked as though the result would be a draw. Glancing across to where the play was taking place, I could see Eddie Hapgood waving his arms. Then I saw Len Goulden, our inside-left, dart across the field with the ball at his feet. He was making for me. When he slipped the ball to me, I cut inside and down the wing. I felt I must be dreaming. I saw the sturdy form of our centre-forward, Tommy Lawton, rushing goalwards. Then I felt the ball stick in the mud. *I must get this ball off the ground,* I thought, *and try and drop it on Tommy's head.* I looked towards Lawton once more to get his speed and distance from goal, then I got the ball on the move again. I saw the Scottish defenders closing in on me in close formation, but I never took my eyes off that ball. I centred it just before the defenders got at me. They—and I—stood still and watched the flight of the ball as it sped towards the goalmouth. Up went Tommy Lawton, and his shining black head nodded the ball into the net. For a second or so I couldn't believe it; then, as I saw some of the England players running to me, I knew it was true. Eddie Hapgood, our captain, normally undemonstrative, was dancing on the pitch. The Hampden roar ceased, the bagpipes stopped wailing. At long last we had silenced them. The final whistle went almost before the game had restarted, and it was a happy England team that followed their captain back to their dressing-room, with the result England 2, Scotland 1. Every man in the England team got nothing but praise from the newspapers. It was the most popular victory for years.

CHAPTER X

ITALY AND THE BALKANS

THE Sunday after the international match at Hampden Park it was our turn to entertain our in-laws. We had just finished our tea, and Betty was over in a corner of the room attending to young Jean, my mother was on the point of clearing away the dishes and the remains of the meal, and I was sitting at the table with my father and Jimmy Vallance.

My father-in-law, who had spent most of his playing days with famous Scottish clubs before he became the trainer at Stoke City Football Club, was holding forth with regard to the recent match at Hampden. I sat staring at him. He was a dour Scot and a loyal one and at last came to the end of his praise of the virtues of Scottish football. He certainly knew his football. My eyes left his face for the first time. I picked up my cup and sipped my tea.

Then my father said, "In other words, you are saying that England was lucky to win?" My father-in-law replied in his Scottish accent, "Of course they were. I've just explained why, haven't I? What more proof do you want, man?" My father replied: "You don't know what you are talking about." That did it. I just sat back and enjoyed the fun. What better entertainment could you have after tea on Sunday than an argument between a Scot and an Englishman who, despite what they say about each other's knowledge of football, do in fact know quite a lot.

I used to pick up a lot of useful information listening to these arguments and was always sorry when at last they came to an end. This one petered out after a while, because Betty was going to bath the baby. This they couldn't miss, football or no football. She was the apple of their eye.

Stanley Matthews with the Stoke City directors. Left to right: Walton, the author, and Alderman H. Booth.

In a Glasgow hotel—May 1947—Stanley Matthews signs to play for Blackpool. The transfer fee was £11,500.

After the baby had been safely tucked away for the night my father came out with a remark that made me remember that particular Sunday for ever.

My mother-in-law, Mrs. Vallance, had left the tea-table as soon as the meal was over to visit a friend who lived close by. She returned to the house after about an hour to find us sitting round the fire. She said to my father, "You must be very proud of Stanley, he's done about everything there is to do in football." My father gave a short grunt. Mrs. Vallance looked at him in surprise and said, "Well, hasn't he?" "He's got to do one more thing before I am satisfied. I want to sit at Wembley and watch him win a cup-winners' medal." My father hesitated and a far-away look came into his eyes. He continued, "Aye, that's what I want him to win most of all before he finishes playing football."

We all looked at him in silence. Then Jimmy Vallance got to his feet, "I expect he will," he said, and then, "Well, it's time we went home."

A few minutes later they had all left the house, and Betty and I were alone. I closed the front door and said to Betty, "What do you think of my father's ambition?" She said, "We all have our secret ambitions, and we know now what your father's is." "Well, it was a surprise to me," I said; "but if that's what he wants, then I'll have to try and make it come true." Betty nodded, then we both sat down and picked up the Sunday papers.

The 1938–39 season came to an end, and almost at once I was informed by the F.A. that I had been selected for the Continental tour in May. I was thrilled with this good news. Millions of young men my age would have given almost anything to be in my shoes, to have the chance to see new lands and faces, and above all the wonderful scenery.

Our first match was against Italy at Milan on May 13th. During that uneasy spring of 1939 the political scene had been so delicate that the F.A. came close to cancelling the tour following consultation with the British Government, but it was decided to let it stand. Nevertheless, as we neared Stresa, our first stopping-place in Italy, we were beginning to worry.

D

The political situation was even worse than it had been the previous year in Germany. By now, Mussolini was openly talking war and screaming for Nice, Corsica and Tunis. Furthermore, he had the backing of millions of fanatical Fascists who, with their cries of "Il Duce", indicated their willingness to march behind their leader and alongside Hitler.

We had long, sober faces when the train slowed down to enter Stresa station, but when it came to a standstill we got the shock of our lives. As the Italian customs officials boarded our train we found ourselves the centre of a battle of flowers. Scores of beautiful Italian girls, carrying baskets of flowers, appeared on the station platform and made for us. I had never seen so many flowers before, nor thought girls in flocks could be so beautiful. They threw the flowers in our compartment; then they sang and giggled and chattered, and every now and then one of these gorgeous creatures would sing out in a lovely musical voice, "Viva Inglese!"

Within minutes of stopping our hearts warmed towards these lovely ambassadresses, and towards the Italian people in general. This was really something we hadn't expected.

Our welcome in Stresa was put in the shade by the welcome we received in Milan. As our train drew into Milan's modern marble station, the sheer magnificence of it took my breath away. The station itself was packed by cheering and whistling men, women and children. Then they started to sing as they waited for a glimpse of us. If we had been the first men to touch down on earth from outer space we couldn't have had a bigger welcome. The noise was terrific. The streets were packed for miles, and when at last we reached our hotel we found another enormous gathering there.

When, at their request, we appeared on the hotel balcony they cheered and whistled and sang once more. The happy hotel manager fussed around us as if he were a mother hen and we his chicks. They liked us all right, and we them.

We were a happy bunch of men wanting nothing more than a nice cup of tea, and much to our surprise we got it—and very good tea it was. As I sat sipping mine a small dark man came to my side and said in perfect English, "Are you Stanley Matthews?"

As I glanced at his unsmiling face my mind was in a whirl, I thought what is this all about. However, I forced myself to smile, and answered, "Yes, I'm Stanley Matthews." He quickly explained to me that he was a Maltese and was one of a large party from Valetta, in Malta, who had made the journey especially "to see England beat Italy".

I listened to him intently, and when he had finished talking I promised him that we would do our best to win the match, and told him that we always did our best to win every match we played. He urged me to make a special endeavour in this one. We shook hands, and as I watched him leave the hotel lounge I thought to myself, *What is all the fuss about?*

Malta didn't mean a great deal to me then, as I sat there drinking my tea. Furthermore I did not appreciate how very serious that Maltese was when he asked for a football victory over Italy. Looking back now, however, I can see the reason why, and I feel proud to have had the honour of meeting that day a representative of Malta, and to have later fulfilled my promise not to let the Italians beat us.

Milan is a wonderful city; and as we had three days to spend sightseeing before the match, we decided to spend a day at Como, which stands on the edge of the beautiful lake of the same name. But it was not to be; in May 1939 sunny Italy was anything but sunny. It started to rain, and it kept up for three days nonstop. The torrential rain kept us indoors, and, as you may guess, the whole England team got very disgruntled. I couldn't get any outside training at all, so I had to do the best I could indoors, and this rather got me down.

We did realise, however, that the more it rained the more likely it was that the pitch was going to suit us on the day of the match. We hoped that the San Siro Stadium would be like a glue-pot.

When we ran out of the tunnel to start the game on the day of the match the pitch *was* like a glue-pot. Would the Italians start the rough stuff they used in England, when I played my first match against them?

Everything began well, with Ken Willingham and Joe Mercer taking complete control of the Italian wings. I found the unorthodox methods of Rava, Italy's left-back, very difficult to overcome, but the rest of the English forwards were doing well—except scoring goals.

The English exhibition of football must have looked good from the stadium because the Italians clapped and shouted "Bravo" as we worked the ball along the "carpet" and to and fro like clockwork. England was easily outplaying Italy, but the first, all-important goal would not come our way. The game up to now had been played in a clean but keen spirit by both sides, and the spectators were loving every minute of it. Meanwhile my brain was ticking over, trying to think of a move that would baffle Rava, the left-back. Near to half-time I found one. I managed to slip past Rava and dribble towards the goal. Seeing Tommy Lawton running into position near the goalmouth, I centred and Tommy's priceless head did the rest. The ball flew off it into the back of the net. After that important goal it was my guess that we would settle down in the second half and give Italy a lesson in shooting as well as football.

We were very confident in the England dressing-room during the interval. We returned to the field determined to enjoy and play good football and score a few more goals. The whistle blew and the second half was on. And we soon got a surprise! The Italians threw aside their defensive tactics and tore into us like a lot of tigers. The crowd stood up and urged them on, delighted that their sleepy team had shaken off its lethargy, and we were caught napping by this sudden burst of energy.

Within five minutes of the restart Bievat, their outside-right, paralysed our defence with a wonderful run almost the length of the field. He completed the move by cutting in and sending in such a powerful shot from close range that Vic Woodley hadn't the slightest chance of saving.

This goal put the Italians on level terms. The spectators screamed, shouted and sang with joy, and urged their team on to yet greater efforts. Following this goal, the Italians threw caution to the wind; they got "stuck in", and their sliding tackles and rough play caused us great concern. We were back to Highbury, November 14th, 1934.

We took all they gave us and managed to keep them at bay.

Fortunately for England, there is always at least one man at hand to pull us together when we are rattled by methods to which we are not accustomed back at home. This time it was Joe Mercer, of Everton, who acted on behalf of England.

I dread to think what would have happened in the first twenty minutes of the second half if Joe Mercer hadn't come into his own. He played the game of his life. He started to tackle the Italians with uncanny speed, and after getting the ball he would always push it to a fellow player with a word of encouragement. By his sheer determination and rallying powers he pulled us through that black twenty minutes. Footballers don't come much better than Joe Mercer.

Slowly but surely we started to get back into the game, and from Mercer's passes our forwards began to shoot again, and they brought the best out of the Italian goalkeeper, Olivieri, the most graceful and daring goalkeeper I have watched. Two great drives by Tommy Lawton, a high shot by Frankie Broome, and a ball that had been packed with dynamite by Willie Hall were all kept out by the astonishing Signor Olivieri. I watched him in amazement. Anyone who was lucky enough to get a ticket to see this match must have had enough excitement to last them the rest of their football-going lives.

The stadium was in an uproar. The spectators could sense that they would never see anything like this again, and they made the most of it. I am sure the noise they made could be heard twenty miles away.

Thanks to Mercer, the game soon got back on an even keel, but it wasn't to stay that way for long. The ball came twisting into our goalmouth from the Italians' right wing. Piola, Italy's centre-forward, came charging into the England goal head first, like a wild bull. George Male hurried in to beat the Italian centre-forward to the ball. Piola slipped slightly, but as he was falling he showed ingenious speed by *cracking the ball into the net with a straight right-fisted punch* that would have floored most of the leading heavyweight boxers of that time. As Piola's wonder punch followed through it came into contact with George Male and hit him in the eye. He dropped like a log. Poor George Male, he was out for the count.

After we got George to his feet again, we stood waiting for the referee to award a free-kick to England and were flabbergasted when he turned dramatically to the centre of the field and pointed, indicating Italy had scored. We hadn't even bothered to protest, so obvious was the foul. When we saw that Doctor Bauwens, the German referee, was in earnest we descended on him as one body to make what we considered a justified protest.

The referee left us and ran across the field to consult a linesman, but, to our disgust, he did not alter his original decision. This was terrible.

The crowd had suddenly gone very quiet. Perhaps the Italians who stood behind the English goalmouth had passed the word round that we were right in protesting as we did.

When we were walking back to the centre of the field to take up our positions for the re-start after the unfair goal we heard the clapping of hands. It was Eddie Hapgood, our captain, who was clapping. He told us that we mustn't lose now, and if we worked together we could still make it. Our dignity had been hurt and our sense of justice injured, and as the referee blew his whistle we heard the Eddie Hapgood clap again, which, interpreted into words, meant "get cracking".

A wonderful fighting spirit swept through the English team. Mercer came up with the forwards, so did Willingham, and with the help of some good solid shoulder-charging we had the Italians worried. Five minutes remained and we were still a goal down. Then that great centre half-back Stan Cullis, his chin jutting out at a dangerous angle, and a fighter if ever there was one, came up to make it an eight-man England forward line. The Italians wilted before our blitzkrieg. Time was running out fast when Willingham came through, juggling the ball like the master he was. I called to him and in a flash the ball came along the carpet to my toes. Away I went at top speed goalwards until I heard a Cockney voice call, "O.K., Stan." I knew that voice; it was Len Goulden. I passed, and Len shot. The ball struck the Italian left-back Rava and rebounded to where Willie Hall was waiting. As quick as a flash, Willie cracked the ball goalwards, and the bewildered Olivieri dived seconds too late. We had saved the day. It was a body blow to Italy and the goal was received in a deep silence. To us that goal meant everything. We left the field with heads held high.

We were not without casualties. My hip-bone was chipped, Willie Hall was limping, and of course George Male had a black eye that made him a target for wisecrackers for a long time after.

I was told the Crown Prince of Italy felt so incensed and embarrassed at the gross miscarriage of justice that he expressed his willingness to consult the German referee immediately and have the goal decision reversed. He was dissuaded by our Football Association secretary, who explained in a most tactful manner that in sport the decision of the referee must be accepted even though the official might make a blunder. It is this spirit that makes an England team welcome all over the world.

.   .   .   .   .   .

We were leaving Milan for Venice *en route* for Yugoslavia. When I joined up with the rest of the team I found they were in a serious mood. The result of the match with the Italians was not to their liking, or mine for that matter, and already our thoughts were on the forthcoming match in Belgrade against Yugoslavia in a few days' time.

The Slavs were an unknown quantity at football, and deep in our hearts we would have liked to know a bit more about them. I suppose it was that fact that troubled us.

When we left the hotel, however, we forgot everything except the Italian people. There they were in their thousands, waiting to give us a regal send-off that was every bit up to the standard of the welcome they had given us on our arrival. They had such a natural and simple way of showing their friendship for us that by the time we had boarded our train and it was pulling slowly out of the station I doubt if any of our English party was sitting in his seat. We were all leaning out of the windows waving and shouting back at our now quickly receding fans.

It was 6.30 a.m. when the train started to slow down to pull into the station at Belgrade. As we got to our feet and prepared to leave the train I popped my head through the window, to see how far we were off the station platform. I took one look, then ducked back into the compartment and said to one and all, "Just take a look at this lot." Everybody made for the windows and looked out. They saw a tremendous crowd of people waiting on the platform.

At that early hour we hadn't expected anyone to be there. When the train pulled up and our party alighted an official came forward and began his welcome speech with "This is an important and proud day for Yugoslavia. Your visit cements the friendship of our two countries . . ." I remember thinking to myself as he went on with his speech that it was good to know that a handful of professional footballers were doing what the politicians at that moment were failing to accomplish—achieving goodwill between nations.

As I glanced around me at the masses of smiling Slav faces—many I found out later had taken up their places on the platform before dawn—I couldn't credit the fact that there were men at this very moment planning and plotting to bring ruin and disaster to these and other simple folk.

We left the station for our hotel, and another welcome given us by the thousands of Slavs which lined the route. At last we got to our rooms and to bed; but the reception had been too much for me, and I am afraid that I tossed and turned for hours before I eventually fell into a fitful sleep.

During the days prior to the match the Slavs fêted us wherever we went, and we were closely followed by a van with a leading radio commentator to give an eye-witness account of our movements. If I visited a public building or cinema it was reported in the newspapers. Nothing was too much trouble for anyone if it made us happy.

I quickly found out that at that time the country was undergoing a food shortage. The shops were meagrely filled and private homes could offer little variety in only small quantities. Yet wherever we went there was plenty of food, with long courses on the menus. This upset me so much that I asked openly why we could be served with such extravagant meals while the Slavs went short. I was told that Yugoslavia considered the visit of the England team to be of such importance that orders had been given that nothing should be spared to make our visit a happy one. This might be hard to believe, but I can assure you that it is perfectly true.

It was while we were viewing some of Belgrade's picturesque buildings that we first met "Charlie"—or perhaps I should say "Charlie" met us. How he got attached to us in the first place no one knew. He was a queer little chap who knew Belgrade inside out.

With the rest of the English party I found myself listening to "Charlie" when he started to explain, in very good English, the virtues of this building and that street; and although it wasn't very long before we began to suspect that our faithful guide was only expert at the art of story-telling, we couldn't tear ourselves away from him. "Charlie's" profound knowledge, and his style of putting things over in words and phrases and gestures, held us spellbound, and when he attached himself to us on our way back to the hotel nobody seemed to mind.

From then on he became our unofficial courier and went with us on all our sightseeing tours until the eve of the match. We called him "Charlie" because we couldn't pronounce his real name. At times we were most grateful for his talents as a courier, because he knew every nook and back street of the capital and would rattle off some amazing stories. Every mountain, every lake, every paving-stone had a legend attached to it. We really enjoyed this fluent story-teller when he related the story of how King Alexander of Yugoslavia had been assassinated when driving through the streets of Marseilles some seven years earlier. He told how the young King Peter had his English education cut short by the call to return to Belgrade to rule a nation shocked by the assassination of its previous king.

We followed "Charlie" to Oplenae, where the beautiful church had been built as a memorial to the martyred king, and "Charlie", with his free-flowing patter, made past events come to life with such reality that we began to look upon him as something of a genius. There was no doubt that "Charlie" had by this time got us all in the palm of his hand; we never tired of his tales.

Then, on the eve of the match, when we had to say good-bye, "Charlie" started to talk of the next day's game. We gathered round him to shake his hand and wish him all the very best of everything in the future. He shook hands with all of us and turned to go. He took a few steps, then turned and held up his right hand. "Gentlemen," he said in a sad voice, "I feel it is my duty to tell you that not one of our boys really knows how to kick a football . . ." He paused, and during the pause we looked at each other. Although most of us thought that this must be an exaggeration, the fact that "Charlie" had spoken these words made us feel easier in our outlook towards next day's game, after our hectic struggle with Italy. Charlie then continued with, "Our boys are so slow in the tackle that I can say with the utmost confidence that you will win by eight or nine goals, so therefore you will be able to settle down and treat the match as an exhibition. Gentlemen, it is with deep regret, as a loyal subject of Yugoslavia, that I am forced to confess my countrymen have not even a sporting chance of beating England tomorrow." He made a very slight bow, then went on, "As footballers we are no more than clowns." His face broke into a sad smile.

He turned and walked slowly away from us. At the corner of the street he stopped, turned, and waved. We waved back. He disappeared from view and we stared after him for a few seconds, as if hoping "Charlie" would show himself again. Nothing happened, so we walked back inside the hotel, each of us feeling that we had lost a well-loved and trusted friend. I noticed, however, that the rest of the team were in good spirits that night. "Charlie's" farewell speech had done a power of good. I felt rather uneasy myself.

I reported to Tom Whittaker on the day of the match and told him I was fit. I had spent several hours testing my damaged hip. I sprinted, twisted and turned without getting any pain. Tom Whittaker, who was then the England trainer, took my word for it, and the same eleven that drew with Italy was put on the field.

The match started before a huge, excited crowd. The Slavs were not only quick in the tackle but were also a first-class team, and they were on the attack from the moment the whistle went. "Charlie" had let us down good and proper. It would take us all our time to beat this team. I received the ball after the game had been in progress for five minutes. Slipping it beyond Dubac, the Yugoslav left-back, I attempted to sprint past him. To my horror my damaged leg didn't respond, it felt as heavy as lead. I was useless for the rest of the game, just a passenger.

To break down after five minutes' play, after telling our trainer that I was fit, made me feel terrible, and the fact that I had proof that my leg had stood up to a most severe test before the game didn't make me feel any happier. It was a complete disaster as far as I was concerned. To make it worse Eddie Hapgood had the misfortune to tear a ligament in his ankle and had to go out on the left wing, so it meant that England were without wingers. When Yugoslavia scored after fifteen minutes' play my cup of bitterness was full to the brim, and I thought that the crowd would never stop cheering. They kept it up for a full five minutes.

After tasting first blood, and encouraged by the cheering of their fellow countrymen, the Yugoslav team put on the pressure and became a fast tackling, fiery set of patriots. They launched attack after attack on the English goalmouth. How we managed to keep them out up to the interval, I shall never know; but somehow we did. When the whistle went for half-time I gave a gentle sigh and limped off with a weary England team to get a well-earned rest.

Eddie Hapgood and I received treatment during the break, and we both insisted on returning to the field for the second half with the rest of the team. I was not in great pain with my leg, but it was stiff, and this enabled Dubac to spend some of his time over on the other wing to help his right-back. He had, however, to keep a watchful eye on me, so perhaps I was of some help.

With grim faces we battled against the odds; then suddenly the ball went to the feet of Frankie Broome, and without wasting a second he slammed it into the back of the net. A great first-time goal. We were back in the game with a fighting chance.

The excitement was intense as both teams battled for another goal. The nine fit men on the English side ran themselves into the ground. Eddie Hapgood and I did all we could to be a nuisance to the Slavs.

As the tempo of the game quickened, so did the cheering of the spectators as the game flowed from one goalmouth to the other. With the game drawing to a close I thought we were going to hold them out, and every minute seemed to be an hour. Then, out of the blue, Perlic, the Yugoslav outside-left, cut in with the ball and scored a lovely goal. The crowd stood up to him and cheered and cheered, and were still yelling their heads off when the final whistle blew. And so the result was Yugoslavia 2, England 1.

I do not wish to make any excuses for this defeat, because the Slavs were such a good team; but if Eddie Hapgood and myself had been fit for the whole of the game I would have felt more satisfied with the result. If "Charlie" had walked into the England dressing-room after the match I don't know what would have happened to him. I suppose he was leaving the ground with the rest of the spectators chuckling to himself. He must have known all along.

We were not a particularly optimistic or happy party that set off for Bucharest next day for our third and last match of the tour—against Rumania. Our defeat at the hands of Yugoslavia, coming on top of the not too successful display against Italy, made it imperative that we should win the last match, otherwise the English sportswriters would give it to us good and hot.

However, by the time we had embarked on the river steamer we felt much better and very excited. As a special treat it had been arranged that we made the trip to Bucharest by sailing down the River Danube.

It would take us fourteen hours to reach our destination. One of my favourite waltzes is the "Blue Danube", and I found myself humming this whilst I sorted myself out on the steamer. Here was I all set to cruise down this beautiful river, and when I went up on deck I expected to watch the famous blue water flow past the steamer.

I have never seen so much dirty brown water churned up as I did during that trip down the Danube. No, not even from the River Trent as it passes through Stoke. At first I couldn't believe it, but there it was—just plain brown water.

A cherished dream had been blown sky-high, and I thought very bitterly that when Strauss had been inspired to compose his great work he must have been wearing blue glasses.

The welcome we received when we disembarked at Turnu-Severin at 7.30 a.m. the following morning was the best ever.

We were not only greeted by sprays of flowers and flags, and the usual huge crowd, but by the town band, which played "John Peel" and as many other British tunes as could be packed into the short time we were there.

We laughed our heads off when they finished up playing "Loch Lomond" at such a fast tempo that it left all the Rumanian musicians out of breath. I'll bet it's the only time in history that an English party has been greeted by a Scottish tune in Rumania. When they saw our smiling faces they were well satisfied with their efforts to please us, and made way for our passage through their ranks to continue our journey to Bucharest.

In Bucharest there was more band-playing, more speeches, more flag-waving, and more flowers. It was simply wonderful, and our hearts went out in friendship to these generous people. Wherever we went we were followed as though we were supermen.

The thing that impressed me most was the fact that our defeat at the hands of Yugoslavia didn't appear to make us any less important in the eyes of the Rumanians; indeed I can only surmise that these people had been educated to the fact that England was the home of football. If this was true, then somebody made a good job of it, because the Rumanians just couldn't do enough for us. They even had a sightseeing tour arranged for us, and I can assure you that this had been planned with the utmost care. Weeks of hard work must have gone into it.

I was particularly interested in our visit to Ploesti. Ploesti in 1939 was a wonderful place. It is an oil town. You find yourself gazing at a huge forest of towering derricks. The proud Rumanian officials who showed us round this masterpiece of engineering answered all our questions most fully, and indeed took a great pride in doing so.

We were also taken to Pelash Castle, the magnificent home of King Carol and Madame Lupescu. As soon as I saw the castle I stood spellbound. My mind went back to my boyhood days, when I spent hours looking at the fairy castles that are illustrated in the Hans Andersen books. Until this moment I had never once thought that such castles really existed. Pelash Castle showed me that I was wrong. Here was one before my very eyes. I felt very lucky to be able to have the chance to explore it.

When we entered the castle and walked through the various apartments my eyes grew bigger and bigger. The rooms were beautiful, and filled with the most expensive furniture and carpets, and the décor was indescribably wonderful. Imagine my surprise when a shrill Cockney voice called out, "Cor, lumme, that ain't the wye to prune roses. Gimme the scissors." We went over to the open window and looked out, and there he was in the garden —a real Cockney. He was delighted to meet us, and told us that he had a very good job on King Carol's household staff. He liked his job immensely. It struck me as being very funny that I should be walking round the fairy palace of a real king hundreds of miles from England, my mind in a whirl from the beauty of my surroundings, then in a flash be brought back to earth by the sound of a Cockney voice in a place you would least expect to hear one.

I reported along with the other England players on the morning of the day the match was to be played. The selection of the England team took some time. It was discovered then that I had a chipped hip-bone, so I was out of the team.

Later I was joined by Hapgood, Willingham, and Willie Hall, all out through injuries. It was decided to put Frank Broome in my place on the right wing. Leslie Smith, who was then with Brentford, received his first "cap", being brought in at outside-left. Len Goulden went to inside-right, and Don Welsh, the Charlton forward, came in as inside-left. Morris, of Wolverhampton Wanderers, took Eddie Hapgood's place. Wilf Copping was at left-half, with Joe Mercer crossing over to the right.

When the England team took the field for the start of the match, I sat in the stand together with my injured team-mates. England badly needed one win on this tour, but with all the changes that had taken place in the England side I felt a little dubious about it all. Before a huge cheering crowd the match started and both teams settled down, but it was not long before it became obvious that England was the better side.

With Cullis playing at his best, England gained a 2-0 win, thanks to a first-half goal by Goulden and a second-half goal by Welsh.

I am not going to say that it was a great performance by

England, but it was a win, and we closed the tour with lighter hearts than we should have if we had failed to register a win during the whole tour.

Even after the match these wonderful Rumanian people kept up their hospitality, and the send-off they gave us was just as friendly and cordial as their welcome had been. We had made many friends during our stay.

A great restlessness stole over me when we left Bucharest; I wanted to get back to Betty and baby Jean as soon as possible. It was a wonderful sight to see the white cliffs of Dover come into view three days later.

There were no lovely girls to meet us. No bands to play for us. No flowers, and no flag-waving. It was so quiet I doubt whether anyone in England knew we had arrived home.

Be that as it may, I know that when my train pulled into Stoke Station, and I popped my head out of the carriage window and saw Betty with young Jean in her arms waiting for me on the platform, my restlessness left me and a deep peace stole into my heart. I was home again.

CHAPTER XI

THE WAR YEARS

SHORTLY after I had reported for training at the Stoke City ground, ready to start the 1939–40 season, my by now usually contented outlook began to get a wee bit ruffled. I noticed that some of my team-mates were talking as if war had to come. Indeed, one or two had, in all seriousness, mapped out which branch of the services they were going to join.

Then when the playing season got under way in August that year the papers came out with the threat of the invasion of Poland by Hitler. When I arrived home that evening Betty, with an anxious look on her face, said, "Have you seen the papers, Stanley?" I nodded. "Yes, Betty. But I still think that Hitler is bluffing; people don't want war." Betty said, " But suppose he goes into Poland as he says—won't we have to go to war against Germany again?" I smiled. "Now don't get upset, Betty; it won't come to that. You mark my words." Betty said, "I hope not. But I've been thinking that our happiness was too good to last for ever."

I didn't answer; instead I walked over to the cot in which Jean was playing. She looked up at me and gave a little gurgle. I bent down and rubbed my nose against hers; she laughed and her little hand shot up and grabbed my tie. Betty came in from the kitchen and laid the table for tea. We passed a rather flat evening.

When I finished training next day I walked round to my father's shop. He was just closing for lunch. I sat down on a chair. My father had brought his lunch with him—a packet of sandwiches. He filled his small kettle with water and popped it on the small gas-ring. "What's brought you round at this time of day?" he asked. I got up from the chair and said, "I've come for your opinion, Father. Do you think there is going to be a war?" He bent down and peered under the kettle, as if to make sure that all the eyelets in the top of the gas-ring were alight, then he straightened up and turned to me and said, "Yes, son, I do." I sat down again on the chair and said, "I can't believe it. I just can't believe it."

My father said thoughtfully, "I know you can't believe it, son, and I know why you can't believe it. You have just returned from visiting countries I have never seen, and I doubt if I ever will see. You have met the ordinary men and women in these countries, talked to them, and found that they are no different from us. They think more or less on the same lines as we do. They are content with the same things that we are, and they don't want war any more than we do. You told me all this when you returned home this summer, and you more or less told me the same thing when you returned home last summer. But don't you see, son, that just as you and I can't leave this shop now and go to London to tell the powers-that-be to stop this war from starting, neither can *they* do the same. Hitler's got the war fever, and nobody is going to stop him from trying to rule the world. He should have been stopped at the very beginning."

Father poured the boiling water on the tea. I watched him in silence. He poured two cups and brought one over to me. I thanked him, and took a sip at the piping-hot liquid. My father insisted I share his sandwiches and we sat together, discussing what might happen in the near future.

I walked home in a serious frame of mind, and each day after that the news got worse. Then, on that fateful Sunday morning in September, Mr. Chamberlain came over the B.B.C. network and told us all that we were at war with Germany.

When he had finished his speech I looked at Betty in silence, and then at young Jean. I picked up a paper off the table, and saw that it gave instructions where you had to apply for gas-masks if war were declared. There was a special notice with regard to children; special masks had been made for them according to their age. When I read that I walked out to the garden at the back of the house. I felt sick. I don't know how long I was outside, but when at last I re-entered the house and sat down in an easy chair my thoughts went back to the people I had met in the countries that were now at war with us. I wondered if any of them would at this moment be thinking about the English football team they had fêted.

.   .   .   .   .

My shirt was wet through with sweat; it clung to my body like a leech. I wiped the sweat from my brow with one hand, then shaded my eyes with the other and glanced upwards at the sun in the clear blue sky. It was a day in July and I was dead beat and very thirsty. I should have been hungry, but I wasn't. I was just tired and thirsty. Mostly thirsty. As I forced my aching legs forward, step by step, pictures of streams and waterfalls and the snowcapped mountains of Switzerland came before my eyes, and I licked my lips in anticipation of drinking a glass of ice-cold water. Yes, it must be just water. It suddenly became the dominant thing in my life at that moment. A glass of cold water.

I had ceased to be a professional footballer and was now A/C 1361317 S Matthews, Royal Air Force. As I held the lowest possible rank in the R.A.F. I didn't evoke any jealousy amongst the rest of my fellow servicemen. I had just been posted to Blackpool, and was on my way to report for duty in that town. When, at last, I finally arrived, I made straight for the buffet on the station and drank glass after glass of water. Then I walked on the promenade. I took in several deep breaths of the gentle north-west wind that was coming in from the sea, and as I gazed at the miles and miles of sandy beach and filled my lungs with the clean, invigorating air and sensed the feeling of well-being that swept through my whole body I fell in love with Blackpool on that warm sunny day in July, and that love has never wavered. Blackpool has everything I could wish for, but on that July afternoon I never dreamed that one day I would make it my permanent home. I glanced at my watch and saw that it was time I reported for duty, so very reluctantly I left the promenade and turned my footsteps in the direction of the reporting centre.

CHAPTER XII

I MAKE A PROMISE

BLACKPOOL was being used by the Government as a reception centre for the thousands of new recruits who arrived every week for service in the Royal Air Force. To keep these men occupied during their off-duty time became a vital matter, so sport of all kinds was brought to them. The favourite sport of 80 per cent of these men was football, and every effort was made to enable them to enjoy it, either by playing or watching the game.

When I arrived in Blackpool I didn't know what job I would be put to, but it wasn't long before I found out that I was expected to play in a R.A.F. services team for the entertainment of the men. I didn't argue against this. In the first place, I was in the services, like millions of other men, to serve my country and fight the enemy. I was willing to do whatever I was told to do and help to get the war over as soon as possible so that I could return to my family and live in peace once more. In the second place, it didn't take me long to find out that it doesn't pay to argue in the services. I will admit, however, that I was delighted more than anything else when I walked into my digs and met other footballers, some I knew, some I had never met before.

I got out of bed very early the following morning, and after going through normal routine exercises I slipped out of the house and made for the promenade and in an easy jog-trot I covered about two miles. I had the promenade almost to myself, the air was fresh and clean, and as I pumped it in and out of my lungs I felt ready to tackle anything.

I returned to my digs, had a shave and a quick shower, changed into my uniform, and went down to join the other boys for breakfast. After breakfast I went along to the mustering point and met the rest of the men in the flight to which I was now attached.

We stood chatting until our N.C.O. came along to take charge. I heard a voice call, "Fall in, you lot, on the double." I looked round and saw to my surprise that our N.C.O. was none other than Sergeant Powell—Ivor Powell, the Aston Villa and Welsh international wing-half. He didn't seem to be surprised to see me, and, what's more, he didn't make a move towards me. I was just 1361317 to him.

Left-right, left-right—form this, form that—look where you are going—pick your feet off the ground—do this, do that—what do you think you are doing. . . . Ivor was a strict N.C.O. and I am afraid, so far as drilling went, I was one of his worst men. He never let up, and showed us no mercy.

When our training finished I was able to take it easy for a day, and take it easy I did. At the same time, during this off-duty spell I noticed the difference this hard training had made to my general condition—and I had thought I was fit before reaching Blackpool. It taught me a lesson I have not forgotten, which is never to rest on your laurels when you feel you are as fit as it is possible to be. By hard work you can get that little extra fitness which, when called upon to help you out of a tricky situation, is worth all the slight extra effort you have made to attain it.

Slowly but surely I settled down in Blackpool and made many friends amongst the men I met. All of them had come from different walks of life, and all had different jobs in civilian life.

I started to play a lot of football again and after a short leave I was instructed to report for training with an R.A.F. unit. I was delighted to find out that this unit was composed mostly of professional footballers from all parts of the country. I started to travel again as we played all over the British Isles.

The months slipped by and the years also. I had several amusing times during that period. In the very early days we had to report very early one morning in Blackpool to get an early start to be in time to play against an R.A.F. unit team a good distance away. We clambered into the waiting bus. The C.O. arrived, took his seat, and gave the order to start the journey. At that moment it was discovered that "Jock" Dodds and Hugh

O'Donnell, who shared the same digs at Blackpool, were missing from the party. The C.O. ordered the driver to go to their digs. The driver left the bus and started to bang on the door. After some time Dodds, who had overslept, and who was still in his pyjamas, leaned out of a bedroom window and in a sleepy voice asked what all the row was about. The C.O., who was standing on the pavement outside the house, told him in no uncertain manner. Dodds vanished from the window and in record time came through the front door partly dressed, followed by O'Donnell in a similar state of dress. You can guess what happened. During the match, however, Hugh O'Donnell scored a smashing goal from twenty yards out. He still had his R.A.F. boots on.

I have always had a horror of being late for an appointment or reporting late for training or a match. Jock Dodds and I were in a train bound for Leeds. The R.A.F. were due to play the Army, which had in its ranks a wealth of famous footballers. A fog came down and held up our train for a considerable time. I began to fidget. Dodds, knowing how much I hated to be late, tried to console me, but it was no use. We arrived in Leeds station just five minutes before the kick-off, with the ground still some way from the station.

Dodds and I dashed out of the station to grab a taxi, but to my dismay there was a long queue in front of us. My heart sank. Jock turned to me and said, "Come on, Stan, we're not beat yet." He dashed to the head of the queue, rushed to the first taxi, and said, "Footballers! We've got to get to the ground in five minutes." He opened the taxi door and jumped inside and I followed in a flash. The taxi-driver let in his clutch and away we went. I think the onlookers were too surprised to protest.

We changed our boots and stockings in the taxi. As we arrived at the ground the R.A.F. team, with nine players, walked out, followed by the Army. "The King" was being played while we were completing our change of clothes, but we ran onto the field just in time for the kick-off. It was the nearest I have been to being late, and I never want to be so close again. It upset me for days. It's better to be one hour early than one minute late.

To make my day complete the Army beat us.

After another R.A.F. *v*. Army game—this time at Edinburgh—Peter Doherty and I were attempting to catch an early train back to Blackpool so that we could arrive in plenty of time to report for ordinary duties. We had arranged for a taxi to be waiting outside the entrance to the dressing-rooms immediately the match was over. Half dressed we dashed out, to find that the taxi hadn't arrived. We waited a further five minutes, then realised that we had been let down good and proper.

It was then that Peter spotted an R.A.F. car waiting. An attractive W.A.A.F. was sitting at the wheel, and we explained our position to her. She said she was sorry she could not help us, as she was waiting for the C.O.—a Group Captain—who would be coming out of the club in ten minutes or so. Peter turned on all his charm and appealed to her again, saying that she could be back in time. She weakened and told us to jump in, at the same time warning us that we would probably get her shot if the C.O. ever found out. We got into the car, only to hear a gruff voice at the back of us shout "Get out". It was the Group Captain, who had arrived sooner than expected.

We appealed to him to help us, but all we received in return was a first-class dressing down, in which he included the unfortunate W.A.A.F. When we explained the whole incident was entirely our fault he ignored us completely and drove off. Peter and I looked at each other in dismay; we both felt sorry for the girl.

Then a Scot came to our rescue. He had been standing on one side and had witnessed the scene. He volunteered to drive us to Princes Street Station; and thanks to his most timely help we just made the train.

I had done hardly any flying before joining the R.A.F., but such were the demands for the services of the football team I played with that after a comparatively short time I got to accept it and enjoy it. We flew to most of the matches that were any distance from Blackpool. In war-time, of course, you are always in some danger when in the air, but the only time I was really close to death was on a return flight from France with a Combined Services team after having played a match there for the troops in the front line.

We flew back to England in a thick fog. On landing we learned from the pilot that we had missed colliding with another plane by fifteen yards over the Channel. Big Frank Swift, who was our goalkeeper in that game, immediately fell on his face and kissed the ground. We all felt the same way.

Among the many friends I made in Blackpool the one who helped me more than I can ever tell was the late Colonel W. Parkinson, chairman of Blackpool F.C. He was a man who called a spade a spade. A real man's man.

It was Colonel Parkinson who asked me to play for Blackpool when I first arrived in that town as an R.A.F. recruit. I duly obliged. During the war they called it being a "guest" player. Scores of footballers "guested" with other clubs.

Whilst playing as a guest for Blackpool I played with the finest side in my career. It was as follows: Savage (Queen of the South); Pope (Hearts), Jones; Farrow, Hayward, Johnston; Matthews (Stoke), Dix (Spurs), Dodds, Finan, Burbanks (Sunderland). The players with no team against their name were Blackpool players.

This Blackpool war-time eleven won the League North Cup, beating Sheffield Wednesday in May 1943, and went on to beat Arsenal (who had won the South Cup) 4-2 at Stamford Bridge. Hubbick played at left-back against Arsenal. George Farrow, the Blackpool right-half, was one of the greatest footballers who *never* played for England.

When 1945 came round I realised that I was only a month off my *thirtieth* birthday. It gave me quite a shock, because when that birthday is reached the average professional footballer starts to think about his future and a new job. You don't find many players in first-class football above that age.

After thinking things over I decided to buy an hotel in Blackpool, bring Betty and Jean over, and settle down after the war to run it. I could think of no better town to settle in.

I wrote to Betty and told her of my plans. She agreed so I got the whole thing fixed up and became an hotelier. I never regretted the move. I didn't know, of course, that they were going to drop the atom bomb in 1945 and suddenly bring the war to a close.

I also didn't know about a lot of other things that were going to happen to me in that year. In fact my life was only just beginning and as for being then in my last few years of first-class football, I was miles off the beam in even thinking so.

I was in London when an urgent phone call for me arrived from Stoke. As soon as I came off I was informed that my father was seriously ill in hospital and had been asking for me. My mind had been constantly on my family for the past few days, my premonitions had been right after all. As I hurried to Stoke as fast as it was possible to do so, my thoughts were with my father. The war had kept us apart for longer periods than before, and although as time went by I had noticed that he was looking more tired and old than usual I put it down to war worries. When I arrived at Stoke I made straight for the hospital. On the way up to the ward he was in I was told that he was dying and only the determination to see me once more before he died was keeping him alive. This news knocked me for six. My father dying: it couldn't be true. I stopped in the corridor leading to his room and in a dull voice asked someone if what they told me was true. Again I was told there was no hope, and that it was better for me to know the truth before I entered the room.

When I reached the door of the sick-room I stopped for a few seconds to pull myself together, then I opened it very gently and went in. I saw the bed in which my father lay. On one side of the bed was Betty and on the other side my mother. They both looked relieved to see me. I closed the door, then walked very hesitantly to the foot of the bed. My father seemed to be asleep. I gave Betty and my mother a wan smile and asked, "How is he?" My mother turned her tear-stained face towards me and said, "He seems to be asleep at the moment, Stanley, but he keeps asking for you." I walked round the side of the bed and put my arm around my mother's shoulders. Looking across the bed at Betty, I said, "This is a bad do, Betty. I never——" My father's voice cut in with, "So you have arrived, son, at last. Where have you been all this time?" He tried to raise his hand to touch me. I sat down on the bed rather quickly and took his hand in mine. Then I managed to smile at him and said, "I was a long way from here when I received your message, Father, but I got here as soon as I could." He looked at me for some time, his hand still in mine, then he looked at my mother and said, "I told you, Mother, it wasn't like him to be late. I taught him——" His voice trailed away, he gave my mother a weak smile, then he looked into my face once more.

For minutes we stayed like that, just looking at each other. The only sound I could hear was the quick ticking of the bedside clock. I thought, *This can't be real, I must be dreaming!* The ticking of the clock seemed to be getting faster and faster. I looked up quickly. There was Betty standing at the bedside. Then I felt my mother's hand touch my shoulder. It was then that I realized that this was no nightmare. I was watching my father die. Suddenly my father said, "Son, I want you to promise me something." I turned to him quickly and said, "Yes, Father, what is it?" He tried to speak but the effort was too much. He stared at me for a few seconds, then with an effort said, "Will you look after your mother for me when I go?" I managed to say, "Of course I will, Father. I give you my word. But you are not going yet—you'll get better——" My father broke in with, "Thanks, son; that's a load off my mind. Now, there is one more thing." He stopped talking once again and lay back on his pillow. His gaze was still on my face. It was at this moment that I knew for certain that he couldn't last out much longer. I said, "Now, Father, don't talk, just take it easy." He managed to give Mother a quiet smile and she bent down and wiped his forehead with her handkerchief, then kissed him on his lips. My mother straightened herself up, and when I saw the look in my father's eyes I knew then for the first time in my life what these two had meant to each other. I was proud to know that I was their son: I also felt very humble.

A few seconds later a change came over my father's face, a look that I had seen so many times before. It was a determined look. He said, "Lift me up, son." I didn't argue. I slid my arms under him and lifted him into a sitting position, then I sat at the side to support him. My mother and Betty sat at the foot of the bed and looked at us. My father seemed to be breathing better, and when he spoke his voice sounded stronger. He said, "Listen, son.

I had only one more ambition to fulfil before I died, and that was to see you play at Wembley in a Cup Final and see you at the end of the match receive a winner's medal from the hand of our king. I shan't live to see that, but don't retire from football until you win in a Cup Final at Wembley."

I was flabbergasted. Imagine my father having that in his mind. In a fortnight's time I would be thirty years old. Time was running short—or could be—for me as a player. But I said then that I'd get that cup-winner's medal—and I meant it!

CHAPTER XIII

MY HAPPIEST NOVEMBER

ON the 3rd February, 1945, I played for England against Scotland at Villa Park, Birmingham. England won 3-2. I was thirty plus two days. No caps were awarded during the war when you played for your country, but that didn't worry me that day. I was only too pleased by the fact that after the game I was going home to Betty and Jean for a few days. As soon as the game finished I changed in record time and just made the train that took me north. A few hours later I was being greeted by Betty and young Jean, who had been allowed to stay up to wait for me.

During the next few days I just relaxed with my family and I felt the strain and tension that I had built up inside me since the death of my father a week or so earlier gradually thaw out, and when the time came for me to rejoin my unit I felt better than I had done for some time. I had felt the death of my father very much indeed, and I had Betty to thank for getting me back on an even keel.

A few weeks later she broke some news to me that really put things back in their proper perspective. She phoned me one day and asked me if I could meet her for a few minutes. I told her I could take her out for afternoon tea. When we met I could tell by the look in her eye that she had some important news for me, and also that it was good news. However, it wasn't until I had refused a second cup of tea, at the small table in the corner of a nice little café, that she opened out. She turned to me and said, "Stanley, I have some good news for you." I looked out of the window, then looked at her. "I hope you have, Betty. Now come along, don't hold me in suspense any longer. What is it?" "Hold your breath," she said. "You are going to be a father for the second time." I sat and stared at her for a second or so. "It's wonderful news, Betty, wonderful. . . . When?" She could see by my face that her news had given me a great deal of pleasure. Tapping the back of my hand with her finger-tips, she said, "This time I think we will have a boy, and about November." I threw back my head and laughed until tears came in my eyes. The tone of voice Betty had used in saying it was going to be a boy was really funny. I managed to gasp out, "Betty, you can't just say you think you will have a boy." She gave me a scornful glance and said, "It's all right you laughing. Just you wait and see, that's all. Just wait and see." I said good-bye to Betty shortly after and walked back to my unit feeling better in spirit than I had done for some time. I remember thinking to myself that it would be nice to have a son, then I decided I was thinking too far ahead and turned my mind to other channels.

From that day on things seemed to take a brighter turn. I played for England against Scotland at Hampden Park on the 14th April. England won 6–1. On the 5th May I played for England against Wales at Cardiff. England won 3–2. Then on the 26th May I played for England against Free France at Wembley. This was a drawn game, with the final score England 2, France 2. It was the first time I had been on the Wembley turf since the death of my father, and all through the game the promise I had made him was in my mind.

The Americans dropped the first atom bomb on the Japanese. Then came the first gleam of a coming peace and our spirits rose high like a tidal wave. The war was soon over. No more bombs. No more sleeping underground. No more innocent children maimed or killed. Like millions of other servicemen I started to work out how long it would be before I was discharged. My thoughts were miles out. The R.A.F. proved in no great hurry to dispense with my services.

In no time at all after the war finished, football came back in a very big way to entertain the people. The first big wave of excitement came early in November, when the Russians sent a football team to this country for the very first time. The name of the team was, of course, the Dynamos. From the moment they touched down in their plane at Croydon until the moment they said good-bye at the farewell party there was intense excitement in every branch of the football tree. The sports writers had a story every day, there was never a dull moment. As they were an unknown quantity, speculation as to their capabilities was rife. Chelsea were chosen as their first opponents. Many people in the football world said it wasn't fair to put the Russians against a First Division English club, it was too big a test. It was the Russians, however, who had insisted on playing their first match against a well-known club. When they found out that the match had been fixed for a Wednesday they went up in the air. They considered it an insult. They argued that Saturday was our big football day. Even when the Football Association secretary pointed out that he didn't have the power to disrupt eighty-eight League matches they replied with, "If a British team played in Moscow, all other games would be stopped." It was only when it was pointed out to them that many international matches are played in Britain during the week that they calmed down.

Yes, football was front-page news once more. When the day of the match arrived all London wanted to see it. Eighty-five thousand human beings packed themselves into the Stamford Bridge ground that afternoon, and I was one of them. Cars caused traffic blocks miles from the ground. Before the kick-off thousands of spectators broke on to the pitch. The police were helpless; in fact they decided it would be safer to let people remain on the touchlines. The crowd was stunned when each member of the Russian team walked on to the ground carrying a bouquet of flowers. They lined up opposite their opponents and with great dignity stepped forward and presented a bunch to each Chelsea player. The crowd yelled its head off in appreciation of this gesture of friendship. This was something new. The Russians waved their thanks to this warm welcome. Then we all settled down for the match.

The whistle went and the Russians played at a terrific pace, demonstrating in the first few minutes the important part fitness plays in the game. They played some of the most attractive football seen for years, and their ability to pass the ball to each other at great speed was astonishing. They had that huge crowd mesmerised. All they lacked in the opening half-hour was shooting ability. Goals were missed one after the other, and when Leonid Soloviev, the left-half, missed a penalty and covered his face with both hands I really thought the Russians would never score. At half-time Chelsea were leading 2–0 with goals scored by Goulden and Williams. During the interval at half-time I could hear people all round me discussing the merits of the Dynamos. The Russians most certainly made a good impression on their first British audience. The second half of the match was chock full of shocks and thrills. The game had hardly been resumed when Karsev, Dynamos' brilliant inside-right, crashed in a great goal from thirty-five yards, just to prove how wrong we were in thinking they couldn't shoot. It was a peach of a goal. A few minutes later Archangelsky, a late right-wing choice in the Russian team, scored a lovely goal that put the scores level. The crowd went wild. They just rose to this great Russian team, who were showing the true fighting spirit every British soccer fan loves to see. When Tommy Lawton, the Chelsea centre-forward, slipped by Semichastny, the Russian captain, to head Chelsea's third goal, nine minutes from time, the crowd groaned in sympathy with the Russians. The Russians fought back tooth and nail, and four minutes from time Bobrov equalised. The final result was Chelsea 3, Dynamos 3. The scenes at the end of the match had to be seen to be believed. I am sure that the Russian team, as they left the field, must have thought they were just finishing a match in Moscow, so great was the reception given them by the British spectators.

On the following Saturday it had been arranged for them to play Cardiff City at Cardiff. The Russians didn't relish the idea of leaving London or playing a Third Division side. But the papers played the match up to the full and said that the young Cardiff side would give the Russians a good run for their money. In fact, Cyril Spiers, the Cardiff manager, thought his club would put up a better show than Chelsea. The Russians finally agreed to the match. Off to Cardiff they went. The result of the match was Dynamos 10, Cardiff 1. Which proved beyond any doubt that only the best we had was good enough opposition for them.

I felt a sudden urge to play against this fabulous Russian football machine. As no match had been arranged for them against

England, and as it was most unlikely that they would visit Stoke, I couldn't see my wish being realised. The next two fixtures arranged for the Russians were against Arsenal and Glasgow Rangers. The Dynamos had particularly requested a match against Arsenal. Mr. George Allison, the Arsenal manager, found himself in a bit of a jam; he pointed out to the powers-that-be that he couldn't raise a strong team. He sought permission for Leslie Compton, Reg Lewis and Bernard Joy, on service duty in Germany, to be brought home for the match. Then I had an idea. I had a chat with Neil Franklin, the Stoke City centre-half. The result of that chat was that Franklin and I went along to have a word with our manager, Bob McGrory. I asked him if he would ring Mr. Allison to offer our services. He did so right away and the Arsenal manager was delighted, but pointed out that he had just had word that Bernard Joy would be able to get home from Germany, which meant that Neil would not be required at centre-half, but he could make use of my services. I was delighted at this good news and went down to London for the match. The Arsenal [sic] team that day was: W. Griffiths (Cardiff City); Scott, Bacuzzi (Fulham); Bastin, B. Joy, Halton; Matthews (Stoke), Drury, Rooke (Fulham), Mortensen (Blackpool), Cumner. As you can see, the team had five guest players in it. It was, however, a very useful side.

After having looked forward to this game for several days, it was just my luck that one of London's thickest pea-soup fogs should come down on the day of the match. The 54,000 fans who paid £10,000 in hard cash hardly saw a thing. Nearly everyone agreed that the game should never have been played. It started, and—what is more surprising—it finished. I myself never saw more than three yards in front of me, so you can guess what the spectators saw. The Russians scored in the first minute, but at half-time Arsenal were leading 3-2. In the second half the Russians scored two more goals, and ran out winners by 4 goals to 3. The conditions under which the match was played was bound to have an effect on the crowd, and a bad one. There was a lot of booing in the second half from the now irate spectators and I am afraid quite a lot of fouling went on on the playing pitch. I had my shirt pulled out of my shorts twice, but I had no complaints. A Russian explained to me after the match that shirt-pulling is not considered a foul in Russia. I let it go at that. The papers had a lot to say the next day. In fact I thought they said a bit too much. My name was mentioned in more than one paper and they stated that I had been roughly handled in the second half and that I had been subjected to all kinds of fouls by the Russians in their endeavours to stop my progress down the right wing. The people who were responsible for allowing the match to be played in such appalling conditions got it in the neck.

The outcome of it all was that after the Dynamos had finished their next game against Glasgow Rangers at Hampden Park they were called home from Moscow. They played before 90,000 spectators at Hampden, and after a very hard fight they held the Scottish club to a 2–2 draw, thereby retaining their unbeaten record in Britain. Following the Hampden match, arrangements had been made for them to play an F.A. XI on the Aston Villa ground on the following Wednesday. This was, of course, cancelled; indeed by then the Russians were back in Moscow. In the four games played in this country by the Russians 260,000 British football fans had paid to watch them. The consensus of opinion was that the Dynamos were the finest team to have visited this island. I think if we had had the luck to have had a fine day for the match at Highbury they would have stayed longer. It was a great pity the tour was cut short.

During the early part of this month I was in constant touch with home and Betty, as she was expecting to go into the nursing-home to have the baby at any moment. Out of the blue a message came for me that the time had arrived and Betty was away. I hurried home at once. I remember that I took the news much more calmly than I had done when Jean was born, but all the same I did a tiger-in-a-cage act in the lounge at home until the phone rang and a voice informed me that I was a father for the second time, only this time it was a boy.

CHAPTER XIV

PROMOTION

CHRISTMAS 1945 was memorable for families all over the world. It was the first peacetime Christmas for many years and although rationing was still in full force most people had made up their minds to have the time of their lives. The Matthews home was no exception. Although I was still in the R.A.F., my home was now in Blackpool at the hotel I had bought, so I had little difficulty reaching home for my Christmas dinner.

In the 1945–46 season more people attended football matches than ever before and new football names were coming into the game. I was selected to play against Belgium at Wembley on the 19th January, 1946, and the sports writers really went to town over me. This match would be the forty-fourth time I had been selected and played for England. Eddie Hapgood held the record at that time with forty-three appearances. This was a good story for the papers and they put it over in a big way. It created such a stir that 85,000 people paid to watch the match, and that is an enormous crowd for that time of the year.

In case anyone thinks that being selected for a match like this gave me special privileges in the R.A.F., I should relate what happened the week before. I was put on night duties, which meant that I was called out of bed at all hours of the night and morning, and that year we were having an unusually bitter spell of weather. On the Thursday before the international I caught a really bad cold. My duties finished that day, so before I went to bed to get a full night's sleep I took some hot milk and whisky in the hope of fighting it off. I have never smoked and never been a drinker, but this night, in desperation, I thought that the whisky might do the trick for me.

I felt much better next morning, and when I boarded the

London train at Blackpool I thought I was over the worst.
However, after I had been on the train for an hour I became very
ill. My head seemed to be going round and round like a round-
about, my breathing became difficult and I nearly fainted once
or twice. Betty had packed me a few sandwiches but I couldn't
touch them, and by the time I reached London, after a nightmare
five-hour journey, I had given up all hope of playing in the match
on the following day. After a brisk walk in the fresh air I began
to feel a little better and walked into the lounge of the hotel
where the England team was staying and met Bill Voisey, the
England trainer. He looked at me in sheer amazement. He said,
"You look terrible. What have you been doing with yourself,
Stan?"

Bill Voisey was one of the nicest men you could wish to
meet. I looked back at him through watery eyes and said, "I've
caught a bit of a cold, Bill. I'll get off to bed right away. I'll be
fit for to-morrow." Bill gave me another piercing look, then
growled, "Just a bit of a cold, eh? I should say so, laddie. You've
got the 'flu. Now get up to bed and I'll get you something to
make you sweat those germs out of you. We must get you right
for to-morrow." I made my way to my room, and it was a
blessed relief to get between the sheets and close my eyes. I woke
some time later to find Bill Voisey at the side of my bed with a
glass of hot milk in his hand. "Here, Stan, take this. I've managed
to get you a spot of medicine that will do the trick." I downed
the milk, to find that it contained a stiff dose of whisky. Anyway,
it put me to sleep. Hours later I woke to find the bed wet with
perspiration. Bill was still by the side of my bed, and although
I felt ill I must say I found Bill a great tonic. He must have been
a natural psychologist and thought that if he left me on my own
I would get depressed and lose interest in everything. He told
me several stories of the old-timers, and even persuaded me to
take some food. About 9.30 p.m. Bill gave me a good rub-down,
another drink, tucked me back in bed with a reassuring wink and
bade me good-night.

Thanks to Bill, I got a good night's sleep and woke the following morning feeling much better, except that my throat was
sore. Bill came into the room to see how I was, and he seemed

pleased with my condition. I had no idea how much trouble my cold had caused until Bill told me the reporters had been ringing the hotel continually to find out whether I would play or whether I would have to postpone the breaking of Hapgood's record of forty-three appearances for England. Bill Voisey eyed me up and down, then asked, "What shall I tell them?" My answer should have been "No", but in view of all the publicity given to the match the word "No" stuck in my throat and I found myself answering Bill's question with, "Tell them I'm playing." Bill disappeared, but he was not away for long; he came back into the room and gave me another good rub-down and then I had some breakfast. I was feeling much better, but far from feeling fit to play at all, and it was hours before a really important match!

When the time came for me to leave for Wembley I wrapped up well, and with a good thick scarf round my throat I was driven to the ground in a taxi chartered by the Football Association. Whilst I was changing in the England dressing-room just before the match someone came in the room with a set of track suits for the English players. The suits consisted of a blouse and long trousers in sky-blue colour. This was something quite new, and as I ran on to the field with the rest of the team I was particularly thankful because on this bleak January day the snow was still on the playing pitch in patches and there was a biting wind. At last our captain, Joe Mercer, lined us up to present us in turn to the Prime Minister, Mr. Clement Attlee, after which we took off our track suits and went to our positions to start the game. The line-up of the England team was as follows: Swift (Manchester City); Scott (Arsenal), Hardwick (Middlesbrough); Wright (Wolves), Franklin (Stoke City), Mercer (Everton) (captain); Matthews (Stoke), Pye (Notts County), Lawton (Chelsea), Brown (Charlton), Mullen (Wolves).

The game was in no way a classic, but it was an enjoyable one for me because as soon as the referee blew his whistle to start the game I forgot all about my 'flu. It was big Frank Swift's quietest international: he had hardly any work to do all afternoon. On the other hand, the Belgian goalkeeper, Françoise Daenen, had one of his busiest international matches. The England forwards kept up the attack all afternoon. Although Daenen was only five feet six inches in height, it was astonishing to see the way he jumped up to a high ball and the uncanny way he had of anticipating the best position to deal with any shot that came at his goal. After thirteen minutes' play Billy Wright brought off a long throw-in twelve yards inside the Belgian half and, with the opposition too surprised to move, Brown ran round Pennaye, the Belgian right-back, and left Daenen without a chance to save his shot, which entered the net like a bullet from a distance of twenty yards. Ten minutes later Jesse Pye sent the ball out to where I was standing some forty yards from goal. I took it past Pennaye to within two yards of the goal-line and made a backward pass that hovered above the goal area. Tommy Lawton went up to head it, but was inches short. The ball went on to Pye, standing about three yards behind Lawton and about twelve yards from goal. The Notts County inside-forward steadied himself, then with all the confidence in the world he shot hard and the ball went well and truly into the back of the net. The Belgian goalkeeper had been distracted by Lawton's attempt to head the ball and the ball was in the net before he could recover himself. That goal of Pye's gave me a great deal of pleasure because in the opening minutes of the game Pye had missed a sitter. This could have ruined him, as it was his first international match, but scoring as he did a little later in the game showed that he had the right temperament for a big game. It was a very fine effort on Pye's part and after his second goal it was England all the way. At half-time fog descended and more or less ruined the rest of the game. We managed to play out time and the final score was England 2, Belgium 0. I had topped the Hapgood record and as I ran off the field I received the congratulations of my colleagues and we made our way to the dressing-room.

After the game there was a banquet in the evening. I had to give it a miss. Now that the game and the excitement was over I felt ill again. In fact, within a couple of hours of the match finishing I was back in bed again at the hotel. I refused all food and spent a wretched night. I could hardly speak on the Sunday morning and I had a nightmare journey back to Blackpool but I somehow managed to get home, but I spent the next four days in bed. I felt sorry for Betty that week. She had to look after a sick husband, a two-months-old baby and Jean; but she did a good job and by Friday evening I was on my feet, though still weak.

The next Saturday Stoke City had an important cup-tie against Sheffield United. Bob McGrory, our manager, wanted me in the team if at all possible, so I reported to the Stoke ground on the Saturday morning after getting up from bed, but by the time I arrived I was certain that I hadn't the stamina to last out for ninety minutes. So I told Bob McGrory I was not fit. Bob seemed worried at this news, and he telephoned a specialist at the Royal Infirmary and asked if he could prescribe something to keep me going. As I had no fever and I was suffering through lack of exercise and missed meals, the specialist gave me two capsules which he described as pep pills. The specialist told me I would be fine if I took the pills an hour before the kick-off. I decided to play and took the pills as instructed. They did the trick and gave me the necessary stamina to pull through and help Stoke City to beat Sheffield United, so everybody was happy.

That evening I sat relaxing before the fire, feeling very tired after the hard game in the afternoon and I was just on the point of dozing off when suddenly I felt wide awake and bursting with energy. I was so keyed up inside that I had to pace up and down the room; in fact I felt so good that if anyone had asked me to play another game right away I could have gone out and played for another ninety minutes. It took me all night to get to sleep. Ever since then I have referred to those pills as D.A.P.s—delayed action pills. I woke the next morning feeling more like my normal self and I was able to get back into my usual training routine. When I returned to my unit, fit and well once more, I had a surprise waiting for me. I had been promoted to corporal. I never discovered what I had done to receive this honour. Could it be that someone felt a shade guilty for the rough fortnight I had just passed through?

CHAPTER XV

MY MOST TRAGIC MATCH

THE dressing-room door opened and in came the Stoke City manager, Bob McGrory. He glanced round the room, saw that we were ready to take to the field, and called for our attention. In his broad Scotch accent he said, "We're two down, lads. Get out and throw yourselves into the game from the kick-off. By doing this we have nothing to lose and we might gain a lot. Good luck, boys." He left the room and we began talking between ourselves.

We were in the visitors' dressing-room at Burnden Park, Bolton, and it was the 9th of March, 1946. This was the second leg in the cup-tie with Bolton Wanderers. In those days two games were played, and the team with most goals when the total was added after the two matches had been played were the winners. On the previous Saturday, on the Stoke City ground, the first leg had finished with Bolton two goals in the lead. However, we felt very confident in the combined strength of our team and we were hoping to-day at Burnden Park to wipe out the lead and leave the field one step nearer to Wembley and the Cup Final. I am sure that as we left the tunnel to run on to the playing pitch every Stoke player had only one thought in his mind—to give all he had and with the help of his colleagues win this important match. As I ran around on the pitch to get the feel of it I noticed the huge crowd (some 70,000). I knew that this match had caused wide interest, so I didn't think any more of it than being a cup-tie.

The game started and for the first ten minutes our team had the best of it. Then in the middle of play there was a terrific roar from the crowd. I glanced over my shoulder and saw a sight I shall never forget. Thousands of fans were coming from the terracing from behind the far goal on to the pitch. We didn't feel at all worried as we had seen tightly packed crowds invade the touchlines before to see the match better, and to get more comfortable conditions. This crowd, however, didn't stop at the touchlines. It came right on to the playing pitch. Then I got the feeling that there was more in this sudden invasion than met the eye.

It was, of course, impossible to continue the game with spectators on the playing area, and I wasn't surprised to see Mr. Dutton, the referee, blow his whistle to stop play. He hurried over and asked the police to push the invading spectators back over the touchline, then came back and bounced the ball where play had stopped, and the game continued. A few minutes later we were surprised to see a police sergeant walk on to the playing pitch and speak to the referee. Play stopped once more, and the police sergeant and Mr. Dutton continued to talk in the middle of the pitch. The referee then turned round and motioned to the two captains to join him. Our captain, Neil Franklin, and Harry Hubbick, the Bolton Wanderers captain, joined Mr. Dutton and the sergeant. The group broke up and our respective captains ordered their teams off the field until order was restored.

When we reached the tunnel which led to the dressing-rooms we found it packed with spectators who had not been able to see the game, and I recall hearing a broad Lancashire voice call out, "Ee, lad, but that was a quick first half." We managed to push through the crowd to our dressing-rooms and five minutes later George Mountford, Billy Mould and Alex Ormston, who had travelled to Bolton as reserves, brought us the tragic news that two or three people had been killed in the crush. We sat in our dressing-room for twenty-six minutes before Mr. Dutton came in to tell us that the game was to be resumed on the advice of the Chief Constable of Bolton. We got up and sadly walked down the tunnel on to the field once more. One angry spectator, who must have been told about the deaths. caught hold of Frank Baker, the outside-left, and shouted, " 'Tis a crime to carry on." This was silly talk, we were doing our job. As footballers we came under the orders of the referee; and if he said play, then play we did. When we once more got on to the playing pitch we could see that thousands more of the spectators had come on to the field. A fresh line had been made with sawdust, which meant we were now playing on a smaller pitch.

Once the match started we forgot about the stoppage and the tragedy. Our thoughts went back to winning the match. Stoke had a big share of the play but the ground was soggy and our forwards, including myself, could not get set to put in the really dangerous shots that would give us the goals we so desperately needed. When the whistle went for half-time not a goal had been scored by either side, and as we turned to walk off the pitch my mind went back to the tragic news we had received in the dressing-room. Mr. Walter Rowley, Bolton's secretary-manager, was standing on the touchline. He asked the referee to carry on and not let the players off the field. It was feared that a ten-minute break would have a depressing effect on the players and that as the news had by now been whispered all over the packed ground it would be better to keep the spectators' minds occupied with the match. The referee agreed to continue, and so this tragic game was resumed at once. Sure enough, as soon as the whistle went and the second half commenced, for the next forty-five minutes I had nothing on my mind but the winning of the match. I am sure that all the other players had the same experience. We tried with all our might to score; but although we did most of the attacking, the goals would not come. The nearest we came to scoring was fifteen minutes from time, when one of our players struck the crossbar with the Bolton goalkeeper beaten. After this narrow shave we piled on the pressure more and more. The Stoke wing-halves ran themselves into the ground. The forwards did not spare themselves. I roamed from the right to inside-left. But it was all in vain; it just was not our day.

When the final whistle blew we walked dejectedly from the field, realizing that Stoke had been knocked out of the Cup. In those first fleeting seconds that was the chief thought so far as I and the rest of the Stoke players were concerned. Only when we reached our dressing-room and heard more about the tragedy that had visited Bolton on that black Saturday afternoon did we realize for the first time what a disaster this match had brought to many homes in the town.

I motored back to Blackpool that evening in a very subdued mood. It was not until I came down to breakfast the following morning and picked up the Sunday papers that I read the true facts. The papers stated that 33 spectators had been crushed to death and 500 injured as a result of several hundred gatecrashers forcing their way into the Bolton ground.

· · · · · ·

In March 1946, the city of Stoke paid me the great honour of requesting my presence at 2 p.m. on the 28th in the Chambers in the Stoke City Town Hall to receive from the hands of the Lord Mayor, Mr. Percy Williams, an illuminated address in recognition of my forty-four appearances for England. This was indeed a high honour, because the only other sportsmen who had been presented with similar addresses by the Stoke Council were Lievers and Wainwright, the wonder swimmers. You will readily understand how deeply I appreciated this honour from the people I was born amongst and had lived with all those years. I was surprised and humbled that I should be asked to accept such a rare honour. As these thoughts passed through my mind I was getting near to home, and I felt as I always did when I came off my early training stint—hungry.

It was after young Stanley, my son, had emptied his bottle of milk, been put in his pram and wheeled out into the back garden that Betty dropped the bombshell. She came back into the kitchen and asked me just one question—"Oh, Stanley, have you decided what you are going to say?" I stared at her in amazement and muttered, "What I am going to say?" Betty said, "You know what I mean, don't you? At the presentation on the 28th at Stoke you'll have to make a speech, you know." "Make a speech?" I repeated. "What speech?" Betty stopped sorting out the baby's nappies and looked at me in amazement. "When they have made the presentation they will expect you to reply and thank them for it, won't they?" Of course they would, and I had never made a speech in my life! Ask me to play in front of 100,000 people and I wouldn't turn a hair, but to get up in public and make a speech! The thought sent me into a blue funk. Whatever would I do or say? "Betty, what am I going to do?"

I asked. "You're going to make a speech," she said. "All you have to do is be natural and just think of three things—the honour, the Stoke people, and your thanks." I said, "Look, Betty, I'll never make it. I never have been a talker, you know that."

Betty could see by now that I was really upset at the thought. I also knew that she wished she had never mentioned the speech. It may sound silly, but it spoiled the next few days for me, until Betty convinced me that the best way out was for me to make it as short as possible and get the three main things fixed in my mind. We left it at that, and never mentioned the matter again. I, however, gave it a lot of thought and each passing day gave me the shivers. Then, as so often happens, an incident occurred the day before the presentation that put all thoughts of the coming speech right out of my mind.

Bob McGrory had given Blackpool permission to play me in the League game against Manchester United at Blackpool at the week-end I was to travel to Stoke for the presentation. The game started off in the usual manner, and I had one or two runs with the ball. Then, out of the blue, fate struck me a cruel blow. I put my left foot out to block a pass and as I made contact with the ball, I felt a terrific pain shoot from my knee down my leg. They had to help me off the field. My heart was as heavy as lead, because I suspected I had torn the ligaments of my knee. In all the years I had been in football I had never felt a pain as bad as this one. In fact, only once before in my playing career had I been forced to leave the field through injury. As I was helped to the dressing-room my thoughts were on Hampden Park. Would this injury keep me out of the England team to play Scotland the following month? Why this should have been my chief worry I don't know to this day, because I knew that it was impossible to find out the full extent of an injury of this kind until at least two days after it had happened.

After I had the knee strapped up I returned to Betty with a long face. I thought, *What a mess! Hampden in a fortnight, a journey to Stoke to-morrow and the speech to follow.* Betty, however, suggested that we should go to Stoke overnight and show the injury to a manipulative surgeon who had a reputation of working "miracles" with his hands. I took Betty's advice and after a good meal we left for Stoke. I had treatment the following morning and took it easy all day. The next morning my knee was rather stiff and sore, but no swelling had developed, so I drove round to the Victoria Ground to report my injury to the Stoke manager. From there I drove to keep a luncheon date with the City Councillors.

Nearly a hundred people were gathered in the Chambers at 2 p.m. Betty, my mother, my daughter Jean and myself all sat close together. During the many speeches that were made I found my thoughts going back to my father's little shop in Hanley. How proud my father would have been if he could have sat with us in the Chambers. The speeches were too flattering to be repeated in this book. Although I felt nervous I found myself amused by the expression on young Jean's face as she stared fascinated at the Lord Mayor's chains. The moment came for me to speak. I stood up and my nervousness left me. I was amazed. Betty didn't say anything after, so I couldn't have been too bad.

CHAPTER XVI

MY BATTLE AGAINST TIME

I RETURNED to Blackpool after the presentation ceremony at Stoke full of confidence that I was going to make the Hampden game. My knee felt much better and, with two weeks to go, everything pointed to the leg being fit by then. I didn't want to miss this great tussle against Scotland, and I did everything I could to ensure that I was perfectly fit. I put myself in the capable hands of Alan Ure, a retired Blackpool trainer, and Johnny Lynas, the current Blackpool trainer. Both worked hard to get me fit. I took long walks along the promenade, and apart from a little stiffness, which made it difficult to bend my left leg, after a day or so the knee started to stand up pretty well. I was delighted. The trainers took another look at the knee, and after a searching examination they gave me to understand that they could have the left leg loosened up in good time for the match. Then I made a fatal mistake. In my eagerness to help I started to apply some liniment that I had brought back from Stoke. The liniment was very good, but I overdid the applications, with the result that I burned the flesh and caused severe inflammation. This meant the loss of the eight precious days' work that had been put in on the leg, and now the trainers were helpless. All I could do was to bathe the swollen knee with hot fomentations all day.

It made me ill to think that a bottle of liniment had put an end to my long run of appearances for England. It wouldn't have been so bad if I had been crocked and had no chance at all of playing in the match, but having won that battle and to mess it up myself when there was no need for me to interfere was indeed a very bitter pill. Fancy being put out of the England team through a bottle of liniment! I just couldn't get over how foolish I had been. Perhaps it was this disgust that I felt for myself that made me pack my bags with still a week to go for the match and motor over to Stoke. When I arrived I explained my position to Dr. Spark, the club doctor, and Hubert Nuthall, the trainer. They promised to do all they could for me in the next four days. So now it was a battle against time. They worked like trojans to get me fit, but the most important part of the treatment was the constant application of hot fomentations. The knee, however, seemed to retain some stiffness. In the evenings, I went on long walks, and then I had sessions on a rowing machine to try and free the stiff leg.

Thursday arrived and I had to make my final test. Hubert Nuthall said he thought I had a good chance of coming through it. I changed and took a ball on to the ground. At the first kick at the ball I felt a sharp pain. It wasn't too bad but it was there. I continued with the practice. I kicked. I twisted. I ran and I dribbled. When I had finished the tryout I knew that the leg was not strong enough, but that I could get by at a pinch. My mind was in a whirl. What should I do? Suppose I reported fit and played in the match and after the first few minutes the leg broke down? It is tough enough to win at Hampden with eleven fit men, but with ten fit men . . . I shuddered at the thought. I left the field, changed, and phoned the Football Association to inform them that I was unfit for the match. Now the matter was finally settled I felt much better and returned to Blackpool to find as a guest in my hotel Mr. Jimmy Davies, manager of Greenock Morton. He handed me six tickets for the match at Hampden and reminded me that he had promised me the tickets months before. They were very welcome.

On Friday I motored up to Scotland with two friends, and when I arrived I found the Scots very sympathetic over my bad luck. I have many friends in Scotland, and of course my wife and father-in-law are Scots, but I always cheer for England. The luckiest man in Glasgow on the eve of the match was a young Englishman who had travelled up to Glasgow to see the match without a ticket. He came to see me at the hotel and his face was very familiar. It turned out that he had been stationed with me in the R.A.F. at Blackpool. I couldn't tell him that he hadn't an earthly chance of obtaining a ticket for the match, so I handed him one of mine. He deserved it for coming all that way on chance.

If the thousands of people who had come to Glasgow that day for next day's match could have seen me at 8 p.m. that evening they would have thought I was mad—and no-one could have blamed them. I was sprinting up and down the corridor in my hotel. I had bumped into Mr. George Max, an osteopath, and at that time a director of Millwall F.C. He had come up with a party of Millwall directors who never missed a Hampden match. He told me quite definitely that he could get me fit for the Hampden match the next day. I thought he was joking; then one or two of our party went along to Mr. Max's bedroom and I went too. I stretched myself out on the bed. He pushed my left leg backwards and forwards, finally cracking it back with such force that I let out a yell. I lay there for some time and as the fierce pain died away my leg seemed to be free of all pain. I got off the bed and to my delight I found I could bend my knee more freely than before. I opened the bedroom door and sprinted up and down the corridor. I felt fine. When I got back to the bedroom I thanked Mr. Max, but at the same time I explained that it was too late to do anything about playing in the England team on the following day. Billy Elliott had been selected to play and I couldn't, under any circumstances, take his place at this late hour. In fact I had handed Billy the two tickets each player receives from the F.A. for the match, and to tell him now that I was fit to play would break his heart. So we left it at that. During the night the leg, or rather the knee, became painful again, no doubt due to the exertion I had put on it running up and down the corridor; and although it felt better than ever in the morning, I doubt if it was strong enough for ninety minutes of international football.

It was raining on the morning of the match, but as I took my seat in the stand just before kick-off the sun was shining and it looked like being a lovely afternoon. Joe Mercer led the England team out to receive the usual generous Scottish ovation. When, however, the Scottish team appeared the noise was terrific. There were 135,000 spectators that day, and when the referee blew his whistle to start the game the cheer that went up could be heard miles away. Right from the start Scotland never allowed England to settle down; in fact in the first five minutes of the game they just plastered the England goalmouth with shots. The England defence was startled at this fierce onslaught by the Scots and wavered slightly in the first minute or so, but Joe Mercer pulled them together and they made a quick recovery to a very solid firmness. The Scots kept up a ceaseless attack, but they failed to find a weakness in the England defence.

After the first fifteen minutes had gone by the Scots had a fright. Denis Compton got the ball, ran forward and sent a beautiful ball over to Tommy Lawton, dead on the target. Believe me, when Tommy Lawton really hits a ball as he did this one I doubt if there is a goalkeeper in the world who would know what to do with it. The Scottish goalkeeper, Bobby Brown, was beaten hands down, but the ball smacked the cross-bar and rebounded into play. A good hundred thousand Scots sighed with relief when they saw Husband, their left-half, whip the ball downfield out of danger. If Lawton had had the luck to score the game might have taken a different turn. As it was, Scotland put the pressure on again, and attack after attack surged down the field in the direction of the England goalmouth; but Scot and Hardwick, the English full-backs, held firm, and back would go the Scottish forwards to plan another raid. Out of the blue, Billy Elliott, England's outside-right, received the ball and took it down the wing. He cleverly slipped round Jock Shaw and centred across the Scottish goal. Up went Tommy Lawton to meet the centre. He jerked his head and hit the ball to Brown's right. Bobby Brown couldn't do a thing and the ball fell down towards the goalmouth. I was all set to yell out, when, to my dismay, I saw the ball hit the foot of the post and roll round it over the line to safety. Two inches the other way and it would have been in the net. Scotland breathed again. If Lawton had had better luck with either of his two wonderful attempts I am sure that England would have settled down and played exhibition football.

England were coming into the game more and the excitement was intense as the play switched from one end of the field to the other, both sides trying to get the first vital goal. Then England had a stroke of bad luck. I had noticed that Joe Mercer, the England captain, instead of giving his usual polished display, seemed to be struggling. As the game went on it became more noticeable. I couldn't put my finger on it at the time, but from my own experience it seemed to me that he had taken a hard knock and was trying to hide the seriousness of it from the Scottish players.

When the game was resumed after the half-time break not a goal had been scored by either side and the grim struggle continued. I admired the Scots for their determination. This was the best side they had had out since pre-war days, and as they hadn't beaten an England side for the past four years they seemed bent on doing it now. The England side, however, was also a strong one and I couldn't see much wrong with it. In fact, if Joe Mercer had been on form I think we should have beaten any team. Then, as the end of the game was in sight and people were leaving the ground to avoid the rush after the game—it happened. The referee glanced at his watch and was feeling for his whistle to blow for time when Jimmy Delaney, the Scottish centre-forward (who had played a splendid game), managed to trap a ball near the England goalmouth, and before anybody could get at him he calmly tapped the ball into the England goal. It was the last kick of the match. For a split second there was silence, then came the Scottish victory roar. It was still gathering strength after I had left the stand and pushed my way towards the exit gate.

The Scots won on their merits, for they never let up; but all the same, I felt sorry for our boys. The result, of course, was Scotland 1, England 0. It had been a grand game, but it was disappointing for England after the hard-worked defence had tried so valiantly all afternoon to keep the Scots at bay. It turned out that I was right about Joe Mercer: he got a knock on his left knee in the first few minutes, but he gamely stuck it out the full ninety minutes. Believe me, that takes a lot of courage, but Joe Mercer always had that. The next day he couldn't walk properly and an examination showed he had cartilage trouble. The England team came in for a lot of severe criticism from the sports writers, but I, for one, couldn't agree with them.

A few weeks later the first post-war football season came to an end. The 1945–46 season was over. Shortly after I was discharged from the R.A.F. at Burtonwood Camp, near Warrington, and from corporal I became plain mister. I didn't argue about this change. I had all the time I wanted now to get into top gear for the start of the 1946–47 season.

CHAPTER XVII

MY TOUGHEST SEASON

I WAS only a couple of yards from the players' entrance to the Stoke City Football ground and the new season of 1946 was under way. A chubby-faced lad about nine years old was standing alone near the entrance. His bottom lip was quivering and he was gazing wistfully after his pals, a gang of small boys about his own age, who were scampering away in the direction of the boys' entrance. It still wanted an hour to go by before the kick-off. Then I remembered—he was one of a small gang of boys who had pulled me up a few minutes ago for my autograph. I recollected noticing his face as they pushed their books at me. It was rather a sensitive one, with a certain shyness written on it. He had been the only one without an autograph book. I had held my hand out to him, but he had blushed and backed away. A passing friend had called out to me and I had waved to him, then started to walk on again to the players' entrance. Now I met the lad again, and this time—as before—he had his head down and was stubbing the ground with the toe of a well-worn shoe. From the look of him I imagined him to be one of a large family, for he was obviously wearing a hand-me-down suit. Nevertheless, he was very clean and neat in appearance. He looked up at me in astonishment when I said, "I'm sorry you forgot your book, so the best I can do for you is to write on one of my photographs. Will that be all right?" He opened his mouth, but words wouldn't come, so he nodded vigorously. I pulled a photograph out of my pocket and signed it, then handed it to him. I said, "Are you going to the match?" He found his voice and said in a shy whisper, "Yes, when they open the gates at three-quarter time. My mother hasn't any money this week." After a pause he said, "Thank you for the picture"; and then,

"The big lads won't take it off me, will they?" I said, "Not if you don't tell them until you have it safe and sound at home." His face cleared. "Now come with me. I'll fix it so that you can see the match all the way through." His face shone with happiness. He took hold of my hand in a tight grip as I led him towards the stand entrance and he said something I shall never forget: "Are you what they call a *real* friend?" We walked along a few paces more, then I said, "I suppose so." Only when I ran on the field with the rest of the Stoke City players did I suddenly remember that I hadn't asked him his name. I looked up in the stand and saw him waving at me. I waved back. Then the game started and I forgot about everything but the job in hand. I was, however, going to remember that little boy before this season was over, and the picture of him standing against the wall all alone was going to stand me in good stead.

I was now riding on the crest of a wave. But there was still something I burned to achieve. It was to appear at Wembley in a Cup Final. Then, after a few games with Stoke City in the early part of the season, I hurt my knee again, but very slightly. It wasn't a serious injury, but as I didn't want to lose any chance of playing in the international matches I did not return to the Stoke City side until 21st September, a week before the Belfast game. We played Manchester United the day I returned. It was while playing against Manchester United at the back end of the previous season (I was "guesting" with Blackpool) that I suffered the injury to my left leg that kept me out of the Hampden match. Quite early in the game I went to sprint for the ball, and tore a muscle behind the *right* knee this time. I just couldn't believe it! This was my first game after a lay-off for a slight injury, and I ran right into a really serious one. I had never had such a run of bad luck in my career. All the next day—Sunday—was spent trying to get the knee right, but it was hopeless, and on Monday my fears were confirmed and I had to notify the F.A. to that effect. On the following Wednesday the England team sailed to Belfast. I was in my hotel in Blackpool, cursing my cruel fate and one right leg. At this time there were several up-and-coming young footballers knocking on the England selectors' door for inclusion in the England team, and one of these was Tom Finney, the Preston

North End winger. The England team selectors decided to play him in my place.

On the Saturday I made myself comfortable and listened to the broadcast of the first match against Ireland. A large crowd swarmed onto the pitch before the game started, and only when a voice through the loudspeakers threatened that the game would be abandoned unless the pitch was cleared did they return to the terraces. When Carter scored a wonderful goal for England in the first minute, I could smell victory. And that was how it turned out—England 7, Ireland 2. Finney had a very good game. The next day the sports writers warned me I would have a job to get back into the England side.

The same England team played Eire at Dalymount Park on the following Monday. This was one day when there was a complete understanding between England and Ireland, and I only wish that I could have been there to see it all; for on that day 32,000 Southern Irishmen removed their hats and caps and stood motionless while the band played "God Save the King". Then the English team and officials stood to attention while the band played Eire's national anthem, "The Soldier's Song". Just before this happened an Irish pipe band had been marching up and down the field playing the song of the rebels, "The Wearing of the Green", and to cap it all a Union Jack floated at one end of the ground. After the easy win in Belfast a much easier win was anticipated in Dublin. But the Irish had other ideas. Encouraged by the roar of the spectators, they nearly beat the England team when Alec Stevenson, the Irish inside-left, sent in a smashing thirty-yard shot fifteen minutes from time. It struck the crossbar and rebounded into play and the England back, Laurie Scott, cleared it upfield. Then, with eight minutes left for play, Tommy Finney scored a lovely goal for England, and the final result was Eire 0, England 1. The Irish took the defeat in silence, and according to reporters at the game this was one match that England should not have won.

After this match I caught it in the neck again from the sports writers; they declared more freely than before that Finney had come to stay. There is no need for me to say anything about Tom Finney at this stage. His name is known far and wide these days and will always be mentioned as long as football is played. In those days he was, of course, climbing the ladder of fame very rapidly. Tom lives only a few miles away from me at Preston and over the years we have done quite a lot of travelling together with the England team. Tom, of course, played on the left wing. So if at any time you have heard that there was keen rivalry between Tom and myself—just forget it, because it isn't true.

The next international match after the Irish games was against Wales at Manchester in November, and controversy raged in the press, and indeed in all football circles, asking "Matthews or Finney?" The sports boys had something to write about now and they gave it their all. I got tired of seeing my name in the papers day after day. When the England team was announced my name was missing; the selectors had decided to stand by Finney, who had justified himself in the matches at Belfast and Dublin. Of course I was disappointed. I was now tasting the sour side of the football apple after having tasted the sweet side for so long. In fact I was beginning to think that I had eaten all the sweet part and there was nothing else left. To coincide with my other bad luck I was also undergoing a most disturbing phase with the management of my club, Stoke City. Our difficulties were so complicated that I have written a complete chapter about it, to follow this one, and when you read it you will understand better the state of mind I was in when the selection of the team for the Wales match was coming up.

As soon as Tom Finney's name was published in the England team the writers showed me no mercy. That I was finished with the England team for good became a louder cry, and indeed I was more than a little hurt when the people who once professed to be my friends turned round and began spreading it abroad that I was out for good. At first I was bewildered, then deeply hurt, and I felt so lonely and disheartened that I began to believe it myself. I missed my father then more than I had ever done; if I could have gone to him, he would have put my mind at ease with his sound common sense. On top of all this, I had the bad front-page publicity with regard to my trouble with Stoke City to contend with, and furthermore I could see that Betty was getting worried about the whole business. So one day, leaning against a wall with my head hung down and stubbing the ground with the toe of my right shoe, a sudden thought flashed through my mind. Why was I doing this—who had I seen stubbing his foot recently? The answer came immediately—the little boy outside the Stoke City ground last August. When I thought about him I began to smile to myself. I thought of the battle he had before him to make his way in the world and I thought of his words, "Are you what they call a *real* friend?" As his words went through my mind I could see again his shy smile and I thought of the faith he must have had in human nature and how I was on the point of losing all mine.

From that moment I ceased to worry, and also at that moment I decided to go to Manchester to watch the international match. England beat Wales 3-0 that day. I left the ground with Billy Meredith and before we parted he promised to look me up in Blackpool in the near future.

I was again passed over for the England-Holland game at Huddersfield. The amateur Dutch XI was completely outclassed and beaten 8-2. There was a long break before the next international match, which was against Scotland at Wembley on April 12th, 1947. To my surprise, and to the confusion of all writers who had predicted I was out of the England team for good, I was recalled.

This game was hard-fought. McLaren scored for Scotland in the first fifteen minutes and the Scots led at half-time 1-0. In the second half we tried to break through the Scottish defence the instant the referee blew his whistle to restart the game. Our attacks were repulsed by the Scots time and time again. When we were beginning to tire, success came. The ball once again landed in the Scottish penalty area, and this time "Raich" Carter managed to get it into the net. This gave us the incentive to launch more attacks, but still to no avail. The Scottish team really put on the pressure, but the English defence stood firm, and, hard as they tried, the Scottish forwards just couldn't get the goal that would put them in the lead again. As time was running out an incident occurred that I had never seen before or since on a football field. "Raich" Carter took a perfect through

pass in his stride, ran forward and stood unchallenged apart from
the Scottish goalkeeper, Miller. The 99,000 got ready to yell
"Goal", but, to their astonishment, and ours, Carter pulled up
dead, and with one foot on the ball looked round in the direction
of the referee. The referee waved him to play the ball, but the
chance of scoring a certain goal had vanished, and the ball was
whipped away by one of the Scottish defenders. Carter believed
that he had been given off-side, but the whistle he had heard
had not been blown by the French referee, M. de la Salle; it had
been blown by an unknown spectator in the huge crowd. So
instead of winning the match, as we might have done, we had
to be content with a draw—England 1, Scotland 1. I need hardly
mention that the above incident gave all the sports writers a
wonderful story. For days after, readers of the national newspapers in all parts of the country scanned the sports columns to
see if the man who blew the whistle had been discovered. He
wasn't, of course, but it made a good running story.

As I reflected on the game on my way back to Blackpool I
didn't feel too happy about my own performance—maybe I had
tried a little too hard—so I was not surprised when the selectors
recalled Tom Finney for the match against France at Highbury
a few weeks later. I didn't worry about this, because in my
League matches I was getting back to concert pitch now that I
had two sound legs again. I was also in rigid training once
more. England beat France 3-0 at Highbury. During this
match Gregoire, the French centre-half, collided with Tommy
Lawton, the England centre-forward. After treatment Gregoire
finished the game on the wing. As this was the first time England
had beaten France in their last three meetings, it must be assumed
that the injury to Gregoire badly upset the balance of the French
team. England never expected such an easy victory, although
they played very well indeed. Incidentally, both Lawton and
Gregoire had to leave the field to have stitches in their cuts.

The 1946–47 season was now almost over, and I wasn't a bit
sorry to see the end in sight. It had been one of the unluckiest
in my career. For years I had never had such a poor season with
regard to international appearances. However, there still remained one very important international match to be played in

this country before finis could be written to the season. Just a
week after England had beaten France, Great Britain was due to
meet the Rest of Europe at Hampden Park, Glasgow. The date,
10th May, 1947. Nine years earlier I had played for England
against the Rest of Europe at Highbury. This match, however,
was far more important, as the Great Britain team was to be
chosen from England, Ireland, Scotland and Wales. It was a
special match arranged to celebrate the return of the Football
Association to the International Federation after a break of
eighteen years, and the full glare of publicity was focused on it
even before the England *v*. France match had been played. The
result was that the football public of Great Britain thought themselves very lucky to get tickets.

With the England *v*. France match out of the way the papers
gave the coming match the strongest treatment they could and
everyone waited with impatience for the Great Britain team to
be announced. The selectors had the cream of the star players of
England, Ireland, Scotland and Wales to chose from, so it should
be a great team. At last the editions came on the streets announc-
ing the Great Britain team. It was as follows: Swift (Manchester
City and England); Hardwick (Middlesbrough and England)
[captain], Hughes (Birmingham and Wales); Macaulay (Brentford and Scotland), Vernon (West Bromwich Albion and Ireland), Burgess (Tottenham Hotspur and Wales); Matthews (Stoke
City and England), Mannion (Middlesbrough and England),
Lawton (Chelsea and England), Steel (Greenock Morton and
Scotland), Liddell (Liverpool and Scotland). Yes, I was in the
team, and what a pleasant surprise that was. It pleased me in
more ways than one, because it showed that the England selectors
must have been more than satisfied with the recent form I had
been showing. Furthermore, I deemed it a very high honour to
be selected for my country in such a match as this, and, of course,
my selection would put an end to all the talk that I wouldn't
make the England team again. Betty was highly delighted at the
news and she was of the firm opinion that this good fortune
would be the turning-point in my general affairs that had been
unsettled for so long. I agreed with her and said I hoped she was
right.

Karel Lotsy, of Holland, was in charge of the Rest of Europe team, and Jack Carey, the Manchester United and Irish international right-back, was chosen to captain it. The Rest of Europe team, when finally selected, read as follows: Da Rui (France); Peterson (Denmark), Steffen (Switzerland); Carey (Eire) [captain], Parola (Italy), Ludl (Czechoslovakia); Lemberechts (Belgium), Gren (Sweden), Nordahl (Sweden), Wilkes (Holland), Praest (Denmark). It was arranged that the Great Britain team should wear dark-blue jerseys, the Rest of Europe Cambridge blue.

Hampden Park was packed with 134,000 spectators on the day of the match, and you could almost taste the fever of excitement in the air. As I changed in the Great Britain dressing-room prior to the match it amused me to hear the various accents. Our team consisted of five Englishmen, three Scots, two Welshmen and one Irishman. When we had finished changing we sat around in a happy group chatting away, and it seemed next to no time before we got the signal to take to the field. Both teams got a tremendous reception as we ran out of the tunnel on to the field, and when the game started the spectators set up a roar which never let up until the final whistle. The game had been in progress a few minutes when I got the feeling that we were going to have an easy win. I felt this from the way the British forward line was moving—in complete harmony. Wilf Mannion, who played at inside-left in the England team, had been switched to inside-right for this match, and he kept me supplied with a perfect stream of passes all through the game. I was feeling very happy and enjoying the match a treat. With the forward line playing like it was, we were unlucky not to have been a goal up in the first few minutes. The first goal eventually came after twenty minutes when Mannion scored. Then, as so often happens in football, the Rest of Europe got on level terms almost immediately. Praest, the Danish left-winger, received the ball and dashed off down the wing at great speed. With a lovely display of dribbling he rounded Hardwick, our captain, and passed to their centre-forward, Gunnar Nordahl, who equalised the score from a few yards out. It was a well-taken chance. The Great Britain forward line swept into action once more and Mannion sent a lovely shot goalwards; the goalkeeper was beaten. However, Ludl, the Czech left-half, diverted the shot with his hand. Mannion then scored from the penalty spot. After this goal there was no stopping our forwards. Billy Steel collected the ball and after a most amazing run down the centre of the field, in which he beat three Europeans, he crashed the ball into the back of the net from thirty yards out. He surprised everyone by doing this, even his own teammates, as we all expected him to pass. So half-time came with the score 3–1 in our favour.

In the second half, Tommy Lawton, our centre-forward, came into his own. He scored two wonderful goals. One came from my centre. I had received the ball and shaken off all opposition, then, giving a quick glance towards the goalmouth, I saw Tommy Lawton's shining head of hair. I centred and Tommy made no mistake, his head connected with the ball and it flew into the back of the net. We kept up the pressure until Parola, the Italian centre-half, who had played a great game, had the misfortune to turn the ball into his own net. This was very bad luck, and I felt extremely sorry to see him do it. That was the end of the game, with the result Great Britain 6, Rest of Europe 1. Everyone who saw this game agreed that it was wonderful entertainment, and so was the sportsmanship. There wasn't a serious foul in the whole of the match.

CHAPTER XVIII

MY FAREWELL TO STOKE CITY

FOR the next part of my story I go back seven months to October 1946. After I had hurt my knee playing against Manchester United on the 21st September I had to drop out of the England team that visited Ireland to play in Belfast and Dublin, and Tom Finney took my place. On October 19th Stoke were due to appear at Highbury to play Arsenal. As I was now perfectly fit, I was looking forward to making my comeback in London, and above all against Arsenal. I saw the Stoke manager, Bob McGrory, and reported fit for the Arsenal match. He didn't appear to be at all anxious to include me in the team. In fact he suggested that it might be as well for me to have a run with the reserves. I told him that I couldn't take his suggestion seriously and we had a few hard words to say to each other. As he did not order me to play with the reserves, but only suggested it, I was not defying either the Stoke manager or the directors. The outcome of my talk with Bob McGrory was that I was told I would not be included in the team to play against Arsenal and I told McGrory not to put my name on the reserve team sheet. How the press got to know anything about the nature of this meeting I still don't know, but the following morning I awoke to find that all the national newspapers had the story. To make matters worse, one report stated that the Stoke players had sent a deputation to the management requesting that I shouldn't return in place of George Mountford. I was deeply hurt when I read that, and at the same time I was getting hammered by the press with regard to Tom Finney and the coming international match against Wales at Manchester in a few weeks' time.

The next few days were a nightmare. I went about my normal

business attending to the correspondence at the hotel and training on the Blackpool ground each morning. I never spared myself in the least, and I knew that I was as fit as ever. The phone rang incessantly and the sports writers began to waylay me because they couldn't get me on the phone. To cap it all, the postman began to deliver poison-pen letters, some accusing me of poor sportsmanship.

Football is my living, and I knew that if I agreed to play with the reserves and the Stoke first team continued their winning ways I might have to remain in the reserves for months or the whole season. I couldn't afford that. I knew I was perfectly fit and experienced enough to play with the first team, and if I had thought for one instant that I was slipping I would have got out of the game there and then. Then the papers got on to the transfer angle, although I had not even thought of asking for one. One paper said I was going to Blackpool. Others said that Chelsea, Arsenal, Newcastle and Aston Villa were after my transfer. Headlines stated that if I was transferred £20,000 would be asked. I have never thought myself to be worth all that money —big money in those days. In fact I was getting more space in the newspapers than Hermann Goering, who that same week had cheated the Allied hangman out of a job by swallowing a phial of cyanide of potassium a few hours before the time fixed for his execution. I had had enough and slipped away from the hotel and hid myself until I received word from Betty that it was quiet enough to come back home.

When I was at my lowest ebb I received a letter from Neil Franklin, the Stoke and England centre-half. In this letter he denied that there was even a grain of truth in the published reports that the players were against me. Neil had resented this smear, and he called all the team together and asked if any player had approached the management. No one had. Neil then asked if he could deny the statement on behalf of the team. They all nodded agreement. He put all this information in his letter to me and it was written with such obvious sincerity that by the time I had read it through my eyes were full of tears. I shall never forget that gesture. It was like taking a knife out of the small of my back.

Stoke went to play Arsenal without me. I stayed in Blackpool. Stoke were strongly fancied to beat Arsenal, who hadn't won a home game that season. However, Stoke did not have a good day and Arsenal broke their home duck with a 1–0 victory. I was sorry for George Mountford, he is a grand fellow and a good footballer. As I had no quarrel with him it was unfortunate that he should also become a victim of publicity. Perhaps that is why, along with several other Stoke players, he didn't play up to his usual standard against Arsenal. Too much bad or good publicity can upset a player's form more than most people imagine.

After the Arsenal match Bob McGrory contacted me at Blackpool, and I agreed to go to Stoke on the following Tuesday to meet the directors. Even that reached the papers, and one report said that Alderman Harry Booth, our seventy-year-old chairman, was going to reprimand me and inform me that in future I must train at Stoke. I motored over to Stoke on the Tuesday with an open mind. I knew that a terrible fuss had been made over nothing at all, and I was more than eager to get the whole wretched business settled.

I met my directors behind locked doors and for two solid hours the whole business was sorted out. The directors agreed to my request for a week's rest and they also agreed that I should be allowed to continue to train at Blackpool as my business was there. There was no ultimatum from either side and we finished up with handshakes all round. Reporters and photographers were then admitted, and photos were taken of me shaking hands with the directors. Then an official bulletin was issued to the reporters, which read as follows: "The differences between the board and Stanley Matthews have been amicably settled, but because of the publicity of the last few days Matthews has asked the board to grant him a week's holiday. This has been agreed."

When I arrived in Blackpool I entered the hotel by the back entrance. October was well out of season and business was at a low ebb. As I walked down the footpath leading to the back door I could see a light shining through the window of the small private sitting-room which I reserved for the use of my family. I walked up to the window and peered in. Everything looked nice and cosy. Betty was sitting by a cheerful coal fire with young Stanley on her knee, and Jean was on a stool reading a book. From the look on Betty's face, it seemed to me that Jean was reading her mother a story. A few seconds later I was in the room, and after the first flush of excitement had died down I sat down with my family and told Betty the good news. She was delighted. There and then we made plans to get away from Blackpool for a few days.

After my holiday I resumed my duties with the Stoke team in my usual position and everything seemed to settle down again. The only fly in the ointment was the uncertainty of my future in international football, and I ceased to worry about that after my trip to Manchester the following month and the delightful afternoon I spent with Billy Meredith. The winter months seemed to speed along, and on the 1st February 1947 I celebrated my thirty-second birthday. It was in the first few days of April that the trouble at Stoke flared up once more. I was chosen to play for England against Scotland at Wembley on the 12th April, and the week-end before this match was the Easter week-end. Stoke City had three matches to fulfil over the Easter period. They were due at Grimsby on Good Friday, at home to Huddersfield on the Saturday, and at home to Grimsby on Easter Monday. As I was anxious to be at my best for the Wembley match, I had a word with Bob McGrory and asked him if he could rest me in the match at Grimsby. He agreed, but stressed the fact that he would expect me to report at Stoke on the Saturday to play against Huddersfield. I assured him that I would be there and thanked him for helping me with regard to the Good Friday match.

On the evening of Good Friday I motored to Stoke from Blackpool and reported at the Stoke manager's office at ten-thirty on the Saturday morning. Stoke had gained a convincing win over Grimsby on Good Friday, so as I walked along to the manager's office it occurred to me that Bob McGrory might want to stick to a winning side for the game against Huddersfield. I made up my mind that I would fall in with him if this was his decision, and stand down. However, when I entered his office he informed me that he wanted me to play and told me to be at the ground at the usual time. I arrived at the Victoria Ground forty-five minutes before the kick-off and entered the dressing-room to get changed. Bob McGrory popped his head inside the room and called me out. He told me that my services were not required as he had changed his mind and decided to field the team that won at Grimsby. I said I thought that was fair enough, but I couldn't understand why I hadn't been told in a more straight-forward manner a few hours earlier. I stayed to watch the match, and Stoke beat Huddersfield fairly easily. As soon as the match was finished Bob McGrory sought me out and informed me that the same winning team would be fielded against Grimsby at Stoke on Easter Monday. I said that it seemed to be a very sound policy, and as my services would not be required I would get back to Blackpool.

On the following Saturday, whilst I was engaged in the inter-national match at Wembley, Stoke City played Blackpool at Blackpool and won the game. A week later Stoke were due to play Brentford at Stoke, and on the Wednesday before the match my name was included among six other forwards on the team sheet. I reported at the Stoke ground on the Saturday morning and was told I was playing. Much to my surprise, George Mountford, who had been successfully holding the out-side-right position, was moved to the inside-right position to partner me. After the match I got the shock of my life. I found out that the only reason I was included in the team was because another player was unfit. I saw the directors right away. They denied it. I pulled out of my pocket a Stoke City programme for the Brentford game, and the evidence in the programme showed beyond any shadow of doubt that my name was missing from the Stoke team printed in it.

For the first time in my life I really had my back up. I lost confidence in everybody connected with the club. Every foot-baller must feel that he has the confidence of the club behind him—directors, manager and players—otherwise his own con-fidence will go and his game will rapidly deteriorate. I knew at that moment that the time had arrived for me to leave Stoke. I asked to meet the directors, and a date was fixed for the 23rd April. At the meeting I told them how strongly I disliked what I thought was the underhand work that was going on, and that through no fault of my own I was being made to suffer once more from bad press publicity. The directors seemed to be sympathetic and offered to do what they could to avoid my being unsettled, but I had heard all this before. One paper had said I had refused to play on Good Friday. Another said that I had been dropped from the Saturday and Monday games at Easter as a disciplinary measure, owing to my refusal to play on Good Friday. Another announcement stated that I would have to play inside-right to Mountford. I claimed that the directors knew, and I knew, that these reports were not true, but what about the British public at large? Did they know?

I told the directors that I wanted to leave the club. Their first reaction was to refuse my request; but when they saw that I would never be at home again with the Stoke City team they softened and agreed to a transfer. They asked me which club I would like to go to. I said Blackpool. They then agreed that I could go there. Once this had been agreed, a condition was made that was to bring me yet more trouble. The condition was that nothing that had been decided at this meeting should be told to anyone outside the room. It was urged that it would be disastrous to let the press get the slightest inkling of what was decided. In fact a pact of secrecy was made. Alderman Harry Booth, the chairman, bound all those present in the room at this meeting to secrecy, and everyone pledged on his honour that not a word would pass his lips until the matter was finally settled. It was then decided that I should remain a Stoke player until the end of the season, and negotiations with Blackpool would be opened in July. This suited me, and provided that all of us kept his promise there was ample time for this incident to be forgotten and negotiations with Blackpool could be opened in July in the right atmosphere. The meeting closed in harmony with handshakes all round. It was now only a matter of everyone keeping his mouth shut.

A few days later I left with the Football League XI to play in Ireland and I looked forward to spending a few enjoyable days amongst the many friends I had in that lovely country. The boat docked and I hurried off with the rest of the players to meet our friends whom we could see waving to us from the dockside.

Imagine my surprise when, instead of being greeted by my friends, I was surrounded by a group of reporters who asked me to tell them all about the news which I had up to that moment believed to be a secret. I kept my bargain and refused to comment. This, of course, made matters worse. Somebody had broken his word, and once more I was going to get it in the neck.

The rest of the day was ruined for me, and when I went down to breakfast the next morning there it was in all the newspapers. The first thing I did after breakfast was to phone Betty in Blackpool. She was completely in the dark, so I knew it was only fair to tell her not to worry, and that I had given my word not to tell anyone—and that included my wife. After I had put Betty's mind at rest I settled down to read the papers. One paper said I had handed the directors an ultimatum and had told them that if they refused to transfer me to Blackpool I intended quitting football and they would lose a five-figure transfer fee. Another paper said this, another said that. . . . Well, why go on? They were all wrong. One fact was true—someone in that room had betrayed a trust. Someone had let the whole board of directors down and had severed for ever the final link that held me to Stoke, and that person had every reason to be disturbed by the trouble he had dropped into my lap.

My trip to Ireland was ruined, and on my return to Blackpool I found insulting letters from Stoke supporters, and their contents cut me to the quick. I was accused of being all kinds of things, the least of these being that I was swollen-headed and a bad sportsman. These people had the facts wrong, of course; but to receive such letters from my own townsfolk, who had watched me play for seventeen seasons, made me feel ill, as there wasn't a thing I could do to convince them that they were wrong. However, the breaking of the news certainly speeded up my transfer to Blackpool. The chairman of Blackpool, the late Colonel Parkinson, contacted Stoke and began negotiations. These were held up by Stoke asking for more money than Blackpool were prepared to pay. Colonel Parkinson told Stoke that they should be more reasonable about the fee, in view of the fact that I had made the request to go to Blackpool, and that he was not prepared to pay a record fee, as no other clubs were bidding for my services.

F

Meantime I had been chosen to play in the Great Britain team at Hampden Park on the 10th May, and it was while I was resting quietly with the rest of the Great Britain team at beautiful Aberfoyle, at the foot of the Trossachs, overlooking Loch Ard, that the Stoke and Blackpool officials decided to meet in Glasgow to watch the match and try to get the terms finalised. I believe it was the night before the match when the parties came to terms. A fee of £11,500 was agreed upon after negotiations had all but broken down. It was, I think, the late Sir Francis Joseph, the Stoke City president (who always had my interests at heart), who stepped in and closed the deal for Stoke. So a few hours after I had helped Great Britain defeat the Rest of Europe 6–1 I signed the necessary forms in the room of my Glasgow hotel. Blackpool were represented by Messrs. Harry Evans, vice-chairman at this time, and Joe Smith, the manager, who handed a cheque for £11,500 to Stoke City, represented by Messrs. Enshall and Burton (directors) and Bob McGrory. After I had signed Sir Francis Joseph took me aside and wished me all the luck in the world with my new club. A great gesture from a great man. I was glad it was all over.

CHAPTER XIX

MY LISBON STORY

I CAREFULLY removed the crinkly protective covering from a new Dunlop 65 golf ball, dropped the covering in the wastepaper bin at the side of the first tee, then noted that the number for identification was four. I placed the ball on the top of a bright-red plastic tee peg, bent down and pushed the peg into the rich green turf, and then took my driver out of my golf bag. After a couple of practice swings I addressed the ball, took a rather slow swing backwards until I could see it dead in line with my left shoulder and left eye, then started my downward swing. I kept my head down until, I heard the sharp click which denotes a well-hit ball, then, as I followed through and my head came round with the rest of my body, I saw a sight that never fails to thrill me. With a clear blue sky as a background, I saw the golf ball soaring upwards like a wingless white dove—a little white dot standing out vividly against a flawless blue background. I stood fascinated at the beauty of it as it curved its way back to earth, hit the lush green grass, bounded up in the air again, came down and ran forward along the turf in the middle of the fairway. I gave a sigh of contentment but was quickly brought back to earth by the voice of one of the foursome I was playing with, asking me if I was waiting for someone to take my photograph. A few minutes later, amidst lighthearted chatter, the four of us left the tee and walked down the fairway towards the first green.

It seemed incredible that less than a week ago I had been playing at Hampden Park, and that now I was a Blackpool player, here in Zurich, Switzerland, along with sixteen other players, in the England team headquarters at the Dolder Grand Hotel, playing golf on the hotel's private golf-course. This was the first time that I was to represent England as a Blackpool player and it was also the first time the Football Association had flown an English team as far as Switzerland, on to Portugal, and back to London.

After we had finished the game of golf we changed in the locker room and returned to the hotel. I walked across my room to the window and looked out at the breath-taking scenery. I have always liked Switzerland and its people, and a smile came to my face when I remembered my last visit here in 1938, and my tussle with the night-club bandleader who played left-back for Switzerland. After dinner I sat on the verandah of the hotel with the rest of the team, listening to the chatter and the leg-pulling that goes on when the team is on tour, then I turned in for a good night's sleep. I was awake at the crack of dawn and slipped out of bed and hurried over to the window. Throwing it wide open, I took several deep breaths of the cold crisp air, inhaling and exhaling slowly. If I had been blessed with a talent for painting, I would have put on canvas the scene visible from my room and called it "A View From My Window". A few minutes later I was doing a spot of training in the grounds of the hotel.

We ran onto the field that afternoon to the cheering of 34,000 Swiss fans. What a reception they gave us! It equalled the one they gave to their own team. Play started in a happy atmosphere, but there is not a lot I can say about this game, except that we had our chances to score in the first half and didn't take them. The Swiss outside-left, Fatton, however, scored a good goal for Switzerland, and the Swiss held the lead at half-time. Instead of getting on top of the Swiss in the second half, as we expected to do, we found ourselves up against a team that was more confident and faster in tackling than they had been in the first half. Try as we would, we could not break through their defence, and the result of the match was Switzerland 1, England 0. This was a blow to the England team, who hadn't lost a match in the 1946–47 season; but goals count and we didn't begrudge Switzerland their victory. However, I am certain that one of the England players put his finger on the spot when he remarked, back in the dressing-room after the match, that it wasn't Switzerland that had won the game for them but claustrophobia. I think there is a lot of truth in what he said, because a small ground doesn't suit an English international team; we are used to playing on more spacious ones. On the small grounds the Swiss teams use, English players are apt to get a feeling of being closed in and playing on top of each other. I know I got the feeling the first time I played against Switzerland in 1938, and we also lost that day—by two goals to one. When I played for England against Switzerland at Highbury eighteen months later we ran out easy winners by six goals to nil, so there must be something in the size of the playing pitch, because I am sure the Swiss in that match found the Highbury pitch much too vast for them.

After losing 1–0 to Switzerland we moved on to Geneva for a match against a Swiss "B" team. There were five changes made in the England team for this match, and I for one was rested. This match ended in a draw. The next day we left for Portugal.

We had a good flight to Portugal and made a perfect landing at Lisbon. On leaving the airport we were put into cars and driven to a luxurious hotel in Estoril, about eight miles away. During this eight-mile journey I realised why the Portuguese people are so rightly proud of Estoril. If you close your eyes for a few seconds and try to imagine a blue sky merging into a lighter-blue sea on the horizon, beautiful snowy white buildings set amongst exquisite displays of geraniums, dotted with miniature palm trees and gardens that must be classed among the finest in the world, you will have a good idea of the picture I had that day from the seat of the car. I was thrilled with it all, and I could understand why it was called the Millionaires' Playground. The millionaires had to pay to be there, but I was getting it all for free, and I appreciated it all the more.

It was decided by the powers-that-be to drive the England team out to the National Stadium to look it over before the match took place. I was looking forward to this trip. You see, I had already played once before on this famous ground and so had two other members of the present England party, Laurie Scott and Neil Franklin. The three of us had been members of the R.A.F. team that had been flown over to Portugal to play the Portuguese Army team in 1946. The game had ended in a draw, but the Portuguese would argue that they had defeated England—or nearly defeated them. Even when it was pointed out to them that although the R.A.F. team was a strong side, it should not be compared with a specially selected international England team, they still didn't want to know. They had got it firmly entrenched in their minds that they had held the might of England at bay when they played the R.A.F. Scott, Franklin, and myself knew that in the coming match the Portuguese really fancied their chances. We also knew that our recent defeat in Switzerland by the Swiss team had made them more confident than ever. Therefore the three of us had made up our minds that if we were selected for the match we would run ourselves in the ground, if necessary, to prove to the Portuguese that a full England team is a much harder nut to crack than a R.A.F. or Army team.

I noted with pleasure the look of wonderment that came over the faces of the English party who were seeing this fabulous stadium for the first time. This magnificent white-marbled stadium is a show piece treasured in such a manner by the Portuguese that they allow only special matches to be played in it. It cost £350,000 to build during a period when unemployment was rife in Portugal. Allowing for the fact that the white marble came from Portugal, it was built very cheaply. To build such a stadium in England would be almost impossible; the white marble would have to be imported, and all the other overhead expenses would, in my opinion, bring the cost to well over a million pounds. The playing pitch is one of the finest in the world. It is every bit as good as the Wembley pitch, as it is composed of the finest Cumberland turf imported from Britain. The Portuguese football fan never stands to watch a match, he sits through the game on the white marble benches. There is no overhead covering at all, but with the almost perpetual sunshine the spectator seldom requires cover. At the back of the stadium there is a beautiful white balcony supported by the most extravagant pillars; this balcony of rare beauty is reserved for the President and his friends.

The selection of the England team for this most important match was delayed by the selectors until they received the final fitness reports on Phil Taylor, the Liverpool wing-half, and Bobby Langton, Blackburn Rovers' left-winger. Both had been injured in the Geneva game. Neil Franklin was also suspect owing to a knock he had received on his ankle. All were receiving treatment from Walter Max, physiotherapist of the England team.

After taking the advice of Walter Winterbottom, the F.A. team-manager, the selectors decided that only Franklin was fit to play. Stan Mortensen was brought in to partner me at inside-right, and Tom Finney was selected at outside-left in place of the injured Langton. This was the first time that Tom Finney played in the outside-left position for England. It was not going to be his last by a long way.

On the day of the match the teams lined up as follows— PORTUGAL: Azevedo; Cardozo, Feliciano; Amaro, Moreira, Ferreira; Correira, Araujo, Peyroteo, Tracasos, Rogerio. ENGLAND: Swift (Manchester City); Scott (Arsenal), Hardwick (Middlesbrough) [captain]; Wright (Wolverhampton), Franklin (Stoke City), Lowe, E. (Aston Villa); Matthews (Blackpool), Mortensen (Blackpool), Lawton (Chelsea), Mannion (Middlesbrough), Finney (Preston North End).

The game didn't start on time owing to an argument about the size of the ball to be used in the game. The Portuguese wanted to use their size 4 football, which is smaller than ours and more like the size used by school teams in England. The England officials wouldn't agree to this.

While this matter was being sorted out we were left kicking our heels in the dressing-room. This can be most upsetting to a bunch of footballers all keyed up to start a big match, but we didn't have to worry. With Frank Swift and Stanley Mortensen in the dressing-room, it was impossible to get nervy. These two England players kept us entertained until we received the order to take to the field. We ran on to the cheers of 60,000 Portuguese football fans, who were still yelling their heads off when the game started—with the full-sized ball. The English officials had won the argument.

Ten seconds after the start Tommy Lawton headed the first goal for England. As Azevedo, the Portuguese goalkeeper, bent down to pick the ball out of the net you could almost feel the silence that had fallen on the ground. For a couple of seconds everybody in that wonderful setting seemed to have turned into marble, like their surroundings. It wasn't until Azevedo booted the ball upfield in disgust that we rushed to congratulate Tommy Lawton as one man. This was a magnificent start.

Portugal kicked off again, and a couple of minutes later Laurie Scott noticed that they had somehow got rid of the large ball and had kicked off with the smaller one. We decided not to protest, and we played as if we hadn't noticed the switch. All the same, I couldn't help but admire the person who had made the switch, it had been done so deftly.

However, when the game had been in progress just seven minutes Stan Mortensen received a lovely pass from someone just behind him; he quickly trapped the ball and crashed it past Azevedo into the back of the net. As Stan trotted back upfield the grin on his face seemed to say, "Now they will put the big ball back."

They didn't oblige. Just on four minutes after the Mortensen goal Tommy Lawton let fly with a good twenty-five-yard drive, and the ball shook the back of the net like an angry wasp. England were leading 3–0.

Twelve minutes after the Lawton goal Tom Finney, who had settled down in the outside-left berth as if that was his regular position, received the ball in his own half and dribbled it at remarkable speed down the left wing, beating all opposition. He capped a remarkable exhibition of ball-control by slamming the ball into the back of the net. This terrific solo effort of Finney's brought the now dispirited Portuguese crowd to their feet, and they cheered Finney all the way back to the centre of the field.

Then the storm broke. The cheers turned to whistles as the crowd turned their anger on poor Azevedo. They never let up until Capela, the second-string goalkeeper, came rushing onto the field and Azevedo, with head bowed, left in shame. This was against the pre-match agreement of substitutes, because Azevedo was not injured; however, we let it go.

A few minutes later Lawton cracked in another great goal. There was also a second substitution when Cardozo, the right-back, was replaced by Vasco. So half-time arrived with England leading 5–0.

In the terrific heat on this Sunday in May, we started the second half of the match determined not to let the heat tire us and rob us of clear-cut victory. We had no need to worry on this count, however. It was the Portuguese team that started to tire, and I soon found out that Feliciano, the left-back, had given up hope of stopping me and it was only too easy to run round him. This enabled me to lay on some good passes to my centre-forward and inside man, and before long Mortensen had cracked home another couple of goals and Lawton scored his fourth. Then shortly after Lawton's goal Mortensen scored another, which meant that he and Lawton had scored four goals each, and Finney one, making the score 9–0.

It seemed to me that at this point the spectators had a change of heart and realized that they were watching an England team who on this form could probably have beaten any team in the world. The crowd began to show, in no uncertain manner, their approval of the fine exhibition of football the English team was giving.

Just before the end of this enjoyable match I received the ball on the right wing and made up my mind to go all the way through to the goalmouth with it. I pulled out all the tricks I knew and found myself right on the goal-line with only the Portuguese goalkeeper, Capela, in front of me. Before he could size up the situation I gently tapped the ball over the line, to bring the England total to double figures. Soon afterwards the final whistle blew and we left the field, with the final result Portugal 0, England 10.

At the banquet given in our honour that night the Portuguese team didn't turn up, and they were later suspended by the Portuguese F.A. We eventually found out that it was genuine shame that had caused them to slip off to their homes, and when our own F.A. ascertained this was true they made a special request for the suspension to be lifted. I was glad to learn this, because the players had shown wonderful sportsmanship throughout the game.

CHAPTER XX

BLACKPOOL F.C.

I HAD reported for training with my new club Blackpool and life had entered a new phase. When I reported to the manager, Joe Smith, I had the feeling of starting a brand-new football career, and in a way I was. Everything was fresh. A new club, new players and ground, a different routine, and of course different supporters.

Everyone was so kind to me on my first day, and when work was over and I returned home I had the feeling that I was going to be happy at Blackpool—and I wasn't wrong. The 1947-48 season turned out to be one of the best the club had enjoyed for a long time. On top of this I was chosen for England in all the internationals in that season; the only game I missed was against Sweden at Highbury in November, when, at the very last minute, I had to be excused from playing owing to a leg injury. This good international luck meant that I broke the Billy Meredith record, as that great winger had said I would. Furthermore I was receiving very good press reports, all the sports writers were good to me and wished me luck in my first Blackpool season.

Blackpool started off the season in grand style, and by the time the cup-ties came round they were near to the top of the First Division. We had fought our way to the fifth round when we met the Cup giant-killers, Colchester United. The sports pages in the national newspapers were full of praise for the then non-League club. Colchester had the old West Ham United centre-half, Ted Fenton, as their player-manager; he was known as the "Man with a Plan." They had created a sensation in the third round by knocking out Huddersfield Town, and in the fourth round they polished off Bradford, who had defeated Arsenal at Highbury. Ted Fenton claimed to have spotted weaknesses in the Huddersfield and Bradford teams and had staged dress rehearsals, behind locked doors, before the matches. After the Bradford victory Ted was mobbed by 16,000 delighted Colchester fans, and this little club made big headlines when they were drawn against us in the fifth round at Bloomfield Road, Blackpool. Ted said right away that he had a secret plan to beat us, and the papers played the match up in a big way. There was no doubt about it, Ted Fenton was a man everyone in the football world was talking about, and not only did he get Colchester voted into the Football League at the end of the season but, because of the fine showing they put up in the Cup rounds, he must at the same time have put up the sales of Colchester oysters to undreamed-of figures. He put Colchester on the map in more ways than one that season.

A few days before the match Ted Fenton brought his players to Blackpool and they stayed at my hotel. More publicity followed. Then he asked Joe Smith's permission to train on Blackpool's ground. This request was granted. Still more publicity. Then on the eve of the match he brought out the "F" for Fenton Plan to beat Blackpool, so it is little wonder that on the day of the match the Blackpool ground wasn't big enough to hold all the people who came to see the match. All the big sports writers came along and the press-box was packed like a tin of sardines. I don't believe in putting too much faith in pre-arranged plans, so I wasn't unduly worried when we ran on the field to start the match. Amidst intense excitement the game started, but it didn't take the spectators long to find out that this time the "F" Plan had misfired. We finished easy winners, with the final score 5–1 in our favour. The Fenton boys were in no way disgraced, and I am sure that if we had been drawn to play Colchester on their own ground, which is on the small side, we should have had to pull out all the stops to win. Even after their defeat, the team returned to Colchester in triumph and received a royal reception on their arrival. Incidentally Ted Fenton later returned to his old club, West Ham United, as manager.

After our win against Colchester we went on to reach the Final. Our opponents were Manchester United. This indeed was a good way to finish off my first season with a new club, to play at Wembley in a Cup Final. Indeed things were never brighter. Twelve months ago I was in the dog-house good and proper. Some sports writers had written me off as finished—or at least finished with the England team. Yet here I was with the rest of the Blackpool team looking forward to playing against Manchester United in the Cup Final. In addition I had also enjoyed one of my best seasons with the England team. I felt that I was playing as well as, if not better than, at any time in my football career. This is a feeling only the player himself can get through coming through his private training without any signs of distress, and it was at this point in my career that I realised that I had many years of good football still left in me. I had proved to my own satisfaction that the maxim which held that once a footballer passes the age of thirty his playing days are numbered was wrong, in my case at least. I couldn't tell the world at large this, but I knew it was true, and the knowledge gave me a wonderful feeling.

Every footballer who has had the luck to reach the Final with his team will tell you that the long wait between the semi-final and the Final at Wembley is a nightmare. As the weeks go slowly by, the chances of meeting with a serious injury on the field during the League matches which have to be completed before Cup Final day comes along loom uppermost in any player's mind, and indeed the more he tries to avoid such an injury the more effect it has on his playing abilities. This was the first chance that I had had of a Cup Final appearance at Wembley, and in view of the fact that I wanted so badly to win a medal as much for my father's memory as for myself I suppose I could have been excused if, although experienced, I felt the waiting as great a strain as any other player. However, in my case I was lucky, because a fortnight before the Cup Final was played I had an important date to keep with the rest of the England team.

On the 10th of April, 1948, England was due to meet Scotland at Hampden Park, and a victory for England meant the International Championship for England. This match was of the greatest importance, not only for England but for each player that had the honour to be chosen to play. Therefore, so far as I was concerned it didn't seem long after the semi-final had been played that I was packing my bags to join the England team, a few days before the match, at Troon, in Scotland. There under the watchful eye of the F.A. team manger, Mr. Walter Winterbottom, we commenced serious training. We had a few minor casualties. I had a slight bruise on the ankle, Mortensen had a sore throat, and Tommy Lawton had a grazed knee. But with the expert treatment we received from the England trainer Jimmy Trotter we were all fit and well for the final training bout on the Ayr United ground. I had been hoping that Harry Johnston, the Blackpool captain, who had been playing well all through the season behind Mortensen and myself, would be selected for this match, to complete Blackpool's right triangle, but it was not to be. Naturally I was disappointed. When I told Harry so, he just smiled and said, "Better luck next time." Those few words sum up Harry Johnston. He knew how to take the rough with the smooth, and he certainly knew how to captain a team.

For a full week before the match was played the full glare of publicity was turned on the game. The newspapers gave every particle of news a story, so by the time the day arrived you had only to walk down a Glasgow street to feel the intense excitement.

In the England dressing-room just before we took to the field there was a definite air of quiet confidence. The teams lined up like this—SCOTLAND: Black (Southampton); Govan (Hibernian), Shaw, D. (Hibernian); Campbell (Morton), Young (Rangers), Macaulay (Arsenal); Delaney (Manchester United), Combe (Hibernian), Thornton (Rangers), Steel (Derby County), Liddell (Liverpool). ENGLAND: Swift (Manchester City); Scott (Arsenal), Hardwick (Middlesbrough); Wright (Wolverhampton Wanderers), Franklin (Stoke City), Cockburn (Manchester United); Matthews (Blackpool), Mortensen (Blackpool), Lawton (Notts County), Pearson (Manchester United), Finney (Preston North End).

Both teams came out of the tunnel to the cheers of 135,000 spectators. We lined up in the centre of the playing pitch and glanced towards the tunnel entrance. A few seconds later Field-Marshal Montgomery emerged from the entrance, and as he came into view those 135,000 spectators sounded like a million. How they cheered as the world-famous field-marshal made his way towards us and shook us all by the hand. He spoke a few words to Tom Finney and Willie Thornton, who had both served in the Eighth Army. When we took up our respective positions for the start of the game a silence fell over the ground—the lull before the storm. The referee blew his whistle and the game was on. So was the Hampden roar.

From the start the Scots attacked our goal with a fury that had to be seen to be believed. Our defence fell back in a tight pack and managed to beat the Scots out. Within seconds they were back again, but our defence held firm. For the first quarter of an hour Scotland never let up, and as each attack came forward, so the roar grew in volume. Thank goodness it did not upset our goalie, Big Frank Swift. Although the roar was only a few yards away from him, he played a storming game; always cool, calm and collected, he pushed a huge hand this way and then that and collected some very powerful drives as if it were the easiest thing on earth to do. This example by Big Frank put confidence into the England side, and it knocked some of the fire out of the Scots. My old Stoke colleague Neil Franklin also played a great game in that first quarter of an hour. He protected Big Frank in every way possible and made some magnificent clearances under dire pressure. I felt proud to be in the same team as those two. The other England defenders were also in top form—they needed to be to repel those early Scottish attacks—but I particularly remember the grand work that Big Frank and Neil Franklin put in during that hectic fifteen minutes. Then it was England's turn to have a go. Our forwards bore down on the Scottish goal like one man. The defence pushed us back, but I could feel that we had rattled them with our pinpoint passing. We attacked again. Tom Finney picked up a quick pass, and from a good fifteen yards out he crashed the ball into the back of the Scottish goal. It was a remarkable shot and it really upset the Scots. They tore into us with renewed ferocity but our defence held out.

Both teams were thankful to hear the whistle go for half-time and a well-earned rest, but as soon as the second half started the Scots again attacked. They were determined to get an equaliser. But they soon found out that it was like trying to knock down a stone wall with their feet, and they seemed to tire after a time.

When this happened we put on the pressure. I received a good supply of passes from my wing-halfs, and I made good use of them. I tried to drop all my centres where it would hurt the Scots most—just inside their penalty area. In the sixty-fourth minute of the game Mortensen smashed the ball into the back of the Scottish net to put England two up. We sighed with relief, but not for long. Six minutes later, just twenty minutes from the end of the game, the Scots launched another attack on the England goalmouth, and this time they got through. Billy Liddell, the Scottish winger, bundled Big Frank into the back of the net, but Swift got rid of the ball, so no goal resulted. Then we saw that Big Frank hadn't got up and it was obvious that he was badly hurt. After a few minutes he was on his feet; but when he found out that Hardwick, who normally would have deputised in goal, was also injured, Big Frank refused to leave the field.

The game restarted, with Hardwick limping in the outside-left position for the rest of the match. With twenty minutes to go and two men injured, a two-goal lead was nothing against a team of the strength of Scotland. The only thing we could do was to attack and keep attacking. Those last twenty minutes were a nightmare, but somehow we got through without the Scots scoring, and the final result was Scotland 0, England 2. Big Frank Swift had to be assisted off the field at the end of the match. In the dressing-room an ambulance was called to take him off to hospital for an X-ray on his ribs, which he feared were cracked. The hospital people wanted to keep Big Frank all night, but as Mrs. Swift had come to Glasgow for the match the doctor agreed to let her take her husband back to the hotel and bed. Frank returned to England and Manchester next morning, but the long journey from Glasgow proved too much for him, and on leaving the train at Manchester he collapsed on the platform and was rushed home, put to bed, and for some time needed careful nursing.

Frank Swift was sorely missed at the banquet after the match, and Stan Mortensen wandered about like a lost sheep—he and Frank were the life and soul of any party, and I am afraid the absence of Big Frank made this party fall flat. However, we had

won the match and it was a high-spirited England team that left
Scotland for home the following day. As I sat in the train I
thought, *Now for the Cup Final winners' medal.* The newspapers
went to town on our victory over Scotland and the England
players received nothing but praise.

After spending a quiet day at home with my family I reported
for training at Bloomfield Road, the Blackpool ground. It was
then I noticed the effect the Cup Final was having on some of
my colleagues. There was really nothing you could put your
finger on, but somehow everyone seemed to be a bit edgy. A
few days before the match was due to be played this tenseness
seemed to disappear; and when the team was finally selected,
things seemed to get back to normal. I suppose it is a kind of
strain which could be called pre-Wembley cup nerves.

I didn't have time to get caught up in thinking too much about
Wembley, because, quite unexpectedly, I had a very pleasant
surprise. During the 1947–48 season the sports writers formed an
association which they called the Football Writers' Association;
this association, which everybody knows by now, decided to
elect, by voting amongst themselves, a "Footballer of the Year."
The plan was to hold a dinner on the eve of the Cup Final in
London and invite the footballer to whom they had awarded
the honour to receive a bronze statuette. This was the very
first year of the association's formation and I was voted into
first place, with my club colleague Stan Mortensen in number-
two spot and Frank Swift in the third position. It came as
a great surprise when I was informed that I had won this honour.
I never expected to win it, and I mean that most sincerely.
It amazed me to think that the men who only a little over twelve
months ago were after me good and proper should turn completely round and hail me as the "Footballer of the Year" for the
1947–48 season. I have many friends among the football writers,
and I have always admired them for their frankness in writing
what they think of any match they attend. I have been criticised
by them and I have been praised by them, they can make players
and they can break players; but in general they are a fine bunch
of men, and who can blame them for always being on the look-
out for a good story?

Any footballer who has appeared at Wembley in a Cup Final will tell you that he never knew he had so many friends. As soon as his team win their way to the Final his fan mail just swells and swells; he opens his letters, and money and cheques just roll out. Scores of people he can't recollect meeting claim to be his best friends, so will he kindly buy them a ticket with the money he will find enclosed, and he can rest assured they will yell their heads off for the success of him and his team at Wembley. Of course the poor player can't get them tickets even if he wanted to. By the time a player has fixed up his personal friends and relatives he often finds himself looking for an odd ticket or two for himself. In any case no player of repute would take the chance of being involved in the black-market racket even if he had tickets to do so. You can rest assured that nearly all his spare time in the last week or so before Wembley is taken up trying to return money to the total strangers who sent it to him in the hope of getting a ticket.

The time arrived for us to leave Blackpool for our journey south. We received a terrific send-off, and several hours later arrived at Ascot, our headquarters for the week-end. We quickly settled down in our hotel. The tension of the last few days seemed to slip away from us all now we had arrived at a place that was on the "secret list" to prevent people getting in touch with us. It felt grand to be away from all the hustle and bustle of Blackpool, and this quiet hotel was just what we needed to calm down our nerves. I, however, had to journey to London the day before the Cup Final.

In the company of Mr. Harry Evans, the Blackpool chairman, and Mr. Joe Smith, the Blackpool manager, I motored down to town, and the three of us duly presented ourselves to our hosts at the hotel at which the newly-formed Football Writers' Association were holding their first Cup Final Eve dinner. The ceremony of the presentation of the bronze statuette was to be broadcast. Many distinguished Fleet Street personalities were around those tables that evening, and also many famous people from the football world. The time for the presentation arrived, a signal was given by the B.B.C. producer in charge of the broadcast and we were on the air. One speaker after another got up and said very nice things about me and my football career. I am sorry to say that I blushed continually and sat with my head down to hide the tears that kept flooding my eyes. I do know that it was one of the proudest moments of my life.

At the end of the speeches I was presented with the statuette, and it was my turn to speak. I got up, stood in front of the mike, and for a few seconds just stared at it. I am no great after-dinner speaker, and I could feel the butterflies fluttering around my stomach. But I knew that I would have to say something and I was determined to keep it short. I said in my opening remarks that some of the sports writers present that evening had written from time to time that I could make a ball talk, and went on to say that I would be very pleased if they could find me a ball that could talk for me now. I thanked them for the statuette and then made a polite finish and sat down. It went down better than I expected, although I had kept it so short. With the presentation and broadcast over and done with, the football writers soon got their party going full swing, and I could see that this first big occasion was going to finish up a huge success. Unfortunately I was unable to stay and enjoy the fun, as I was making my first appearance in the Cup Final next day. I was given an early send-off, and with the good wishes of the football writers ringing in my ears I left with my chairman and manager for the return trip to Ascot, and was in bed asleep before midnight.

Except for the singing of the birds all was quiet when I opened my eyes at a very early hour next morning. I got out of bed and a few minutes later I was walking down one of the lanes near to the hotel inhaling the sweet country air deep in my lungs, holding it down for a few seconds, then slowly exhaling it through my mouth. I came across a nice piece of turf, stopped walking, and after a short rest commenced on a series of sprints over various distances. After that I was ready for the afternoon's match. All I could do now was to relax and rest as much as possible before the whistle blew to start the game. Meanwhile in London itself thousands of North Country football fans were walking round the West End.

When the coach in which we, the Blackpool players, travelled to the Wembley ground neared its destination I, for one, thought all the world was coming to see the Final played. There were thousands of private cars and thousands upon thousands of people all making for one spot, and it was nice to see the Manchester and Blackpool colours being worn on the lapels of the majority of this huge crowd. When at last we found ourselves safe and sound in our dressing-room it was so quiet and so remote from the bustle and noise outside that I got the feeling we were miles away from the stadium. Of course I had been at Wembley many times before when playing for England, but the feeling I got on this occasion was totally different from an international match. Around me, getting changed into their football gear, were my own team mates, players that I played with every week, not players whom I saw once in a blue moon, and this made us feel much closer to each other. It was the first visit to Wembley for a lot of the players, and they were feeling nervous. They seemed to look to the players who had played here before to give them confidence, and that is what we tried to do.

The minutes ticked away, then the door opened and on the threshold stood our manager, Joe Smith. Now Joe Smith had played at Wembley in the very first Final held there; his team was Bolton Wanderers and they won the Cup. He must have known how nervous some of the boys would be now that the time had come for us to take to the field; he smiled at us all in turn and then said, "Play football, and do your best, lads." He paused. "I shall not ask any more." We followed him out of our dressing-room and lined up alongside our opposite numbers from Manchester United. Then, ten minutes before the kick-off, Blackpool, headed by Joe Smith, and Manchester United, headed by their manager Matt Busby, walked through the tunnel on to the green turf to be presented to His Majesty King George VI. The roar that greeted our appearance startled us after the quiet of the dressing-rooms, but we soon got used to it. King George came on to the pitch and we were introduced by our respective captains: Harry Johnston for Blackpool, Jack Carey for Manchester United. The teams were as follows—BLACKPOOL: Robinson; Shimwell, Crosland; Johnston (captain), Hayward, Kelly; Matthews, Munro, Mortensen, Dick, Rickett. MAN-CHESTER UNITED: Crompton; Carey (captain), Aston; Anderson,

Chilton, Cockburn; Delaney, Morris, Rowley, Pearson, Mitten.

We lined up in our positions and I saw the referee glance at his watch. I looked around me, and saw a wonderful sight on this lovely May afternoon—masses and masses of faces all around the ground all ready to enjoy the game, and a thought came in my mind—*The first team that gets over the initial nervousness in the first vital few minutes of the game will have a good advantage for the rest of the game.* I hoped it would be us. The whistle went.

From the kick-off the ball ran well for us, and I was more than pleased to see that; furthermore we attacked the Manchester goal for all we were worth, and after fourteen minutes success came our way. Chilton, the Manchester centre-half, made one of his rare slips in the centre of the field, and Stan Mortensen, our centre-forward, took full advantage of it. He quickly got the ball under control and ran down the middle of the playing pitch at great speed towards the Manchester goalmouth. Carey chased him hopelessly, and though Chilton was breathing down Stan's neck he couldn't get at him to tackle. Then, when Mortensen had a gaping goalmouth right in front of him, the desperate Chilton stuck out his foot and brought him down from behind. Mr. C. J. Barrick (Northampton), the referee, came running up and pointed to the penalty spot. Many people who were present at the match said that Mortensen was tripped outside the area, but I don't think many people grumbled when Shimwell scored from the spot to put Blackpool in the lead. Justice was done.

This goal was a big break for Blackpool and we piled on the pressure. I noticed that there was no sign of nerves in the play of any of the Blackpool players. In fact both teams settled down to play a natural game, and the play swung from one end of the field to the other. Then, as often happens in this wonderful game, it swung in favour of United. Out of the blue our defence was caught napping and Jack Rowley, the Manchester centre-forward, practically walked the ball into an empty net. This happened within fifteen minutes of Shimwell converting our penalty award.

Now we were on level terms once more and both teams served up real football in the endeavour to gain the lead. Even to-day

people who saw the match still say it was a classic. Ten minutes
before half-time we scored again. We were awarded a free-kick
and I took it, placing the ball in the goalmouth, but not too near
the goalkeeper. Kelly got his head to it and headed on to Mortensen, a few yards away. Quick as a flash Mortensen turned in
his stride and cracked the ball well and truly into the back of the
net. As the crestfallen Manchester goalie bent down to pick the
ball out of the net Mortensen disappeared under the weight of
his colleagues. This goal marked a wonderful Cup run for him.
It meant he had scored in every cup-tie for Blackpool in the
season—a total of ten goals. A magnificent achievement. I had
a shock when I heard the whistle blow for half-time, I couldn't
believe we had been playing for forty-five minutes.

We started the second half full of confidence and both sides
played wonderful football. Twenty minutes from the end the
score was still 2–1 in our favour and Blackpool seemed to have
the match in the bag. Then Jackie Morris, Manchester United's
inside-right, went through outside the penalty box with the ball
at his feet. Hugh Kelly, our left-half, went into a tackle, and for
a few seconds both players seemed to be in a bit of a mix-up.
Mr. Barrick blew his whistle. I, for one, didn't know who
the free-kick was against, and I am sure our defence didn't
either; but I do know that in a situation like this, when there
is doubt, any player on any side who is nearest to the ball
should kick it away until things are made clear. In this case,
as the ball was near to the Blackpool goalmouth, a Blackpool
player should have kicked the ball away until the defenders
got themselves sorted out. Jackie Morris took a lightning free
kick, and Jack Rowley, the United centre-forward, headed in
a great goal to make the scores level 2–2. Our defence were
caught totally unprepared.

This shock goal of United's turned the game completely round.
Before this they were struggling, now it was our turn to struggle.
The play went from end to end in quick succession but we had
lost the initiative and that goal put new life in the United team.
Then, twelve minutes from time, Stan Mortensen roamed out to
the right touchline. Chilton followed him. The ball came over
in Chilton's direction and seemed simple enough—but Chilton

misjudged the bounce. Mortensen was on to the ball like a terrier, and before you could blink an eyelid he was off in the direction of the Manchester goal at breakneck speed. He sorted out a shooting angle; it was not a good one, but knowing Stan I thought, *This is it.* Stan belted the ball goalwards, but to my dismay I watched it go straight into the arms of Crompton, the United goalkeeper.

What followed lost us the match. Crompton kicked his clearance straight down to Anderson, the United right-half, who quickly slipped the ball to Stan Pearson. Pearson made for goal, swayed as if he was going to the right, which unbalanced our defenders, then instead moved quickly to the left and scored with a terrific shot which passed Robinson, the Blackpool goalkeeper, like a thunderbolt and crashed into the netting at the back of the goal. A few seconds before Mortensen had been shooting at the Manchester goal—and it was those few seconds that cost Blackpool the Cup. A few minutes later we had more bad luck. A thirty-yards drive from Anderson came towards the Blackpool goalmouth, struck Hugh Kelly on the head, and the ball flew past Robinson into the net. It was hard luck on Kelly, who had played a good game. A few minutes later the final whistle went, and the result of the game was Manchester United 4, Blackpool 2. I must confess to feeling a bitter disappointment. I felt as if I had had a winners' medal in the palm of my hand and somebody had stolen it from me.

We all shook hands, and then, just a little enviously, we watched the United captain, Carey, lead his smiling team-mates up to the royal box to receive the Cup and winners' medals from the King.

Then it was our turn. It was good to hear the cheers and condolences of "Well played, boys" by Blackpool fans. We had been beaten but not disgraced.The King seemed to smile at us with understanding as he handed us the runners-up medals.

Back in our dressing-room, Joe Smith thanked us for the good football we had played. He said we had done our best and lost. What might have been wasn't and that was all there was to it. There was not one word of reproach from our manager and directors, and the boys deeply appreciated this.

We got dressed and went along to the Manchester United

dressing-room. Joe Smith was already there congratulating Matt Busby and the players on their success, and we did the same. Matt Busby had given the same instructions to his players as Joe Smith had done to us—"Play football whatever happens."

The accounts we read in the papers after the match confirm that both teams had carried out their managers' instructions to the full, and made the 1948 Cup Final a game to be remembered by all football fans for all time. If any outsider had looked in at our dinner and dance in a West End hotel that evening he would have thought that Blackpool had won the Cup, not lost it. It was a jolly evening.

CHAPTER XXI

MY MATURED YEARS

My two children were safely tucked up in their beds for the night. Turning my head first to the right and then to the left, I could see Jean and Stanley in turn. They were fast asleep. It would be many weeks before I saw them again, so I gazed down at them very intently to carry the picture away with me on my long journey. I left the room and went downstairs to Betty. She gave me an enquiring look, and I smiled at her and said, "They are both fast asleep, so we had better get going."

We left by the back entrance of our hotel in Blackpool, entered the car, and a few seconds later I was driving in the direction of Preston to claim my sleeping berth on the night train to London. As I drove along my mind turned several things over. I was on my way to join the England team who had a date to play Italy in Turin on the 16th of May. After this match I could say that the 1947-48 season was over, and I could return to my family and stay with them until the 1948-49 season commenced in August.

I really hadn't quite got over all the excitement of the Cup Final we had just played and lost against Manchester United; in fact the reporters were still writing about it.

As I drove along some of the things they had written about me went through my mind. I thought, *I can't be all that good*; and then another thought came—I was now fully matured. I knew that my name was on everyone's lips in the football world, but I also knew they had got things out of perspective when they printed and said that I was the wizard of this and the wizard of that. All I had done, from youth onwards, was to take great pains to learn my job properly.

I found it easy to do those things on the football field that seemed to make me a public hero, simply because I had been doing the same things for years and years and had practised hour after hour to ensure that I could do so. I thanked God at that moment for giving me a father who had knocked any ideas which might have given me a swelled head out of me when I was young.

My advice to any youngster who suddenly finds himself a public hero is never believe it! If he does he is lost, because he will rest on his laurels, neglect his practice, find himself in company that will do him no good, and before long he might lose everything he has worked for. One morning he will wake up to find that he has no friends, no more publicity, and a bitterness in his heart against the whole world.

At Preston I sat chatting with Betty in the car for ten minutes, then we said good-bye, I got out of the car and Betty slid behind the wheel. She turned the car round, waved to me through the window, and set off on the return journey to Blackpool.

I stood and watched the car disappear in the gloom, then I bent down, picked up my bag, and made my way into the station. Five minutes later I boarded the train and was shown my sleeper. Ten minutes later I was in bed fast asleep.

I joined the England team around noon on the next day at our London headquarters, and was pleased to hear that Big Frank Swift had made a remarkable recovery from his injury at the Hampden match and would be coming to Italy with us. Furthermore, owing to the fact that George Hardwick, the England skipper, was not fully recovered from his injury, it had been decided to appoint Big Frank as captain of the England team for the match in Italy. This was indeed an honour for Big Frank, and it was also the first time a goalkeeper had captained England. We had a most pleasant trip to Italy and arrived in the best of spirits. My ribs were sore with laughing at the antics of Big Frank and Stan Mortensen. As I have said before, with those two for company there is never a dull moment. A happy team is a contented team.

We rested, as in 1939, at Stresa, which lies on the edge of beautiful Lake Maggiore, and we were all looking forward to the coming tussle with Italy. We knew how seriously the Italians took themselves in games against England, so from a prestige point of view we were anxious to win the match. For myself I hadn't forgotten the match at Highbury in 1934 or Milan in 1939.

The Italians were determined to beat us, because, apart from anything else, they were to get a bonus of £1,000 each if they could do so. We, of course, were paid £20 each—win, lose or draw.

We had a terrific thunderstorm the day before the match. This, in fact, was a bit of good luck, for us. It surprised me to see that fans were coming from all parts of Italy to watch the match and also from many places in Europe.

On the day of the match the atmosphere in Turin was tense. Fantastic prices were being offered for tickets. The black market was busy and huge sums of money changed hands. The Italian team were still tucked away, to all intents and purposes, in their mountain hideout, and the players' names hadn't been announced. Eighty thousand fans began to make their way towards the ground at least six hours before the kick-off, and the rain pelted down, but in no way did it deter them. It stopped just before the match started and the game was played in brilliant sunshine.

The time came for us to take to the field, and we received a tremendous ovation as we followed our skipper, Frank Swift, through the tunnel into the sunshine. The teams were as follows— ENGLAND: Swift (Manchester City) [captain]; Scott (Arsenal), Howe (Derby County); Wright (Wolves), Franklin (Stoke City), Cockburn (Manchester United); Matthews (Blackpool), Mortensen (Blackpool), Lawton (Notts County), Mannion (Middlesbrough), Finney (Preston North End). ITALY: Bacigalupo; Ballarin, Eliani; Annovazzi, Parola, Grezan; Menti, Loich, Gabetto, Mazzola (captain), Carapellese.

The whistle went and the game was on. Encouraged by the roar of the crowd, the Italians bore down on the England goal. They were hurled back. We had been expecting this kind of opening from the Italians, so they hadn't a chance of catching the England defence napping. In fact Frank Swift was magnificent in goal. Perhaps it was the fact that he was captain which made him seem so inspired, and during the first few minutes of the

game the confidence he showed, coupled with the perfect understanding between our full-backs Howe and Scott, did a great
deal to boost the morale of the rest of the England players as we
watched attack after attack from the Italians break down.

The skill of the Italians was excellent and they played good
football, with very few passes going astray; but it didn't take
them long to find out that our defence was as solid as a rock, and
I think this upset them.

The game was just four minutes old when, after repelling
another swift Italian attack, one of our defenders pushed the ball
out to me on the right wing. I gathered the ball and made off
down the wing. The spectators must have foreseen sudden
danger, because the shouting stopped as if it had been cut off by
a tap. Looking ahead, I saw the Italian left-back, Eliani, running
towards me at great speed. I also saw, out of the corner of my
eye, my Blackpool colleague Stan Mortensen running into position goalwards. Instead of trying to evade Eliani, as he expected,
I ran to meet him. He lunged at me, and as he was off balance I
disappeared with the ball and passed to Mortensen, and in a second
or so the ball was in the back of the net.

This surprise goal shook the Italians and their supporters, and
we took advantage of this by going into the attack. It was now
the turn of the Italian defence to do some hard work. We kept
up the pressure and twenty minutes later Neil Franklin took the
ball away from Gabetto, the Italian centre-forward, and with a
neat pass sent me away once more. This time I ran forward a
few yards only and passed to Mortensen, who was travelling
down the field at great speed. He took the pass without slow-
ing down and made a wonderful fifty-yard dribble towards
the goal, despite the fact that Parola was snapping at his heels all
the time. When he reached the goalmouth he managed to slip a
good pass to Tommy Lawton, who promptly put the ball into
the back of the net. It was a great effort of Mortensen's, and by
the time he regained the centre of the field his back must have
been sore from all the back-slapping he got from the rest of the
England players.

Half-time came, and we went off the field to take a breather
with a two-goal lead. In the England dressing-room I think the

proudest man was Frank Swift; he just sat down quietly and looked around the room at all of us. He must have felt proud, because I have never known him to be so quiet.

The second half started with the Italians playing full-out; they seemed determined to get on level terms. For a long time they had most of the play, but they couldn't get the ball into the England goal. Even when, through sheer weight of pressure, they managed to get past the backs, they still had to get the ball past Big Frank, and I doubt if any team in the world could have done that on that day. His anticipation was uncanny, he could smell danger; he shouted out warnings to his backs, and he took those Italian forwards by the scruff of their necks and wrung every drop of confidence out of them. Yes, we all felt very proud of our captain that day. There is not the slightest doubt that a fighting captain makes a fighting team, and I am sure that I am speaking on behalf of all the England team on that day when I say that every one of us gave everything we had to ensure a victory for Big Frank in his first match as captain of England.

Halfway through the second half the left wing of England took command. Mannion took the ball in the direction of the Italian goalmouth, then sent a quick pass to Tommy Finney, and before the Italians could blink Finney banged the ball into the back of the net. Two minutes later it was all over. Mortensen had rushed at breakneck speed towards the Italian goal, and instead of shooting himself sent the ball along the ground to Finney, who slammed it once more into the rear netting of the goal.

After this the Italians gave up hope, and we ran out winners, the final score being Italy o, England 4. Apart from giving Big Frank his victory, we had built up the prestige of English football in Italy to a very high level.

We followed our captain off the ground at the end of the match with heads held high. This was a most fitting end to an undefeated season in international football.

We returned to our dressing-room after receiving a most moving send-off from the spectators, and as we changed I made my way towards Big Frank. When I reached him I had to bite off the words in my mouth before they reached my lips: I just patted his arm and passed on. I had never seen tears in his eyes before. The word quickly went round the room to leave him alone.

That night, however, we had a jolly time, and as usual Big Frank and Mortensen were up to their tricks. I am sure that many of the party felt regret at having to leave each other now that we had come to the end of an international season that England might not experience again for a very long time.

The passing of time has proved that we were not far wrong, and when I read the papers in May 1959 it made me feel miserable to see that after ten years an England international football team is the laughing-stock of the world; to read that countries which once looked up to us with the greatest of respect now call us the world's worst footballers.

I hope most sincerely that something is done very quickly to put England back to where she belongs—right on top. There must be no more excuses, no more copying of other countries' style of play, but a deep determination on the part of players and officials to start from scratch once more and build up an England team that plays the English way. It can be done, and it should be done as soon as possible. I also think that this is the time to mention that tragic Munich crash when a plane carrying the Manchester United team met sudden disaster.

I was ill for days. To think of Frank Swift, as I knew him, dead, was at first unbelievable. It was bad enough to read about all the others, but Frank Swift was the biggest shock. I shall always be grateful for the memory of the match I played when he was my captain. He had the knack of being able to get the maximum effort from his players, and most of all he could instil in them, by his own playing ability, the killer instinct which every successful team must have. Frank Swift was a good man, a gentle man, a firm man, and a great goalkeeper. His name will live for ever in the football world.

It felt nice to get back to Blackpool after our return from Italy, and I spent the rest of the 1948 summer looking after my hotel business and taking out my family whenever I got the chance. I had nothing at all to complain about; indeed I was now enjoying what I term my "matured years" in football. I was in peak condition, and playing more or less consistently and keeping free from injuries.

I was with a team that was on the upgrade, and the papers at that time said that whenever I appeared with Blackpool my name was good enough to fill the ground. Some went further and suggested that I was worth a lot more money, with regard to my drawing power, than I was receiving.

This led to long arguments about players' salaries. Should star players get more? It made very good reading; and although I wouldn't have said no to more money, I refused to comment on this subject when approached to do so, because football, unlike golf or tennis, is a team game, and its star players are in a different situation.

The 1948-49 season came and went. My old club Stoke City knocked Blackpool out of the Cup in a replay at Blackpool, and I appeared in five international games in the season.

The 1949-50 season came along, with my life running along on the same pattern. That season, for the first time in years, I wasn't chosen to play in any of the international matches. I think the main reason was this: the war had been over for five years, and during that time plenty of youngsters had entered the game for a living, and they were knocking on the selectors' door, to be given a chance to prove their worth in international matches.

I was thirty-five years old on the 1st February, 1950, and to some of the budding youngsters in their early twenties I must have appeared an old man.

Apart from myself, quite a lot of the regular international players disappeared from the international scene that season, and most of them never got back. Of the five internationals that I played in during the previous season, England won three, drew one, and lost one—which is not bad going by any standard. With regard to goals, England scored a total of fourteen and had five scored against them.

If you look up the recent records you will find that the England team these days rarely make double figures in goals scored in a whole season, and the average age of the modern England teams is kept down to around the twenty-four-year-old mark. Which surely proves that it takes more than youth and uncontrolled zeal to win international matches. I suppose one of these days the penny will drop, and the present powers-that-be will begin to see the light.

However, in the 1949-50 season I proved in the matches I played with Blackpool that I was by no means finished, and my club enjoyed another successful season. In fact we were very unlucky not to reach the Cup Final again. In the round before the semi-final we were drawn to meet Liverpool away. At this time Blackpool, under their captain Harry Johnston, were playing superb football, and we felt confident we could beat Liverpool. Then, after a long run of being free from injury, I pulled a muscle and had to miss the match. To make it worse, Eric Hayward also had to cry off, and as I sat with Eric on the touchline watching the match I felt as excited as a schoolboy.

It was anybody's game. Eight minutes from time the score was 1-1, then that great Scottish international left-winger Billy Liddell switched places with Payne, and with one of his great shots scored the winning goal. That was the end for us. Liverpool went on to beat their neighbours Everton 2-0 in the semi-final, and met Arsenal in the Final, only to lose to the London team by 2-0.

Shortly after the Final I received a pleasant surprise. I had been chosen for the F.A. party to tour Canada and New York during the summer of 1950, and we were due to sail from Liverpool on the *Empress of Scotland* on the 9th of May, a few days after the Arsenal *v.* Liverpool Cup Final. However, all through the past winter season the word "Rio" had been on every footballer's lips. Also the sports writers had been having the time of their lives.

For the first time England had entered the World Cup series arranged by F.I.F.A., and Rio de Janeiro was to be the venue. With a setting like that to spend a few weeks in, can you wonder that every footballer in England was trying to get into the England party that was to fly to Brazil.

Not having played in an international match in the past season, and having been chosen to go with the F.A. party to Canada, many people, including myself, took it for granted that I would be left out of the more important England party bound

for Rio. Can you imagine my surprise when Walter Winterbottom phoned me at Blackpool and asked me if I was 100 per
cent fit. I assured him I was. He then asked if I would be prepared to break off with the F.A. party at a given spot in Canada
and join the England players in Rio. After recovering my
composure, I managed to say I would be delighted to do so, and
I placed the telephone receiver back in its cradle in a daze.

I spent as much time as I could spare in the company of my
children before I joined the F.A. party at Liverpool, and as young
Stanley was getting on towards his fifth birthday he wasn't taking
my long trips away from home any too calmly. He was beginning to miss me more and more and couldn't understand why he
couldn't come with me. I managed to appease him with a promise
to tell him all about the wonderful sights I would see on the
trip.

I walked right into trouble as soon as we docked in Quebec.
Some reporters came on board and interviewed me. Everything
went along fine until they asked questions about salaries. They
expressed great surprise when I told them what I was paid in
football. The Canadian journalists pointed out that their ice-
hockey and baseball stars would have refused to make one
appearance for what I was being paid for playing for a year.

Then it happened. One reporter asked if I would be interested
in taking a job as coach in Canada for, say, £50 a week. Instead
of giving a blunt "No" to the question, and not wishing to appear
ungracious, I gave him what I thought to be a non-committal
reply, saying that if such an offer was made I would have to think
about it.

I picked up a paper next morning and saw in glaring headlines
that I was definitely coming to Canada to coach for the salary the
reporter had mentioned. It was evident that the reporter was hard
up for a story and hadn't taken much notice of the true facts. I
picked up the phone and killed the story in no uncertain manner,
but by then it had gone all over the world. I was taught a lesson
by this incident—it pays to be blunt at times. However, since
then I have been most careful while being interviewed.

I enjoyed my stay in Canada. We of the England party were
treated royally wherever we went throughout this great

Signing his autograph for two smiling schoolgirls during his tour of Ghana (1957).

Awarded the C.B.E. for his services to Association Football in the New Year
Honours List, 1957, Stanley Matthews is pictured here, holding the insignia.

Dominion, everyone was most kind and did all they could to make us feel at home.

We played our first game in Montreal in great heat and we won the match easily. I shall always remember playing before Canada's biggest-ever Soccer crowd—32,000—at Toronto when we met and defeated Manchester United, who were also out there on tour. Then we reached New York, and from there I was due to fly out to Rio to join the England team.

Before I left I saw the F.A. XI beat America's World Cup team. I didn't play in this match as I was in the middle of packing to leave New York. It gave me a chance, however, to see the team that England was to meet in the World Cup series at Belo Horizonte later on.

When I saw the easy victory the F.A. team scored over them I smiled to myself and thought, *It looks a piece of cake for England to win the World Cup*. So in an easy frame of mind I boarded the plane for Rio. As the plane drew near to Rio I could feel my pulse quicken. I knew that Rio was beautiful from the scenes I had seen in various films, but when I arrived and had got clear of the airport I just stood and gazed around me for a long time.

At the Copacabana Beach where we stayed I used to wait impatiently for darkness to fall. Copacabana is about eight miles from Rio on the coast road. On the top of Mount Corcovado there is a huge figure of Christ poised with outstretched hands as though protecting the whole city. At night twinkling lights are switched on, and a huge floodlight focuses its powerful beam on to the figure of Christ. I have never seen anything so moving in my whole life. I could stand for hours looking at it, it just held me spellbound.

It was the middle of June when I arrived in Rio and it was their winter. To me it was still summer by English standards. England was due to meet Chile on the coming Sunday in the World Cup series. When the team was announced I was not included. On the Saturday, the day before the match with Chile, Brazil played Mexico in the World Cup series, on their new £3,000,000 ground, which they had built especially for the World Cup. The work of building the stadium had started in August 1948, but something went wrong with the time-table.

Twenty-four hours before the first match of the series was due to be played between Brazil and Mexico there were still 7,000 workmen tearing down the scaffolding to get the stadium tidy, and ready for the opening. They made it, but it was a near thing. The seating accommodation was 130,000, with room for 25,000 standing. You will notice that the people of Rio like to watch their football in comfort, and I can assure you it is a beautiful piece of stadium.

It was decided that the England party should attend the opening match to get some of this Rio soccer atmosphere which we had heard so much about. What a day out that turned out to be! We left our hotel in good time, but the traffic jam was so huge that it took us nearly two hours to get within sight of the ground. We passed hundreds of abandoned cars miles from the stadium. Finally the driver of our coach had to call it a day, so we abandoned the coach and pushed our way as best we could through the huge crowd. This was no easy matter, but eventually we got inside and took our seats in the stand, feeling very hot and sticky. We soon forgot our discomforts when the 80,000 Brazilians began shouting and screaming with delight when their team came running on to the pitch.

Within minutes the sky was black from fireworks emitting sulphur and smoke as they exploded. It was like a miniature blitz. Then, before the smoke had time to clear, they sent up thousands of balloons, and as the balloons rose swiftly in the air to mingle with the smoke they released 5,000 pigeons. I stood up, looking dumbfounded skyward; then to finish things off, and to bring the pre-match celebrations to a close, there was a salute of twenty-one guns before the Brazil team kicked off.

I sat down in a daze. Never in my life had I seen or heard anything like this. It was just too fantastic to be true. In the distance, towering over the ground, was the magnificent figure of Christ, with hands stretched out in peace, looking down on the most fantastic scenes I have ever seen on any football ground.

I calmed down and concentrated on the football match. As this was the first time I had seen Brazil in action, and as I had been told that they were the chief danger to England with regard

to our winning the World Cup, I tried to pick out their weaknesses. They were good footballers, but they seemed to have to
put too much effort into beating this weak Mexican team 4-0. I
could see gaps down the middle, and should we meet them in the
series I thought Stan Mortensen would have a field day galloping
through those open spaces.

At the end of the match I was convinced that England would
win the World Cup if Brazil was our chief danger.

On the following day I sat in the stands again to watch England
play Chile. I watched the game in a very relaxed manner and
noted the good and bad points of both teams. England won
2-0, but I was disturbed by the form of the England team; it
wasn't up to scratch by a long way. The Chilean team had only
one professional, and this was George Robledo, an old friend of
mine. George was born in Chile but had lived most of his life
in England (he played, of course, for many seasons as inside
forward in the Newcastle United team). The rest of the Chile
team were part-timers. They consisted of grocers, bookmakers,
accountants, and engineers.

As the match was played under more or less normal English
conditions as far as the weather went, I thought we should have
done much better against the weak opposition. The Brazilians
who were watching the match thought we were taking things
easy, but I knew different. However, we had cleared the first
hurdle, and now we had to tackle the United States at Belo
Horizonte, nearly 300 miles away. I thought this should be easy,
because a week earlier the F.A. XI beat them easily in New
York. There again the Yankee team was more or less composed of part-time professionals and it was a confident England
party who flew out from the Santos Dumont airport for Belo
Horizonte (which means "beautiful horizon" in our language).

It was just over an hour later when we sighted this modern
city of skyscrapers, which only came into existence at the turn
of this century. We received a great welcome at the airport,
and during our stay there we were to be the guests of the St.
John d'el Ray Mining Company, a British firm who had been
mining in the state of Minas Geraes for more than a hundred years.

The owners of the mine put their camp at the disposal of the

England party. It was on an attractive site at Morra Velho, close
to the little town of Nova Lima, sixteen miles from Belo itself.
The Englishmen and their wives at the camp met us with open
arms and their hospitality was the last word. Servants fluttered
round us like flies, and when we wrote home they would not let
us pay for the stamps. The food was cooked in English fashion
and was excellent.

In the friendly clubhouse we sat and talked with the residents
about home, and they leaned on every word. They never stopped
talking of the mother country. It was a perfect atmosphere to
train for the coming match.

Any chance I had thought I had of being selected to play against
the United States was dashed to the ground when it was announced that the selectors had decided to rely on the same side
that had beaten Chile. So for the second game in succession I was
a spectator.

The team selected was as follows: Williams (Wolverhampton
Wanderers); Ramsey (Tottenham Hotspur), Aston (Manchester
United); Wright (Wolverhampton Wanderers), Hughes (Liverpool), Dickinson (Portsmouth); Finney (Preston North End),
Mannion (Middlesbrough), Bentley (Chelsea), Mortensen (Blackpool), Mullen (Wolverhampton Wanderers). You will see from
the above that during the past season many new faces had made
their way into the England team.

It was a laughing and confident team that made their way to
the Belo Horizonte Stadium on the day of the match. I suppose
the England players were thinking that what the F.A. XI team
did they could do better, and nobody could blame them for
thinking that.

I walked along to my seat in the stands and looked around.
The stadium had been specially built for the World Cup, but it
was a small ground, and I thought the pitch was on the bumpy
side. It was a great contrast from the huge arena at Rio.

The match started in much more sober style than the Brazil *v.*
Mexico had, and I was surprised to find that the England players
were allowing the Americans to settle down instead of going
after a quick goal or two. Then the crowd made the Americans
the favourites by cheering them, and the United States team

began playing some good football. I kept waiting for our team to get going but they didn't oblige. They might have been handicapped by the small ground and pitch, but I couldn't for the life of me understand what was wrong with them. They just could not shoot, and they couldn't get the passes going to the right places.

Five minutes from half-time the ball was sent over from the American right wing, and Gaetjens, the United States centre-forward, got his head to it and put it into the back of the England goal. As I waited for the teams to make their appearance for the second half of the game I consoled myself that the half-time talk that must have been held in the England camp would get things sorted out.

Much to my disappointment, the second half started where the first had left off. As the minutes ticked away I felt all tensed up; surely we wouldn't get beaten, it just couldn't happen. But the whistle blew without another goal being scored, and within minutes the craziest result of the series was flashed round the world—United States 1, England 0.

The football fans at home in the mother country were shocked. I sat with bowed head until the players had left the field. I never thought I would live to see this. As I raised my head to look around me I felt a pain in most of my fingers. I looked down at my hands and saw spots of blood on the palms. I had been so tense in the closing minutes of the match that I had dug my finger-nails into my flesh without at the time feeling a thing.

Very reluctantly I left my seat and made my way towards the England dressing-room. I wouldn't like to describe what I met in there, so I will draw a veil over it.

I can say that at the victory party that night, thrown by the mine-owners, little was said, and it was a sad band of footballers who gathered there. To make matters worse, our English friends of the mining camp, who sympathized with us, also told us that it would take years to live down this defeat among the Brazilians who worked with them. This was bad enough to take, but I think the things we worried about most were what the people back home would think after the sports writers had finished with us.

As I lay in bed that night I went back in my mind over the sixteen years I had been connected with international football, and I prayed that this shock defeat by the United States might not be the thin edge of the wedge in the decline of England as world masters at football, but looking back I think it was. Some people say that we started to slip in 1953, but I think we can date the start of the whole sorry business from the defeat by the United States. Even now in the year 1960 we are still floundering, and I hope most sincerely that in the next decade conditions will alter and that we shall build up our lost prestige once more.

We flew back to Rio with the knowledge that we had to beat Spain or bust. If we could beat them we had a chance of playing in the final groupings. A draw or defeat would mean our sudden return to England and disgrace. If we beat Spain we should be on equal points with them and would then be entitled to a second play-off with the Spaniards.

I expected the England team to be reshuffled for the match with Spain, and I was right. Four changes were made. Bill Eckersley, the Blackburn Rovers left-back, replaced Jack Aston; Eddie Baily, Spurs inside-left, took over from Wilf Mannion; Jack Milburn was brought back at centre-forward, to the exclusion of Roy Bentley; and I returned to the right wing, with Tom Finney going to outside-left and Jimmy Mullen dropping out.

I can't say that I jumped with joy when I heard that I was selected to play against the Spaniards. For one reason, I had been a spectator at the Chile and United States match, and I had noticed that the will to win was sadly lacking in the England team. I blame this on the pre-match talk on playing tactics that had been introduced for the first time by our team manager.

You just cannot tell star players how they must play and what they must do when they are on the field in an international match. You must let them play their natural game, which had paid big dividends in the past. Their minds shouldn't be full of *Now I must do this or that* when the ball arrives at their feet.

A natural ball player is synchronized from brain to toes and when the ball arrives at his feet he knows in a split second what he is going to do with it to the best advantage of his team. For this he wants a clear head and an instinctive reaction, not a head full of instructions, because instructions can make him feel uncertain and destroy his powers of concentration. I have noticed that in recent years these pre-match instructions have become more and more long-winded, whilst the playing ability of the players on the field has dwindled. So I say scrap the talks and instruct the players to play their natural game; see that they have a good captain who can use the whip when it is needed to urge the players on to win —like Eddie Hapgood and Stan Cullis did. Then you will see the might of England once more.

The second point I did not like about the approaching match with Spain was the attitude of mind that would accompany the England players when they ran on to the field. Over and above the instructions that would be handed out, the players, with the shame of the United States match still buzzing in their heads, might try too hard not to make mistakes on the field.

The more you try not to slip up the more mistakes you make— it is similar to being accident-prone. I hoped for the best, and the thought that Spain wasn't by any means a first-class team got me thinking that by the time we ran on to the field at Rio on the 2nd July, 1950, we had a good chance of winning.

This time it was the turn of the Brazilian team to sit in the stands and watch us play. The playing conditions were good and the size of the ground well up to standard. The stadium was packed, and amid intense excitement the Italian referee blew his whistle.

The game was on. Spain played some good football, but it didn't take me long to see that if we shaped well we could soon have this game wrapped up.

But it didn't happen. Our shooting was by no means in the international class, and when we did get on the target we found Spain's famous goalkeeper, Ramalets, on top of his form. He dived, jumped and threw himself at every shot, to the delight of the crowd. He made no bones about the way he was enjoying himself.

I was also enjoying myself. I found that after the first two or three meetings with the Spanish left-back I had his measure, so I played on this, and it was not long before he gave it up as a bad job and made only feeble attempts to stop me passing him. Then

I turned on the pressure and sent a centre over to Mortensen, who collected the ball and went goalwards. I thought, *This is it.* He made the penalty area, then he was brought down; but to my surprise the referee waved play on.

A few minutes later Milburn went through, and he too was tripped; but again the referee waved play on. These slips by the referee upset the England team but gave the Spaniards heart. They tried body-checking and got away with that. In England they would have been sent off the field.

Half-time came with the score sheet blank. We attacked from the whistle in the second half but no goals came. Then when the second half was only a few minutes old the Spanish centre-forward, Zarra, scored unexpectedly for Spain. After that goal the Spaniards went to town. I got the ball past a defender, only to feel a hand grab the back of my shirt and pull me back. A few minutes later it happened again. The referee took no action, so I wasn't shown any mercy for the rest of the game. My shirt was nearly off my back.

Then the Spaniards started to use their hands freely and as the game drew to a close they started kicking the ball out of play. In fact they did everything they could to waste time and keep the goal lead.

I know time-wasting goes on in England most winter Saturday afternoons, but in this match the Spaniards put on a show of time-wasting that must still be a world's record, and got away with it—thanks to the referee. As the closing minutes came and quickly passed on for ever, I broke out in a cold sweat. I thought, *It mustn't happen—we mustn't lose this match.* We lost it. England, the masters of Soccer, had failed even to qualify for the World Cup finals.

It was my turn to walk off the field with my head hung in shame. I felt we should have won this match in the first ten minutes, despite the rough handling we received from the Spaniards. To complete the story of the World Cup, Brazil, Spain, Sweden and Uruguay qualified for the finals. The Brazilians routed Sweden 7-1 and beat Spain 6-1. It seemed they were the super team of the World Cup.

Rio went wild with delight, and I have heard that the scenes before the final match was played in the great Rio stadium had to be seen to be believed. The final was between Brazil and little Uruguay, whom no one in the whole wide world appeared to have heard of before this series began. Uruguay, of course, hadn't a chance of winning and great victory celebrations were planned in Rio for the evening after the match. In the meantime we had returned to England in disgrace long before we had expected. I never heard one complaint from a colleague, or from Walter Winterbottom, Mr. Arthur Drewry or Sir Stanley Rous. This gave the impression to one and all that England could still take it.

The sports writers, however, gave us a beating, and I am afraid that those good solid supporters of British soccer who spend their hard-earned shillings standing on the terraces in all kinds of weather in the winter months also had a few things to say, and in a very special language of their own.

Incidentally, the winners of the World Cup in 1950 didn't turn out to be Brazil after all. The world was staggered when the result was flashed through. Uruguay 2, Brazil 1 was the final score. Uruguay, after drawing 2–2 with Spain, beating Sweden 3–2, and beating Brazil in the final by 2–1, collected five points to Brazil's four, and ran out the winners.

There's a good moral in that if you care to think it out.

Down Rio way after the final there were tears and clenched fists and rolling heads. They are a little more temperamental than we British, or you would think so by the way they carried on in that beautiful city after the final had been played. I was reading the full report of the final sitting in a chair at home in Blackpool when I felt a tug. I saw my son standing by my side, and I knew what he wanted. I gathered him in my arms and told him a bed-time story. It was a fairy story—but not half as fantastic as my experiences over the previous few weeks.

CHAPTER XXII

MY FINEST HOUR

THE 1950–51 season was in sight and my summer holiday was swiftly coming to an end. I had enjoyed every minute of it because I was able to spend every day with Betty and the children and join them in everything that was planned for each day. It was a wonderful summer—yet there was just one snag. It concerned the hotel. In the middle of the summer I began to wonder if it was right to bring up my family in an hotel atmosphere. It was rather a tie, as there were so many things to attend to, and as time went on I began to think that we would be better off in a private house with a nice big lawn at the back, with perhaps a tennis-court at the bottom end of the lawn where the children, as they grew up, could practise and play to their hearts' content.

I played a lot of tennis myself, and I wanted to interest the children in the game. As the summer drew to its close I made up my mind to look around for a suitable house. Eventually I found the perfect house (in which we all live today), the hotel was sold, and we moved into our new home. I have never regretted it for one second. I am sure it was one of the most sensible things I ever did at this stage in my career.

When I reported for training at the Blackpool ground I found all the other players just as eager as I to get the coming season off to a good start, and what a season it turned out to be! I should think it was the best ever for Blackpool. Joe Smith, our manager, had the right idea: he never worried us with pre-match plans. He would, of course, talk important points over with us, but generally he would always advise us to play our natural game and never give up trying.

In Harry Johnston we had a captain of a very forceful and direct nature, and so under the guidance of manager and captain the Blackpool team in those days turned in some very good performances. It was in this season that I found myself thinking more than ever about my chances of winning a Cup Final winners' medal. In fact it was becoming an obsession.

The will to win a medal before my football career ended made me keep my nose to the grindstone; and although the draw for the third round of the Cup for the 1950-51 season was still months away, not a day passed without my thinking who we might meet in that round. So great did my obsession grow that I would find myself talking about the subject whenever I got the chance. I soon realised that I was doing this and had to watch my small-talk very carefully.

With regard to international matches, which up to now had always been my main source of interest, I am afraid they ceased to concern me. I knew that after the recent show that England had put up in the 1950 World series there would be a lot of talks about this and that, and that a lot of the regular players would lose their places. Apart from thinking about the ultimate shape of things when the talks had ended, I am sorry to say I didn't worry one little bit about what had happened. Somehow I got the feeling that all was not well between the selectors themselves and that a kind of tug-of-war was going on between the powers-that-be.

In football, just as you can in any other profession, you make many friends without trying, and by the same rule you also make many enemies. Admiration can gain you friends. Jealousy can gain you enemies. The season got under way, and my team made a good start. We were a happy bunch of players and each one of us enjoyed our football for the full ninety minutes of each game. We also enjoyed winning.

I was selected to play for England against Ireland at Belfast on the 7th of October. The final result was England 4, Ireland 1. The score shows that England must have played some good football that day, because the fighting Irish are always a hard team to beat on their own ground.

However, I was dropped from the rest of the international games that season until the very last one between England and Scotland at Wembley on the 14th of April 1951. In that game

Wilf Mannion, who was my partner at inside-right, had a cheek-bone fractured eleven minutes after the start.

I played inside, but try as we did we couldn't overcome this early handicap, and Scotland ran out winners, but not easy winners, with the final score England 2, Scotland 3. I think it was a good effort on the part of the England players, only ten strong, to hold a full Scottish international team to a one-goal lead. Great credit should have been given to the England defence in that match, as they had to play all out to hold off the Scottish forwards.

I knew that my heyday with regard to international matches was over. I had only been selected three times in the last two years. Before that I had been first choice for many years. I could only put it down to the fact that it was my age. When the England/Scotland match was played I was thirty-six years old.

At the same time, however, I was holding my place in the Blackpool team, and that same season we almost won the League Championship. We had a run of twenty games without defeat, and finished third from the top, with fifty points. The championship went to Manchester United, and Spurs finished second from the top.

Then the great day came along, the draw for the third round in the Cup. I was sitting by the wireless ten minutes before the draw was announced and I felt as excited as a schoolboy. At last the voice came through the loudspeaker and told me that Blackpool were drawn away to Charlton Athletic. Now I knew which team we were to play I calmed down for the first time in days. I began to consider how we could beat them. Then just before the match was due to be played I became a doubtful starter owing to a hip injury. I nearly wept. I did everything possible to get my hip right for the match—so much so that I was able to pass the pre-match test.

On the day of the match, however, I had to confide in our trainer and tell him that when I tried to get that extra spurt that is so essential to my style of play my hip caused me pain and slowed me up. It was also preventing me from getting off the mark quick enough. Arrangements were made to give me a cocaine injection at half-time if I needed it. The game started, and to my dismay my hip got worse and it put me right off my usual game. We went in at half-time 1-0 down. I decided to have the injection, and it did the trick for me—the pain vanished.

I played much better in the second half, and we scored, but Charlton also managed to get another goal and keep the lead. With only five minutes' playing time left we were losing 2-1, and people were beginning to trickle out of the ground assured that Charlton were through to the next round. The Blackpool team were fighting to the bitter end, and I still thought we had a chance to snatch a late goal. With three minutes left for play we gained a corner, and I took it. I placed the ball near the corner flag very carefully, as I knew that time was running out fast and that this might be our last chance to score. Glancing towards the Charlton goalmouth, I saw that Mortensen was in a good position. If only I could get the ball to him! I decided to chance it and centred the ball. To my great joy, Mortensen put it in the net. This was a real life-saver, and it affected George Farm, our goalkeeper, so much that he left his goal and ran the length of the field to pat Mortensen on the back.

The final whistle went and we lived to fight another day. The replay was fixed for the following Wednesday at Blackpool. It was a happy bunch of footballers that returned to Blackpool, but I had run into a heap of trouble. My hip started to give trouble again after the match when the effects of the cocaine had worn off, and by the time I arrived back in Blackpool I had also developed a cold.

Betty got me to bed and sent for the club doctor, who diagnosed 'flu. Furthermore, he instructed Betty to keep me in bed until the following Tuesday. Influenza by itself is depressing, but on top of that I knew that I would be out of the replay, and that thought really did depress me. But, thanks to the doctor and Betty, I felt much better on the Tuesday, and as the day drew to a close I began to think I had a chance to play on the following day. Needless to say, I kept those thoughts strictly to myself. On the Wednesday morning I felt better than ever; so, against all the advice Betty gave me, I surprised Joe Smith by turning up at the ground on Wednesday morning. I was given a try-out, and, much to my surprise, my hip never troubled me; the rest in

bed must have done the trick. Joe Smith watched me go through
my paces, nodded his head, and promptly put me in the team.
My return on the day of the replay took everybody by surprise.
The sports writers had printed the usual stories about the coming
replay in the morning papers, and what a pity it was, they wrote,
that I would be missing from the Blackpool line-up.

I played and enjoyed myself like the rest of the Blackpool
players, because Mortensen scored twice and Jackie Mudie once,
and the game ended Blackpool 3, Charlton 0. We had made it
to the next round. In the fourth round we were drawn at home
to Stockport County. On paper this looked an easy match to
win. But you can take it from me that no First Division club
relishes the idea of playing a club from a lower division in a cup-
tie. Many giant-killers emerge year after year from the lower
divisions, and a First Division club has a tendency to play too
cautiously against these clubs to make certain of avoiding defeat.
On the other hand, the lower clubs get into the game from the
start, as they know they have nothing to lose. Furthermore, in
this particular tie Stockport County, who had always been a
hard fighting club, had a very astute manager, a man who knew
football backwards, sideways, and of course forwards—namely
Andy Beattie.

It didn't take us long to find out, when the game was under
way, that Andy Beattie had switched the right-half and captain,
McCulloch, to left-half to watch me. He had also instructed the
left-back to concentrate on breaking up the raids of Mortensen
and Mudie down the middle. But he didn't make the mistake of
telling the players in bulk to do this and that; he just told them to
play their natural game.

He did enough in his two switches to make us fight hard, and
we found ourselves held for most of the game. Stockport County
fought tooth and nail to win. The game was getting towards
its close, and the score was 1–1, when, for a change, I managed
to slip by the defence and slip over a pass for Mortensen to score
the winning goal, which made the final score 2–1 in our favour.
I can tell you we were relieved to hear the final whistle.

Twenty-two very tired footballers trooped off the Bloomfield
Road ground that afternoon, to the cheers of the spectators who

had enjoyed the excitement of a hard-fought battle. I went home a happy man, and I eagerly looked forward to the fifth-round draw.

When the results of the draw came through we were drawn at home once more, for the second time in succession, and the team was Mansfield Town, who had at that time as player-manager my old Stoke City colleague Freddie Steele.

Now Freddie and I, when we played as boys in the same forward line at Stoke, had been great ones for tactics and showing each other our particular style of play, so when I heard the draw I thought, *Here is another manager who will know how to keep me quiet*, because I reckoned he knew every trick I had.

When I ran on the field with the rest of the Blackpool team on the day the match was played I felt slightly worried. But the game had not been in progress more than ten minutes when I discovered that Freddie had made a big mistake—he had instructed Eddie Barks, Mansfield's outside-left, to shadow me all the time. I paid visits to all parts of the playing pitch, and even when I went into the Mansfield Town penalty-box Barks was with me.

This meant that Mansfield had only four forwards, and our right-back, Eddie Shimwell, had no outside-left to watch, which gave him plenty of time to dribble down time after time to the Town's penalty area. We had a 2–0 lead at half-time.

I guessed that during the interval break Freddie Steele would instruct Barks to leave me alone in the second half and line up with the rest of the Town's forwards to try and get on level terms, but he didn't, and when the game was resumed Barks continued to shadow me until the final whistle. The result was Blackpool 2, Mansfield 0. Our goalkeeper, George Farm, had his quietest afternoon of the season.

I walked off the field with a warm feeling in my heart towards my old friend Freddie Steele. We were through to the sixth round.

I was feeling as happy as a schoolboy, and once more I waited impatiently to hear who was to come out of the bag for us to play in the next round. The voice came through the loudspeaker and informed me that Blackpool had been drawn at home against

Fulham. I was delighted with this news, for not only had we the advantage once more of playing on our own ground but our opponents happened to be the one team I had hoped we would be drawn against after I had scanned the list of teams left in the Cup.

I knew them as a good clean-playing team on the field, and I always enjoyed playing against a team of that class. Whichever team won this match would most certainly win a thrilling one.

At last the day of the match arrived, the referee blew his whistle, the crowd roared, and the players went into battle. After just four minutes' play our captain, Harry Johnston, let fly at the Fulham goal with a first-time shot. Joe Bacuzzi, Fulham's right-back, saw that Ian Black, the Fulham goalkeeper, had advanced too far out of his goal, so Joe became the goalkeeper and handled the ball. A penalty was awarded. Allan Brown crashed the ball into the back of the net from the spot, and we were one up.

After that early goal Fulham fought like tigers to get on equal terms, and our defence had a rough time keeping their forward line under. Fulham attacked, then we attacked—and that is how it went until the final whistle blew. That early goal was the only one scored, and it won us the match. I should think that everybody who saw that game must have been well satisfied and wished that they could see a game as good every week.

When we got back to our dressing-rooms after the match and everybody was relaxed, we found out how lucky we had been. Several of Joe Bacuzzi's own colleagues told him that he had no need to handle the ball, as the shot would have gone wide. They asked Harry Johnston to confirm this, and he agreed with them; he said that the ball would have finished up wide of the goal.

Poor Joe! He, of course, would not be expected to know *that* when he had his back to the goal. All he knew was that the ball was going goalwards and his goalkeeper was out of position, and as he couldn't get his head to the ball it was only natural that he instinctively handled as a last resort.

I have told you before that you need all the luck you can get to reach Wembley, and here was proof. I bet it took a long time for Joe Bacuzzi to forget that game. I felt sorry for Jim Taylor, the Fulham centre-half and captain. He had played a big part in keeping our forward line down, and, taking things all round, I don't think any player on either side would have grumbled at a replay. Our stroke of luck, however, saved us that. We had made it to the semi-final.

The news quickly came through that the other three teams left in the struggle to Wembley were Birmingham City, Newcastle United and Wolverhampton Wanderers. I spent the best part of the following day wondering which of these three teams we would be drawn against.

It turned out to be Birmingham City. The semi-finals are always played on neutral grounds, so the ground advantage did not enter into it.

Our venue was at Maine Road, Manchester. The venue for the Newcastle *v*. Wolves match was at Hillsborough, Sheffield. We knew that we were up against tough opponents in Birmingham. They have always been a tough, quick-tackling team and great fighters.

Now I could see Wembley in sight I trained harder than ever, if that was possible, and when the game started at Maine Road I felt as fit as a fiddle.

It turned out to be a real tough cup-tie game. Not for a single second did either side let up. We received a blow that shook us in the first half when Stanley Mortensen injured his shoulder, but despite the great pain he suffered for the rest of the game he wouldn't leave the field.

I can say at this point that they don't come any tougher than Stan. Having a key man injured is no joke, as you cannot expect miracles from an injured man, but I think the courage Stan showed that day helped us to overcome some sticky patches.

Neither side had scored when the last five minutes of the game came along, but it was at this point that the Birmingham forwards really went to town. Until the end of the game they raided our goal non-stop. Two minutes from time Stewart, the Birmingham winger, managed at last to break through our hard-worked defence; he went on goalwards and sent a fine drive in the direction of our goal. My heart dropped to my boots and I closed my eyes, a feeling I cannot attempt to describe ran through my whole body—it was the end! I heard a loud crack, and on looking up I saw, to my amazement, that the ball was still in play and was being scrambled out of danger by the gallant Blackpool defenders. Stewart's shot had struck the bar. What a let-off! Before I could get control of myself again the referee blew his whistle and the game was over. We lived to fight another day.

I was trembling like a leaf when we left the field—this obsession to get to Wembley had me in a grip far tighter than I had realized. When we got back to our dressing-rooms we heard that the other semi-final had ended in a goal-less draw, so it meant a further battle for all of us in the middle of the coming week.

Our replay was fixed to take place on the Everton ground at Goodison Park, and on the day of the match, after taking an early lunch at St. Annes-on-Sea, we left by coach in plenty of time to reach Liverpool. I looked around the coach as it made its way towards the great Lancashire seaport and I could see a few worried faces, denoting pre-match nerves. The knowledge that just one more win can put you in the Final at Wembley is enough to put a frown on the toughest footballer's face. I glanced at Mortensen, who had made a quick recovery from his shoulder injury. He was sitting with the usual half-smile on his face and looked the calmest of the lot. Whether or not he felt the tension in the motor-coach a bit too much for his liking, I don't know; but he suddenly started off on one of his many gags and soon had us all laughing, and certainly more relaxed.

Then we ran into heavy traffic which slowed us down. We thought what a good job it was that we had left in plenty of time, but we quickly found out that we should have left a lot earlier than we did, as the traffic got thicker and thicker. Coaches and cars were making their way to Goodison Park from all directions, and the nearer we got to the ground the worse it became. We finally made Goodison Park, but we had less than ten minutes left to get ready and to be on the field in time for the kick-off. The Birmingham team had been in the ground for over an hour. All thoughts of who we were playing, what we were playing for, and even where we were playing left our heads in the mad scramble to get ready.

We hurried on to the field eleven minutes late, and Mr. A.

Bond, the London referee, later reported us to the Football Association.

At least the thousands who were trying to get in the already well-packed ground must have blessed us for being late. With not having time to think, the Blackpool team settled down right from the start, and in four minutes Mortensen scored when Merrick, the Birmingham goalkeeper, only managed to half stop a stinging drive. The greasy ball was, I think, well over the line, but Perry made sure by cracking it into the back of the net from the rebound. This was the tonic we needed, and we fought like demons to keep the lead.

We started the second half still one up, and then Perry, after taking a pass from Allan Brown, dashed through on his own and made it 2-0 in our favour. However, a minute later Smith, of Birmingham, scored a good goal. Then the battle started in earnest. Despite being knocked out earlier by an accidental kick on the head, our goalkeeper, George Farm, played a wonderful game. At long last the final whistle went and it was Wembley again for us. I walked off the playing pitch on air.

We were almost ready to leave our dressing-room and board the coach to return to Blackpool when we heard the news that Newcastle had beaten Wolves in their semi-final. Now we knew our opponents at Wembley. I felt rather pleased that it was Newcastle, because, despite their good run in the Cup, their League record wasn't any too good—in fact they were going through a bad patch; whereas the Blackpool team was bang on form and in the running for the League Championship.

As stated before, we eventually finished third from the top, so nobody can blame me for thinking that this was the year for my Cup Final winners' medal. I didn't make the mistake of taking it for granted, because bitter experience in the past had taught me not to take anything connected with football for granted; but somehow I felt a quiet confidence, and, if things didn't change, current form must make us strong favourites. The bogey, of course, was injuries to players whilst engaged in the League matches that had to be played between now and Wembley. That is a nightmare period for every team reaching the Cup Final.

Our fans in Blackpool were in high glee. To have their team in the Cup Final twice in three years was something to be proud of, and I must say that at our home matches before Wembley they came along to Bloomfield Road and gave us grand support. There was no doubt in their minds who was going to win the Cup. Then I received a real shake-up. The newspapers got busy and their sports writers got down to getting all the news they could on football's biggest annual event. Now the two teams for the Final were known, everything and every move these teams made up to the great day was news, and the writers couldn't get enough to satisfy the appetite of the football fans.

They scrutinise every facet of a Wembley team to see if there is a big story shining there. This year it was my age. "This is the last chance Matthews will have"—"Will Matthews retire if he wins his medal?"—"Matthews gets his last chance". . . . Headlines similar to the above appeared in most of the papers, and I realized for the first time in my life that from now on I was fighting my age.

My telephone never stopped ringing. Not only were the sports writers on the line but all kinds of people asking if it was true that I was considering retiring. I was hopping mad. What right had these people to invade the privacy of my own home, to make my life almost unbearable—and also Betty's. You cannot ignore phone calls, because of the general calls that are received, and for days I denied that I was going to retire, medal or no medal. Would anyone believe me outside my own family? Not one person! Stories were printed saying that in a recent conversation Matthews had said this to So-and-so—" . . . and you can take it from me . . ."; or, "Despite all the denials by Stanley Matthews that he is not going to retire at the end of the season, I have just received some very reliable inside information that . . ."; and, "In any case he is at the age when he must think of retirement—after all, thirty-six is a ripe old age to be holding a key position in a First Division side!" I couldn't stand any more of it and I went into hiding for a few days, like a wounded animal. I was exhausted in mind, spirit and body, but still they pursued me. You see, I was a big story, and by now it didn't matter a hoot what I said, nobody believed me, so to all intents and purposes I *was* going to retire after this season.

Day after day brought the same type of newspaper story. It made me mad to think that other people felt they had the right to tell me I was getting too old to play football. On top of all this the club itself had some bad luck.

One of our star men at Blackpool in those days was Allan Brown, our inside-left. He was right on top of his form and, like the rest of us, looking forward to playing in the Cup Final. Brown hadn't been with Blackpool very long, but he had fitted into the team immediately; he was a brilliant ball player and had a most powerful shot. He had been transferred from East Fife for a £26,000 fee.

During the dreaded waiting period before Wembley many League matches have to be played, and against Huddersfield Town Allan Brown damaged a knee. Our trainer did all he could to get him fit for Wembley, but it was no use, Allan was a non-starter. Apart from this bitter blow of losing the services of such a great player at Wembley, we all felt sorry for Allan himself. It was the toughest luck that could happen to any footballer. A week before the Final George McKnight was picked as inside-left against Sheffield Wednesday to get the feel of the position. He also received a knee injury twenty minutes after the kick-off and he suffered the same cruel fate as Allan Brown.

When we lined up on the field at Wembley a week later, waiting for the referee to blow his whistle to start the game, Bill Slater, a wing half-back with Wolves and an English international, filled the bill at inside-left in the Blackpool team. As I stood watching the referee, Mr. W. Ling (Cambridgeshire), who was standing in the centre of the field, whistle in mouth and eyes on his wrist-watch, I took a swift glance round the packed stadium. It was a wonderful sight—Wembley always is. *Is this really my last chance?* I thought. *Am I getting too old?* I quickly shook my head to get rid of these morbid thoughts and the whistle blew. After that I was too busy to think anything. I had only a single feeling in the whole of my body, and that was for my team to win. Right from the kick-off "Wembley nerves" stepped in. Much to my surprise, I saw it had both teams in its grip. I was hoping for a quick goal, because I knew we had been playing better football than Newcastle prior to Wembley, and a quick goal would strengthen our confidence and weaken the morale of Newcastle. The first half, however, was as dull as dishwater and both teams went in for a breather still suffering from nerves. I don't know what the Newcastle manager said to his players in their dressing-room, but I do know that Joe Smith came into ours and told some truths. He said that both teams had "nerves", and also that Newcastle never looked as if they would score; so if we could go out and show a little more confidence he thought we had every chance of scoring a quick goal. You will notice that Joe Smith didn't tell us what to do to get a quick goal, nor did he criticise our first-half play in any way; he left us to play our natural game—and that is the hallmark of a good manager.

It was a different Blackpool that opened the second half; you would have thought it was a different team on the field. We attacked from the start and soon had the Newcastle defence in trouble. Then, five minutes after the restart, I saw the opening I had been waiting for. Jackie Mudie slipped me a perfect pass and I brushed past Bobbie Corbett and cut along the line at speed. Out of the corner of my left eye I could see Mortensen making a typical dash down the middle. I waited until he was through, then I quickly cut the ball back to him. It was a shade too fast for him, and he pulled up in his tracks and raced back, but stumbled; and in the split second it took him to recover, George Robledo gathered the ball in his stride and was away. George passed to Jackie Milburn, who ran through, drew Farm out of his goal and scored. He scored the most important goal at Wembley— the first one. Two or three of our defenders, who had been well upfield because we were on the attack, protested to the referee that Milburn was offside. Mr. Ling, however, awarded a goal, and that was that. One minute we were attacking, and ten seconds later the ball was in our net. I stood flabbergasted: I just couldn't believe it. The thought ran through my brain that if I hadn't been too fast with my centre *we* might have scored instead. It was a similar incident to the free-kick in the 1948 Final. Manchester United took a quick free-kick, caught us unawares, and a goal against the run of the play put them ahead. The Newcastle team was jubilant with this success and the players mobbed Milburn all the way back to the middle of the field.

The game restarted and we attacked now with a greater determination than ever. My hopes of getting an equaliser rose. Then, just five minutes after that first Newcastle goal, Ernie Taylor, the Newcastle inside-right, passed a Blackpool player and made a perfect back-heel pass to Milburn, who was running up behind him. Milburn hit the ball first time with his left foot and scored a most spectacular goal from thirty yards out—I should think one of the finest ever seen at Wembley. The ball flashed like a rocket past Farm into the back of the Blackpool goal. The Newcastle fans stood up and roared their heads off. When the Newcastle players withdrew from congratulating Milburn he picked himself off the ground and, with a huge grin all over his face, trotted back to the centre of the field, the happiest man in the world.

Whilst I stood watching Jackie getting the full treatment from his colleagues I was swearing to myself like a trooper. I am not a swearing man, but some primitive instinct must have got the upper hand for those few seconds. I was not annoyed with Newcastle—they fully deserved the goals by taking their chance; it was Lady Luck that I was cursing. I knew from my experience in the game that it was a million-to-one shot to score from such a position, and when I spoke to Jackie after the match he admitted, being the good sport he is, that his shot might have gone anywhere.

When play recommenced I hitched up my shorts and told myself we were not licked yet—but as time went on I could see we were. Newcastle were now playing with the confidence that only a two-goal lead gives any team, and I am afraid that we began to try a little too hard to get on level terms. It was no use, and Newcastle United ran out winners by two goals to nil. So for the second time we followed our captain, Harry Johnston, up the steps to the royal box to receive our consolation prizes—the runners-up medals.

Whilst the Newcastle team stood on the ground surrounded by press photographers and their followers, I followed the rest of the Blackpool team towards the tunnel leading to our dressing-room. I am not in the least ashamed to say that tears clouded my vision and my heart was as heavy as lead. Just as I was about to leave the turf itself something made me stop. I kicked deep into the turf with my right foot and said, "I'll be back. You haven't seen the last of me." Reading this as I write it, it sounds rather childish; but I assure you I was not feeling silly or childish at that moment, I really meant it, and no matter how long it took me, and how much I had to train and fight to make it, I knew I would come back once more—for the third time—to do battle on that famous turf for a cup-winners' medal. I broke into a trot and in less than a minute I was in our dressing-room with the rest of the boys. Joe Smith entered the room. He spoke eleven words—"You did your best, lads, and that's good enough for me"; then he left us to get ourselves sorted out.

When I look back on that day now, I realise what a lot of good I got out of it. I seemed to acquire a new kind of quiet courage that is difficult to explain. It was a kind of anticipation, of looking forward to running on the playing pitch at Wembley once more in some future Cup Final and knowing somehow, whatever people said to the contrary, that, as sure as my name is Stanley Matthews, that day would dawn.

Any down-in-the-mouth feeling that the Blackpool players may have felt on the return trip to Blackpool vanished when we met the terrific welcome we received from our townsfolk. You would have thought we had won the Cup. After this welcome things began to look a little brighter, and when the time came to say good-bye to each other until the 1951–52 season it was a contented bunch of footballers who went their various ways to enjoy the summer break.

In next to no time the summer slipped by and once more we were training hard for the opening of the season in August. The season started off well and I got a very pleasant surprise—I was asked to switch on the 300,000 lamps for Blackpool's Festival Year illuminations in September. This was indeed an honour—so much so that at first I thought it was a leg-pull.

It was a very proud footballer who stood on the Town Hall steps in Talbot Square, Blackpool, on the 7th September, 1951, and it gave me a special thrill when I gazed at the faces of the 8,000 people who packed the square in front of me. When the Town Hall clock had struck the last stroke of eight I pulled the switch and the town became a blaze of lights. The Corporation had promised the sightseers a special surprise, and when this special surprise was revealed it held me spellbound. As I pulled the switch a lit-up football appeared above my head, then a representation of myself scoring a goal was shown in coloured lights. The goalkeeper was spreadeagled and each time the ball entered the net the crowd cheered their heads off in good-natured fun. I took this as a leg-pull, because they knew I didn't score many goals. I was introduced to the crowd by the Mayor, Councillor Joseph Hill, J.P., who told them that in his opinion everybody in the world should see the Blackpool illuminations at least once. I remember thinking to myself how right he was. If a show like this was put on abroad, British people would flock to see it. I spoke a few words and mentioned how proud I was to have had the honour of being chosen to switch on the lights and that it was the third time I had been on the Town Hall steps, having been there twice before with the Blackpool team that had reached the Cup Final at Wembley but had not been able to bring the Cup to Blackpool. I wished the crowd a happy evening, and the fun was on.

What a night that was! The Blackpool Tower with its 520 feet of lights could be seen miles away, and it wasn't long before the promenade was packed with cars and coaches from the South Shore right up to the North. Yes, that was a night that Betty and I won't forget in a hurry.

With regard to football, nothing very much happened to Blackpool during the 1951-52 season. We met West Ham United in the third round and they beat us. It was a good game and we couldn't grumble at the result. Somehow I didn't feel that we had much chance of reaching Wembley twice in succession. It was asking too much, the odds were all against it happening. It shows you how wrong one can be. Newcastle not only reached Wembley again this season but they won the Cup again by beating Arsenal. That indeed was something to be proud of, the odds against a team doing so are fantastic. At the time I thought that Newcastle must be going through one of those lucky phases that now and again happens to some team, and it is when impossible things like these happen that you realise again what a fascinating, unpredictable game football is.

For myself, I had run into a quiet spot in my career. I still puzzled the critics by keeping my play up to standard, but I noticed that when I had a bad day the pens couldn't get to paper quick enough to write me off. Then I might turn out the following week and upset their calculations again. I had, of course, reached a stage in my career when it was necessary for me to turn in a first-class performance every time I stepped on a football field. If I failed to do this, knowing looks would appear on the critics' faces and their heads would shake sadly.

By not conforming to pattern I could see that I was a source of worry to a lot of people. One of the strongest weapons my critics had at that time was the fact that I had dropped out in the international field, and there was surely a reason for this. I suppose there *was* a reason. My answer—in 1960—is this: I was still considered good enough to represent my country in 1957, five years after I had been written off for good.

I have said that the 1951–52 season was a quiet one for me, and have just tried to paint a picture of the general attitude towards my future. In a nut-shell, the general impression was that I had passed my best and from now would just amble along until I decided to call it a day. People now had a tendency to speak about me in the past tense.

Now this is an important point to keep in mind in view of the sudden disaster that was to fall on me and which started in a very simple way.

When the 1951–52 season ended and the summer holiday came to an end I reported for training at Bloomfield Road for the start of the 1952–53 season, which soon got under way. Then trouble walked into my life. I had been out for a run in the car with Betty and the children and was running down a grassy slope after a small ball when suddenly one of my legs gave way and I fell flat on my back. I got on my feet and found that I could walk, but when I broke into a run a terrible pain shot into my instep. I returned home and rested the foot.

The next day I reported for training and saw our trainer, Johnny Lynas, who examined my leg. There didn't seem much wrong with it. After a few days I tried to sprint in private practice but just couldn't get off the mark. The pain was now unbearable around the right thigh, which suggested a badly pulled muscle, it had the trainer and myself puzzled.

The weeks went by and I kept missing the team through this knee trouble. In fact I did not play for three months. That is a long time to be out of football, and as the injury didn't get any better I began to worry. Betty did what she could to cheer me up, and suggested that it might vanish as suddenly as it had appeared. In the meantime I went regularly to the ground for treatment, but it was no use; it would not get better.

It was getting into the third month when I first heard the whispers and saw the funny looks that some people were throwing in my direction. Then I picked up the paper one morning and it was all there as usual—I was going to be transferred to Stoke. I gaped in astonishment at the headline and called Betty in from the kitchen where she was getting some breakfast ready. The look on my face must have been enough—she took the paper out of my hand and read the headline.

After a few seconds she turned to me and said, "Whatever is all this about?" I looked at her and said, "Betty, I haven't the foggiest idea; it's the first I have heard of it. You believe me, don't you?" She smiled and said, "Of course I do. One look at your face convinced me of that." She disappeared into the kitchen and reappeared almost immediately with a cup of tea, which she thrust at me. "Here you are—drink that. It will do you good." I couldn't help but smile. The faith women put in a cup of tea is remarkable. I took the cup and sipped the tea; then we read the paper.

After that I made a few phone calls, and half an hour later I had the true picture of events in my mind. I turned to Betty and said, "So that's it. Half the people in Blackpool think I am swinging the lead. They don't believe there is anything the matter with me, and think that I just don't want to play with Blackpool again. On top of that, they say Stoke City must have heard all these rumours and they have approached

Blackpool with regard to a possible transfer. To make it worse, it seems that the Blackpool directors have agreed to the transfer." I jumped up from my chair and paced the room. What I saw in Betty's face made me calm down. I think that was the first time in our married life she had seen me so upset. She came over to me, patted me on the shoulder, and said in a very low voice, "Don't, Stan. Don't let it worry you like that; it isn't worth it." She paused, then went on, "I should have thought they would know that you couldn't do anything like that. I know how you feel, so take it easy for a few minutes." I looked up at her, then the doorbell rang and Betty left the room.

I leaned back in my chair and tried to pull myself together.

Soon after that I went to see Joe Smith. "I don't like all this talk," I said, "it's gone so far now, I think I had better see whether I could transfer—but I'm not fit yet to play for anyone." We talked it over for some time and finally Joe said: "If you really want to go back to Stoke, I'm sure the directors will let you. There's a meeting next Thursday, will you come along?" I agreed to do so.

I met the directors and told them I would like a transfer but I pointed out that I was still far from fit. We discussed various details together and then I went home.

Next day Joe Smith came round to see me. "Sorry, Stan," he said, "but the directors won't agree to the transfer." So that was that. Two weeks from that time we were due to play Sheffield Wednesday at Sheffield in the third round of the Cup. I must explain this because a couple of days after my request was turned down I met one of the Blackpool directors. I told him how surprised I was at their decision. "Well, Stanley," he said, "we're playing Sheffield soon and they've got a strong side— why not ask again *after* the match?"

During all this time I had been having manipulation and I was now due to go to Manchester for an operation on my leg. I was prepared in the usual manner for the operation, and I remember my last thought before I went under was that it wouldn't be long now before I knew whether I stayed in football or finished.

The next thing I remembered was a parched feeling in my mouth, then I felt someone slide their arm under my body and lift me slightly. I felt something wet touch my lips, and pressed them together to try and get some of the moisture in my mouth. Then everything went black. . . .

I heard a clock ticking and opened my eyes, then I moved my head in the direction of the sound. I was in bed in a darkened room. At the side of my bed was a table with a small table lamp on it, and beside the lamp was a small clock. The hands pointed to two o'clock. Except for the ticking, everything was quiet. Then my memory returned and I remembered where I was. I felt fit and well. For some time I lay on my back gazing at the ceiling, then I put my hand under the bedclothes and felt my leg. I began to wonder if I was cured.

I could soon find out if I got out of bed. Swinging myself to a sitting position on the side of the bed, I very gingerly stood up. So far so good. I glanced at the clock—it was quarter past two— then walked slowly to the foot of the bed and over to a chair, and stopped in front of it. I looked at the hard wooden edge at the front of the seat and thought, *Now for the test. I have only to lift my leg and press my instep firmly on that hard edge, and if a pain shoots up my leg as it has done in the past months I shall know the operation has failed. If I feel no pain the operation will have been a success.*

I lifted my foot and got it within a few inches of the edge of the chair. Sweat was pouring from my body, and I asked myself what I would do if the pain was still there. I grappled with this question for some time, then glanced at the clock again. It was half-past two. Lifting up my foot, I pressed it hard against the chair's edge. I felt no pain at all. Then I tried again. Still no pain. I could have shouted with joy—the operation was a success! I got back into bed, but I tossed and turned until the early-morning light crept through the curtains of my room, and only then fell asleep.

The next thing I remember was someone shaking my shoulder. I opened my eyes and a nurse asked me how I felt. I said I had never felt better. She gave me breakfast after I had washed and the bed had been made tidy. Then the moment I had been waiting for arrived—the specialist walked into the room with a smile on his face. He said, "Well, how do you feel this morning?" "Fine," I said. He gave me a searching glance, then laughed. "So you know the operation was a success."

I was soon on my way home and reported to Joe Smith, and I told him all about my experiences in Manchester, then I went out on the playing pitch and under his watchful eye did a full work-out. I changed back into my lounge suit and went back to the manager's office. Joe Smith was sitting behind his desk writing. He looked up at me and smiled, then he said, "Well, and how do you feel now, Stan?" I said, "Fine, Joe." He nodded and waved a hand in the direction of a chair. "I'm pleased to hear that, Stan; it won't be long before you're back in the team again."

The news that I was in the team to meet Sheffield Wednesday caused a sensation. It also brought plenty of publicity to the match, and when Saturday came and we arrived in Sheffield it seemed that all England was trying to get into the Sheffield ground. I was determined to have a good game, and I will let you into a secret about this match. On my way to our dressing-room I passed a bunch of Sheffield players, but they didn't see me, and when I was almost past them I heard one of them remark, "And you can leave Matthews alone—he won't be much use after a three-months lay-off." I entered our dressing-room and kept this vital information to myself. The Blackpool team that day was: Farm; Shimwell, Garrett; McKnight, Johnston (captain), Fenton; Matthews, Mudie, Brown, Taylor, Perry. The Blackpool left wing was a very useful one; with Taylor at inside-left and Brown at centre-forward we had two ball players who were capable of tearing any defence wide open. Joe Smith had put a lot of thought into the selection of that forward line.

We ran on to the field to a great reception and there were many of our own supporters there. The game started, and I could tell that I was on trial. Each time I got the ball the crowd seemed to quieten down; but what they expected to see I don't know. I foxed for quite a time and then I realised it was true that I was being more or less ignored. When I was sure of it I acted at the next opportunity.

I could see that the Wednesday players knew they would have to watch our left wing, with Brown and Taylor being together, and as I lulled them into false security they thought they had everything under control. Then there was a free-kick into the goalmouth, the keeper ran out, punched the ball out of goal and it landed right at my feet. I lobbed it over his head, and—bang!—the ball was in the back of the net. I had scored the first goal.

I bet Joe Smith in the stand laughed his head off. The Wednesday team were flabbergasted at the success of my effort, and I had a strong suspicion at the time that a few of my own colleagues were also surprised. The fact was, however, that we were leading at half-time 1–0, and I had scored the goal.

In the second half Ernie Taylor scored a second goal for our side, and Sewell scored for Wednesday, so we ran out winners 2–1.

The Sunday papers were full of this match, and a lot of nice things were said about me; but I got the biggest thrill in reading what they said about Joe Smith, because he was the man who had to make the decision to include me in the team. I was also pleased to be on the best of terms again with the Blackpool supporters, who took me to their hearts again after this game. Until this book is published they will not know the real truth with regard to my long lay-off.

We met Huddersfield Town at Blackpool in the fourth round and won 1–0, the goal being scored by Tommy Garrett, our left full-back, from a long free-kick. In the fifth round we met Southampton at Blackpool and could only draw 1–1. In the replay at Southampton we were a goal down at half-time. As we walked back on the pitch to commence the second half I asked Harry Johnston whether it would be all right if I wandered over to the other wing to try and shake off the tight grip they had on me; at least I would take the players with me, and I might make things easier for the rest of our forward line. Harry agreed to the suggestion.

When the second half of the match had been in progress about ten minutes I put my plan into action. I took my time because I didn't want to make it obvious. Slowly but surely I began to wander, and where I wandered so did my bodyguard. I went deep into my own half, then over to the left wing. This relieved our forwards of a lot of unwelcome attention, and at last Allan Brown scored to bring us on level terms. I resumed my rightful position for some time after this goal, then I began to wander again. Jackie Mudie obliged this time with the winning goal, and we left the field with the result Southampton 1, Blackpool 2. In the papers the following day there were reports such as, *Half-time pep talk puts Blackpool on the way to victory*, or *A huddle session at half-time paved the way for Blackpool's win*. What I have just written was the plain fact and nothing but the truth.

When we came out of the hat for the sixth round of the Cup we found that we had been drawn to meet Arsenal at Highbury. When I heard the news I knew that this time we had something on our plate. Arsenal at Highbury is no push-over at any time for any team. In a cup-tie it would take a very good team to come away with a win. So Arsenal were made favourites to win the match, and some critics said they would win easily. However, off to Highbury we went, and after the match had got warmed up I was inclined to agree that they wanted some beating, so I was hoping for at least a draw.

At half-time no goals had been scored, but soon after the game had been resumed Logie scored for Arsenal, and it looked as if they had got our measure. Little Ernie Taylor tipped the scales, however, by scoring a very good goal to put us level. The battle now started in earnest, and the excitement rose higher and higher. Then Allan Brown broke through and scored a lovely goal to put us in the lead. As we ran towards Allan to congratulate him he never got off the ground and seemed to be in great pain. Then it was discovered that he had broken a leg. He was carried off the field and rushed to hospital. This meant that if we were lucky enough to reach Wembley he wouldn't be with us. We didn't look at that angle too much when the accident happened because we were a long way off Wembley, but I am sure it flashed through every Blackpool player's mind. The tragedy at that time was that he would be lost to the Blackpool team for the rest of the season, and no team can afford to lose the services of a player like Allan Brown.

The game restarted, and we managed to stick grimly to our lead, the final result being Arsenal 1, Blackpool 2. Although we had won this important match, it was a miserable bunch who made their way back to Blackpool. Allan Brown was on all our minds all the way home. He was playing right on top of his form when fate stepped in and cut him down. There were plenty of long faces amongst the Blackpool supporters for some time after the Arsenal match. Brown was a firm favourite at Bloomfield Road. Now that we had reached the semi-finals a faint hope started to flower that we might make Wembley again. But when the semi-final draw came out and I saw that we had been drawn to play Spurs at Villa Park, Birmingham, I smothered the flower quickly. Spurs at that time were playing football second to none. With Allan Brown in the team, supported by Ernie Taylor, I would have said we had a good chance of victory, but now . . . I hadn't defeat in my heart, but the facts were that on form Spurs at full strength should win.

I knew that Blackpool would play their hearts out to win, but if they lost it would be no disgrace, because we should be playing one of the finest teams in England at that time. So I didn't get unduly excited about the match; instead I set about making myself completely fit for it. Joe Smith gave the team selection for this vital match a lot of thought, and when the team appeared on the board he had decided to recall Mortensen, who hadn't played in any of the previous cup-ties this season, in place of Allan Brown, who was making good progress with his injured leg.

When the two teams took the field at Villa Park they read as follows—BLACKPOOL: Farm; Shimwell, Garrett; Fenton, Johnston (captain), Kelly; Matthews, Taylor, Mudie, Mortensen, Perry. SPURS: Ditchburn; Ramsey, Withers; Nicholson, Clarke, Burgess; Walters, Bennett, Duquemin, Baily, McClellan.

In the first half of the game Spurs seemed to be all over us and our goal was under constant fire, but somehow our gallant defence held them at bay and in a break-away Bill Perry scored, and we went in at half-time leading 1-0. In the second half Spurs renewed their attack until they reaped their reward with Duquemin scoring a lovely goal. We played ourselves into the ground in trying to keep Spurs from getting the winning goal, and then in a few minutes it happened. Alf Ramsey, the Spurs famous international right-back, stopped a ball that had been booted downfield and decided to pass back to his goalkeeper.

H

But he didn't connect with the ball properly, and as it slowly rolled towards Ditchburn Jackie Mudie nipped round Ramsey and kicked the ball into the back of the net. Ramsey held his head in horror and Ditchburn beat the earth with his clenched fists. A few minutes later the final whistle went, with the score Blackpool 2, Spurs 1.

I rushed to the centre of the field in a daze and shook hands with my colleagues. Even then I couldn't grasp that we were through to Wembley. I have said that a team needs all the luck to get to the Final, and we had more than our share that afternoon. As I saw Spurs walking off the field my heart went out to them; but there you are—it could have been us.

When I reached the dressing-room with the rest of the team Joe Smith was already there waiting for us. He congratulated us, and as he was leaving the room he whispered to me in a low voice, "Remember your wish? Well, you've got it." I turned to speak to him, but he had vanished. It slowly dawned on me that I wasn't dreaming—it *was* Wembley again. 1948, 1951, and now 1953. Would the third time be lucky?

All the way back to Blackpool I sat back quietly listening to the good-natured fun that was going on between the lads. My mind kept flashing back over the years. I thought of my father. I thought of the other two Wembley Cup Finals. I thought of the time when I kicked the Wembley turf in anger.

Only a few weeks before the semi-final against Spurs I had celebrated my thirty-eighth birthday. I decided not to say a word if the sports writers said it was my last chance—three chances in five years is fantastic. At last I closed my eyes and the sudden shock and the following excitement seemed to make me feel sleepy, so, amidst all the laughter and chatter, I dozed off, and when someone woke me on our arrival at Blackpool I thought again for a second that I had been dreaming it all. I gasped, "We are in the Final, aren't we?" Nobody seemed to hear my words in the din that was going on. Then, as the sleep cleared away from my head, I remembered it all. Yes, we were going to Wembley again! And within a few weeks I wasn't going to be allowed to forget that I was bound for Wembley.

The Cup Final was due to be played at Wembley on the 2nd

May 1953. As our opponents were Bolton Wanderers, and Bolton is only about thirty miles from Blackpool, it was an all-Lancashire final. Bolton Wanderers at that time (as indeed they are now) were a hard-tackling and a hard-fighting team. They would take some beating, and should they get behind in goals they would fight until they dropped to get back to level terms—and then find some hidden reserve power to try and snatch a winning goal. That was the team we had to play in the Final. (Incidentally, Joe Smith won his first cup-winners' medal with Bolton in the famous White Horse Final, and he is still held in great esteem by Bolton football fans.) We knew that to win the Cup we should have to get fit, acquire staying power, and have a keen will to win.

It was in early April, a month before the Final, that I found myself pitchforked once more into universal publicity. It started in a small way from a few well-wishers sending me personal letters wishing me success at Wembley. Then one or two people wrote to the papers, and the papers scented a big story. Suddenly everyone in the country became interested in me. They wanted me to win a cup-winners' medal. What amazed me most was the fact that my age wasn't mentioned like it was in 1951, nor was my retirement stressed. The simple fact was that for some unknown reason the people of England, and indeed all the Commonwealth, seemed bent on my getting a winners' medal. The papers started naming the coming Final "The Stanley Matthews Final". My fan-mail was fantastic. People who had never seen me play, or in fact never seen a football match, sent me their good wishes for success. I received hundreds of mascots and thousands of letters. It overwhelmed me; I couldn't understand what all the fuss was about. In the early weeks I thought it would die down, but I was wrong. It got bigger and bigger. It became a kind of a cult. Everyone seemed to be a Stanley Matthews fan. The papers were most kind to me, and fresh stories of my past experiences on the football field were being printed every day. Strangers called at my home, and phone calls came through day and night from all parts of the country. I shall never forget the month of April 1953. I must say that I felt very proud to know that I had the whole country behind me in my third attempt to win my medal. If I had told them about the vow I had made in my father's sick room, I dread to think what would have happened. A story like that would have created a sensation. However, I had no fear of that breaking out in the press, because until now it has always been a closely guarded secret between my mother, Betty and myself.

One of the biggest surprises I got during the period prior to the Cup Final was the number of letters and good wishes I received from the Bolton and Farnworth area. You wouldn't have expected me to get much support from the fans of Bolton Wanderers. I did though, and many of the writers said that although they wanted their team to win they wouldn't shed any tears if they lost—at least not on this occasion; and they finished by hoping that the best team would win. It must have been very difficult to write such a letter.

After the first two weeks of this sort of publicity I began to feel somewhat exhausted—I never seemed to be able to get a minute's rest from dawn until dusk; so the week before the match I was given a few days' leave to get a rest.

I returned to Blackpool and joined the team to travel south to our hotel just outside the city itself. I am sure all the members of the Blackpool party were glad to get away from our seaside resort. The request for tickets had nearly sent most of the players up the wall; everyone they knew thought they should get one. When we reached our destination we relaxed in the quiet of the hotel grounds. It was a relief for all of us to get this breather before the next day's battle began.

I was up early on the day of the Final, and before breakfast I had a brisk walk and flexed my muscles. Then I drove all thoughts of the Final out of my mind and had a quiet nap until we were summoned to board the coach to Wembley. When we got near to the ground the blood started to tingle in my veins. It is impossible to remain calm when you enter the Wembley atmosphere. We changed in our dressing-room without much fuss. Joe Smith popped in to wish us luck, and then the time arrived for us to take the field. We walked side by side with the Bolton team to the centre of the field and Prince

Philip came on to the ground with some of the F.A. officials. In a very relaxed manner he shook hands with all the players, and the linesmen and the referee, and he made us all feel very much at ease. The Queen was also present, and she watched Prince Philip meet us all.

It was a lovely day and conditions were ideal for football. As we took up our playing positions I glanced round the packed stadium. What a sight it was! Although I had seen the same sight many times before, somehow today it looked more wonderful than ever. The referee looked at his watch, put his whistle in his mouth, and it was then that I could hear my name being shouted with good-luck messages from all parts of the ground.

The line-up of the teams was as follows—BLACKPOOL: Farm; Shimwell, Garrett; Fenton, Johnston, Robinson; Matthews, Taylor, Mortensen, Mudie, Perry. BOLTON WANDERERS: Hanson; Ball, Banks, R.; Wheeler, Barrass, Bell; Holden, Moir, Lofthouse, Hassell, Langton. *Referee:* Mr. B. M. Griffiths (Newport). *Linesmen:* Rev. G. S. V. Davis (Oxford) and G. F. J. Sawyer (Somerset).

The whistle went, the game was on, the crowd roared their heads off—and then, before the spectators had settled down after the initial roar, Bolton were a goal up. In exactly one minute's playing time Lofthouse scored a lovely goal for Bolton from out on the right. What a start for any team! A goal in the first minute. The Bolton players overwhelmed Lofthouse with their congratulations and the Bolton contingent amongst the 100,000 spectators went mad. The Blackpool players stood spellbound. We couldn't realise what had happened. I didn't feel unduly worried, because the game had hardly started, and I had seen teams play the rest of the game without another goal being scored. This goal, however, put Bolton on their mettle, and they tried with all their might to increase their lead. The Blackpool defence had now settled down and they held the Bolton attacks. I was being watched pretty closely and was finding it hard to get away, so I decided at this stage to hold my fire and see if I could give my watch-dogs a false sense of security.

After the game had been in progress for thirty-five minutes Mortensen scored, to put us on level terms. Our success was short-lived, however, because four minutes later, in the thirty-ninth minute, Moir scored for Bolton, and half-time came with the score Bolton 2, Blackpool 1. It hadn't been a good first half. Some of the players on both sides played well below form, owing to "Wembley nerves", and most of the others seemed to be rather unsettled. Joe Smith popped in to see us and wished us luck in the second half. We returned to the field, and the game restarted.

I have said before that Bolton were a tough side, very quick in the tackle, and went into a tackle with one purpose—to get the ball. Blackpool played a more delicate game, relying more on the quick-passing positional play and ball play. In the second half Bolton again put on the pressure, and in the fifty-fifth minute Bell scored their third goal.

So with thirty-five minutes' play left we were losing by three goals to one, and it looked as if only a miracle could save us. Then in the sixty-seventh minute Mortensen scored again to make the score 3–2 for Bolton. We now had just twenty-three minutes in which to score two goals and win the match, providing that we kept Bolton from scoring again. It was at this point of the game that I decided the time had come for my all-out effort. I knew that the Bolton men were getting rather tired from the hard work they had put into their game, and I also knew that they were feeling very confident.

I took a deep breath and went into battle. Within minutes, with the valuable help of Ernie Taylor, our inside-right, I gave the Bolton defence their first taste of worry. I pulled out every trick I knew, and after ten minutes I knew they couldn't hold me. I sent centre after centre goalwards. At last Mortensen scored, to complete his hat-trick—and anyone who scores a hat-trick in a Cup Final is the man of the match. Mortensen had scored to put us level with only two minutes' play left.

From the kick-off we attacked once more, and with just over a minute's playing time left I again received the ball. Getting it quickly under control, I ran down the wing, beating first one man and then another. At last I was through, and I could hear the roar of the crowd, who were now on their feet in excitement. They were shouting my name at the top of their voices. Glancing towards the Bolton goalmouth, I saw that Perry had every chance of scoring the winning goal if I could get a perfect centre to him. I pushed the ball forward a little, at the same time praying with all my heart that the years of practice, training and experience would stand me in good stead, for I knew that everything depended on this centre. Then, as I stepped forward with my left foot and raised my right foot off the ground to kick the ball, I found, to my horror, that I was standing in a divot hole and was losing my balance; my shirt felt clammy next to my skin. It was as if an unseen hand held me upright until I kicked the ball, then the hand let go and I fell to the ground. As I rolled over I saw that the ball was in the back of the net. We had made it and Perry had scored the winning goal. Then a bomb burst over Wembley. The next thing I remember was a lot of pain in the small of my back and a stinging sensation in my face, then I saw I was in the middle of a bunch of Blackpool players—they were nearly killing me. The final whistle blew, and then—and only then—did I realise that I had won my medal. My head was buzzing from the roar of the spectators and once more I found myself in the centre of the crowd of Blackpool players. They picked me off the ground and chaired me. I looked across to my left and saw that our captain, Harry Johnston, was in the same position as I was.

Then the great moment arrived. I followed Harry Johnston up the steps leading to the royal box and in next to no time I was in front of the Queen. She shook hands with me and handed me my cup-winners' medal and said, "Well done." When the rest of the team had received their medals the rumpus started all over again—photographs, reporters, and a march of triumph round the ground with the Cup held high, for all to see. Then we returned to our dressing-room and I sat in the corner for some time just gazing at my medal.

After an interview by the B.B.C. television, I changed, quietly left the dressing-room, and made my way back up the tunnel on to the pitch. The vast stadium was now deserted. I walked to the spot where I had kicked the turf at the end of the 1951 Final, looked up in the sky, and held out the medal in the palm of my hand—it was the only way I could think of to show it to my father. As I held out my medal the sun came from behind a small cloud and shone down on it. Standing there, a wonderful feeling of peace entered my body and mind. I felt that all the years from boyhood to manhood in football finished here. I had fulfilled my destiny, and I knew in my heart that from now on, no matter how long I stayed in football, I would never have another day like this. What had they called it? "The Stanley Matthews Final." Well, what a Final it had been, and what a game I had played!

We made our way out of the stadium to meet the crowd who were waiting to see me, then to our victory party, and afterwards back to Blackpool to the biggest welcome any football team has ever had. When the next few days passed by and things got a little quieter, I realised that the season was now over and it was holiday time again. I thought of the Bolton players and knew how they felt, because twice before I had felt as they must now. I hoped Bolton would be lucky in their next attempt, then I took my family away on holiday, knowing in my mind that whatever the future held in store for me I had already completed one full circle.

CHAPTER XXIII

THIS AND THAT

I HOPE you will forgive me if I digress for a little while. I will return to 1953 later and take you through the years up to 1959. I feel, however, that before I do so I must write about 1959. It is June and once more I am enjoying my summer holiday with my family in Blackpool. During the past season (1958-59) Blackpool reached the quarter finals of the F.A. Cup. After making a draw at Bloomfield Road against Luton Town, they beat us in the replay at Luton by one goal to nil. The goal that put paid to our hopes was scored by Allan Brown, who through injury missed two Cup Finals with us. I am pleased to say that Allan played with Luton in the Cup Final at Wembley in 1959, but had to be content with a runners-up medal. So after his bad luck with us he eventually made Wembley six years later. With regard to myself, I have already signed for another season with Blackpool and when this book is published I shall have concluded the 1959-60 season in First Division football. I am feeling completely fit and looking forward to completing another successful season with Blackpool. When am I going to retire? Well, it is eight years since 1951 said good-bye, and in that year everybody said I was going to retire on account of my age. I am now forty-four years old, and I can assure you that I still keep up my regular morning private training and still come through fitness tests with flying colours.

During the six years since I won my Cup medal many things have happened to me. It is odd to think that at the present time there is not so much talk about my retirement. I think writers have tired of the subject. One journalist some time ago called me the Peter Pan of football.

For a few weeks after winning my Cup-winners' medal at Wembley I just relaxed with my family. I needed the rest very badly. The strain I had been under during the weeks leading up to Cup Final day made itself felt now that the ordeal was over. It was, of course, plainly a mental strain. I had to watch my step very carefully, because after the first week I felt myself getting irritated at the smallest thing. Luckily for me I was aware of the tension, and with Betty's help I managed to overcome it. When I arrived home once more, to resume full training in preparation for the 1953–54 season, I decided to get down to sorting out and answering the huge pile of mail that was waiting for me.

I was surprised to find a great number of the letters were from parents who thought that if they could get their son coached by me in the finer arts of football I could make him a world beater. When I read the first one or two I smiled, but when countless others kept turning up I grew alarmed. I know that coaching is a modern craze, not only in football but in all other games, and I also know that there is plenty of money to be made at it. I have strong views on coaching. I know that a boy or girl needs some instruction in whatever game they fancy, and perhaps some advice, but I cannot believe that when you apply the same set of orthodox rules (which coaching is based upon) to a class of youngsters and expect each and everyone of them to soak in the same rules, progress on the same lines, and play in what must be a similar style, you are likely to get much success. I do not believe in trying to turn out a set of human automatons.

I know that many coaches will cry shame on me for saying this, but it is true and I can prove it. Most of the great athletes in the world have done things to get them to the top that the orthodox coach would frown upon, but these champions have something that the coaches never possessed—*natural ability*. This is also true of great boxers, golfers, tennis players, and—last but not least—footballers. Most of our leading players in football today will tell you they have never had organised coaching. Perhaps they have had tuition whilst still at school, but their biggest asset is natural ability. A boy with natural ability for football will succeed, and in nearly every case you will find that he has made the grade through practice, watching others play, and playing against more experienced players. When he has had plenty of practice in trapping and ball-control he will form his own natural style of play. The same applies to dribbling. Once a natural footballer finds out his natural style of dribble he will beat his man, because he has the confidence in his own ability to do so. Without that confidence he hasn't a chance. To force a natural ball player to attend organised coaching classes to teach him orthodox methods is just asking for trouble. He will worry himself to death in trying to do things that are not natural to him. Slowly but surely he will lose confidence in himself and that may mean the end of another promising career. It would be silly of me to say that a natural ball player should never be taught anything at all. I contend, however, that if a player of this class feels at all worried about anything in his play he should seek out a more experienced player and ask his advice on what he is doing wrong. Now the advice he will receive will be based on what the older player can see is wrong in the younger player's natural game, and will be put right on those lines. The older player will not attempt to change the younger player's style of play. Giving advice is as different from coaching as chalk is from cheese. There isn't a coach on this earth who can make a really good player out of a boy who hasn't any natural ability for football.

Most of the letters I received during the summer of 1953 were from football fans thanking me for the pleasure I gave them when they saw me on the playing pitch, and with the usual good wishes they closed with the hope of seeing me for a good many more seasons. Well, I duly obliged them in that respect. I also received quite a number of letters from my critics, and I have indeed quite a number of very stern critics who do not like my style of play. When boiled down, I always find left in the pot the usual three objections with regard to my style of play on the football field. They are: (1) that I am not a match-winner; (2) that I don't get sufficiently "stuck in"; (3) that I don't cut in goalwards and score more goals.

With regard to the first allegation I have always been a little confused by what is meant by a match-winner. Every forward in any team is always a potential winner while the game is in progress. If it means that I do not score winning goals I must agree that I don't score many, but I have made quite a number. I always try and play pure football, to try to reduce the opposing defence to a state of jitters so that, having confused them time after time, it is not long before I find myself in a position to make a favourable opening for a colleague in an easy scoring position to finish off the movement. I suppose that makes my colleague a match-winner, but as long as I see the ball in the back of the net I do not care who scores.

The second allegation is one that I do not mind answering in the least; in fact it will give me the utmost satisfaction to do so. It is a funny thing, but in nearly every match I play I hear a section of the spectators urging their side to get "stuck in". If by any chance the opposing side get "stuck in" from the start of the match, all you hear from the spectators then is "Send him off, ref", "Get off the field, you dirty so-and-so!" From this you can gather that when you get "stuck in" you are heading for trouble. If I had to get "stuck in" to get through a game of football I am afraid that my career would have ended long ago. Any player who has to lower himself by tripping, ankle-tapping or following through with his boot after he has tackled is admitting to the football world at large that he is not fit to be earning his living as a professional footballer. Fortunately for English football, the game is only lightly sprinkled with professional footballers who get "stuck in". The Football Association frown on this type of player, and every footballer in the country knows that if he persists in playing this type of game he will never get the chance to play for his country, however good he may be. This strict ruling on the part of the Football Association has, in my opinion, saved professional footballers from being ruined.

My reply to the third allegation is that when I played for Stoke City as a very raw youngster I did cut in and I did score goals. In fact, so keen was I to make good at my new job that I made it my ambition to score as many goals as I could, thinking that was what the club expected. At one time I was among the club's leading scorers. I soon found out that I was making a big mistake in scoring all those goals. It was at this time I changed my style of play. After all, the ideal winger makes the openings for his inside men to score easy goals. I soon proved to myself that a winger who can make scoring openings for his centre-forward and inside men is as valuable to his team as a winger who scores himself. I would like to add that this style of play makes the winger far more popular with the rest of the forward line than the winger who wants to do the lot. It made me concentrate more than ever on my dribbling and ball-control and make the most of my natural swerve. I worked hard to perfect these, and my future style of play for the rest of my playing career was at last finalised.

Having now answered the three allegations, I do not intend to go deeper into the secrets of my play. I am sure you will agree with me when I say that I believe that this subject should be confined to some future technical book, dealing solely with the method and technique of play.

There was no doubt that my Wembley Cup Final appearance of 1953 had made me a much-discussed football personality as in those days to gain a cup-winners' medal at the age of thirty-eight was, in the eyes of the football fans in this country, something like a miracle. It was generally accepted at that time that any professional footballer over the age of thirty-four was a "has been". Indeed so deep-rooted was this supposition that footballers themselves believed it, with the result that when a professional footballer reached the "ripe old age" of thirty-two he took it as a matter of course that he had only two years in which to fix himself up with a job to see him through the rest of his life. When I proved at Wembley in the 1953 Cup Final that this supposition was all eyewash, as indeed it was and always has been, I opened up for discussion a subject that had been accepted as a cast-iron fact since the early days of professional football; the subject being—"Is a man in his middle thirties too old?"

This question raised a good deal of controversy amongst sports writers and the man in the street. My name, of course, was used all the time as an example. Some people said I was a "freak", others that it was my training methods, and yet others that it was a million-to-one chance against anyone doing what I had done again. They were, of course, all wrong. The simple truth is that

I refused to believe in the supposition. I had set an example to other players and got them thinking, *What he can do, I can do better.* That is what I wanted to happen. I know there are still many people connected with football who think that a footballer in his thirties is on his way out. For their benefit, I would like to draw their attention to the situation as it was in 1959. I will give three examples. First Tom Finney of Preston North End.

During the later half of the 1958–59 season Finney was out of the Preston team through injuries. With Finney out of the team Preston lost match after match and had to fight hard to remain in the First Division. Now Finney is fit again and looking forward to the 1959–60 season. He will be more than welcome back in the team, to all Preston supporters, his team mates, and, of course, the Preston officials. Yet Tom Finney is past his mid-thirties. Does anybody say he is past it, or that he should retire? No! They expect to see Finney at Deepdale for a good many seasons yet, and the people of Preston would be most annoyed with any-one who told them that Tom was too old to play in first-class football. Now if this had been 1948 instead of 1959, things might have been different. The fact is that, despite his age, Tom Finney is still one of the finest footballers in the country, and he proves this every time he runs on to the field; he also knows himself that he still has a lot of football left in him.

I suppose one of the chief ambitions of every professional foot-baller is to captain his country's team in an international match. During the past few years Mr. Walter Winterbottom, the Eng-land manager, has brought about some radical changes in the England team, and I by no means agree with many of them. For one thing, he has been slowly but surely trying to change the England style of play to a style similar to that played by the con-tinental teams—I may add without much success. I firmly believe that we should stick to the style that brought us great success in the past—which is our natural style; the English style. All the continental teams started their careers by copying us, then on their own initiative developed their own style. Remember this, how-ever—the temperaments of these people are different from our own, so it is only natural that, having once mastered the fundamentals of the game, they should allow their natural instincts to mould a style more suitable to them. This they have done with great success. I still think, however, we should hold fast to our traditional English style, because it is our natural style built up over the years on our English temperament. Play a natural game in your native natural style is what I believe. Walter Winterbottom also believes in youth. In 1959 the England team, with very few exceptions, were in their early twenties. I make no comment on that, except to say that it brings me back to the subject under discussion—age. There is, however, one footballer to whom Walter Winterbottom has stuck through thick and thin over the years, and that is Billy Wright of Wolverhampton Wanderers.

Billy Wright played in his hundredth international in 1959. I saw Wright start his international career and have played with him as a fellow international, and under him as captain of an international team. Why has Walter Winterbottom throughout the years always been pleased to see Billy Wright lead the England team on the field as their captain, when in some matches he must have been eight to ten years older than the next oldest member of the international team? Why has Walter Winterbottom time and time again entrusted the most exacting and important job of captain to a player who is now in his mid-thirties? For a man who believes in youth as Walter Winterbottom does, surely there must be only one answer—which is that in Wright he believes he has a player in which he can forget all about age. So you see that in these days it is possible to captain an England side at an age which would have brought all the sports writers down on your neck twenty years ago. How times have changed! Although Billy Wright never inspired me as a captain when I played with him in international matches, he proved by his playing abilities that you cannot tell a man when to finish his playing career by looking at the calendar.

The third and last example is the Wembley Cup Final of 1959. Sid Owen, the captain of Luton Town, one of the finalists, led his team on to the famous turf and played a great game. He was thirty-eight years old—the same age as I was in 1953 when I played in the Cup Final. Beyond saying that this would be his last game (as he would be taking over a job as manager of Luton Town in the 1959–60 season) his age was not mentioned at all— because of the sound displays he gave on the field during the 1958–59 season.

I am convinced that the age bogey has been killed for ever during the past years, and the haunting thought at the back of every footballer's mind—"What am I going to do when I pass thirty?"—is a thing of the past. I say with the greatest confidence to any young professional footballer who is now reaching his twenty-first birthday—get it in your head that you have a good twenty years of football in you. In that time, providing you put your job first by not abusing your body, by being eager to learn all the time, by being a good club man, by undertaking constant and regular private training, by keeping your feet on the ground no matter what honours come your way, you should have saved enough money to make your post-football career bright. The conditions for a professional footballer are first-class now and it is a fine career for anyone who has a natural bent for the game. Now that the game offers a much longer working life I am sure that in the next few years we shall see a wealth of talent come into this game of ours from youngsters who would have shied away a decade ago owing to the uncertain future it then held.

The Blackpool Football Club started the 1953–54 season with a halo around its head. The wealth of publicity given to the club prior to the Cup Final day at the end of the previous season, coupled with the fact that I also got my fair share, had put the name of Blackpool on everyone's lips. So much so that when the first match of the new season was played at Blackpool it seemed to me that all Lancashire wanted to see us play. Many times that season the gates had to be closed at home matches, to the bitter disappointment of thousands of would-be spectators left outside. Bloomfield Road, the Blackpool ground, is not a large ground, with 38,000 spectators inside it is over-full. Still, for all that, if a team could pull that many spectators into the ground for all their home matches I don't think you would get many moans from the directors.

There was no doubt about it, Blackpool had become a very big attraction in the football world. During that period when we played away from home we were welcomed with open arms by the management of the team we opposed, because they knew, no matter how big the average gate was for them at that time, a visit from the Blackpool F.C. would increase it by thousands more. In many cases the "Full" notice would be put outside the ground. When we paid a visit to the really large grounds in this country (and there are a great many of them) crowds of 45,000 to 50,000 were the order of the day.

Now the point I wish to make is this: most of the credit for the drawing power of the Blackpool Club was credited to me. Most people said that I was the drawing card and that without me Blackpool wouldn't draw the crowds they did. It would be stupid of me to deny that people didn't come along to watch me play; but so far as being the drawing card—I very much doubt that. When I didn't appear with the team through a slight injury or some other cause, I noticed that the gates were still big and my non-appearance with the team hadn't made much difference. The Blackpool team played real football, as indeed they do today. Rough play was frowned on by the directors and by our manager, Joe Smith, and to ensure a regular place in the team you had, in every sense of the word, to be the complete footballer. That is the main reason why I have always loved playing for Blackpool and the reason why I shall finish my playing career with them. The Blackpool team has built up a good reputation over the years and are now regarded as one of the best clubs in the country. May this continue to be so for many years to come.

It is only natural when a team is well in the public eye that it should receive many offers to play in other countries in the close season. So when the 1953-54 season ended it was decided by the management to accept an offer that had been made to play a series of matches in Germany during the summer of 1954. It was whilst I was in Germany having a most interesting and enjoyable time with the rest of the members of the Blackpool team that I was suddenly recalled to join the England team who were preparing to go to Switzerland to play in the World Cup series. It was a nice surprise and with the best wishes of my team mates ringing in my ears I packed my bag and made my way home. I duly arrived in Switzerland with the rest of the members of the

England party, and I thrilled again at the wonderful scenery. I got my biggest thrill, however, when we met Switzerland in the series and beat them. This was the first time I had played for my country against Switzerland in Switzerland and finished up on the winning side. It gave me a feeling of deep satisfaction to know that I had been included in an England side that at last had overcome the small-ground bogey. I am sorry to say that we didn't get very far in the series and eventually I returned home with the rest of the party and spent the rest of the close season with my family in Blackpool.

The 1954–55 season got into full swing and again I was feeling fit and well, and enjoyed my football. I was deeply moved on the 1st February, 1955, my fortieth birthday. From dawn till dusk that day I was a very busy man. From all parts of the Commonwealth, as well as from England, Ireland, Scotland and Wales, I received shoals of letters, cards, telegrams, from well-wishers and personal friends, all wishing me a happy birthday and many more years on the football field. I was overwhelmed. Besides the countless messages from home and the Common-wealth, I received congratulations from the Continent, Russia, the Far East, China, Japan, and the U.S.A. It was just fantastic. I also received countless presents from all parts of the world. I think the G.P.O. in Blackpool must have had a special delivery van working solely for me on that memorable day. In the evening, when I said goodbye to the last of the many friends who had kept popping in all through the day to wish me the best of luck, I sat down in the lounge at home exhausted, but the happiest man in the world. I still couldn't get it in my mind that so many people knew me and thought enough about me to go to the trouble they had. It was hopeless, of course, for me to even contemplate trying to answer them, so I take this oppor-tunity of thanking you all for your wonderful gesture and assuring you that your thoughtfulness and kindness did me the world of good and will never leave my mind. The newspapers also went to town on that most fantastic of birthdays, and I wish also to thank them from the bottom of my heart for the good wishes they sent me, because I know they were most sincere.

The 1954–55 season came to an end, and I went to South Africa to play a few matches. The children were now grown up. Jean was sixteen years old, Stanley was nine years old. I used to worry quite a lot when they were young, wondering what effect being brought up in the atmosphere of their home life would have on them when they grew old enough to realize that their father was a famous footballer. There is no need for me to tell you that all children when they are young think that Father is the most clever man alive, no matter what his job is. The trouble is, of course, that as soon as a child realizes that one of his or her parents is a celebrity it gives them an opportunity to show off and brag in front of their friends and the rest of the children at school. I used to shudder at the thought. I am pleased to say that I found the answer to this problem. I found that children copy their parents in everything they do, so if the children find out that their parents are not affected by one or the other being a celebrity, then they are unaffected. If parents live normal and natural lives, so will their children. It worked in my case and I am sure it will work in every case if the parents set an example when their children are young.

In those days both Jean and Stanley were keen tennis players. I also took to the game and became a very keen player. It was in that summer of 1955 that I made a big discovery. You will remember my saying that for anyone to succeed at any game he or she must have a natural gift for it. Many people through their love for a certain sport can become a very good performer, but the person with a love for a sport and a natural gift for playing it is the one who will one day reach the top flight. I noticed in that summer that Stanley, at the tender age of nine, had that natural ability. I was overjoyed, because the one passion in Stanley's life is tennis. Since that summer I have done everything I can to encourage him, and he is all set now for his future career. I shall indeed be the proudest father in the world if in the distant future he makes the final in the men's singles at Wimbledon, and I am in the stands with Betty and Jean to watch him fight for the title.

The 1955-56 season arrived, and once more I was on the move with the Blackpool team, playing away matches in various parts of the country. Since winning the Cup in 1953 we had not experienced much success on the rocky road to Wembley, but our team was still holding its own in the First Division. It was during this winter that television was making its presence felt all over the country. The advent of commercial television had made us all very television minded, and new television sets were making their way into homes all over the country by their thousands each week. Television had come to stay, and indeed it was going to prove itself to be the number-one entertainer in most homes in the country. The B.B.C. and the commercial companies were vying with each other to sign up big names in the entertainment world to attract the biggest viewing audience. I received several offers from both parties, but I did not take advantage of any of them. During the previous summer it had been arranged, unknown to me, for me to appear on the popular B.B.C. television feature "This Is Your Life". However, some newspaper managed to get someone in Stoke to talk, and they published it in the newspaper. I, of course, read this, so the programme was off because the element of surprise on my part was lost.

It was in the early part of 1956 that I was approached by the B.B.C. television to take part in a new series dealing with ball-control and dribbling. I was told that I would be assisted by Wally Barnes, the ex-Arsenal full-back, who is now a B.B.C. sports commentator. I asked to see the script. I liked the idea and I liked the script so I accepted. It was arranged that I should go to London by sleeper from Preston one week-night, rehearse early the following morning with Wally Barnes, and a tele-recording would be made of the quarter-hour script at the Shepherd's Bush Empire, which is a B.B.C. studio, at 3.30 p.m. Any suspicions I had in my mind that this was a cover for another attempt to make me appear in "This Is Your Life" were dispelled because I knew that this programme was broadcast—or rather televised—direct from London on a Sunday evening and that it was a live show.

I said goodbye to Betty and the children, got in the car and motored to Preston. I left the car in a garage, caught the train to London, and enjoyed a good night's sleep. After breakfast next morning I reported to the rehearsal studio, which I remember was well out in North London. From 10 a.m. to 1 p.m. I rehearsed with Wally Barnes. The producer took great pains to get everything just so. I went through routines time and time again so that he could get the cameras just right for the close-ups and the long shots. I worked really hard for three hours, and just as I thought we had finished the producer decided to go right through the whole thing again for timing. Although somewhat tired, I was pleased to see that great pains had been taken to ensure the success of the first spot in the new series, and I thanked the producer for the trouble he had taken to get it perfect.

Wally Barnes, the scriptwriter, myself, and the rest of the party piled into a couple of cars and made for the centre of London's West End. In a well-known restaurant we all sat down and enjoyed a well-earned lunch. I shall never forget that meal. Everybody was so relaxed, and the conversation was light and covered all kinds of subjects. At last the producer remarked that it was time we got going. I glanced at the wall clock and saw that it was just five minutes past three. Laughing and chatting, we left the restaurant and entered the cars. We were back in Shepherd's Bush at 3.25 p.m., and when I passed through the stage door I noticed the corridors were empty. Then the producer, who had slipped in before us, came tearing down some steps. He said, "Quick, change as soon as you can. I have left it a bit late; we are due on the set in a few minutes!" I was hurried off to a dressing-room, and quickly changed into my track suit. A knock came on the door and I called out, "Come in." A man in charge of make-up entered and he quickly but deftly made me up. Just as he had finished the door opened and a call-boy came in. He said, "You are on in half a minute." I dashed down on to the stage. The curtain was down. I took a football from someone and placed it at my feet, then the announcer walked to the mike and made the opening announcement. Suddenly the lights blazed on and with my head in a whirl I started to chase round the chalked circle on the stage with the ball in front of me. I heard applause, but I hadn't any idea what was happening. I had been rushed about so much since I entered the theatre that my brain just wouldn't function. I broke out in a sweat. I thought, *What do I do after this?* Then the music stopped, the applause stopped, and the lights all over the theatre went on. I stopped dead in my tracks and gazed around me. I saw the audience in a gallery and a lot of television cameras in front of me. I thought, *Somebody has messed this up*, then someone walked up to me. It was Eamonn Andrews. He smiled at me, patted me on the shoulder, and said, "Stanley Matthews, this is your life."

I don't know up to this day why I didn't drop down on the stage in a dead faint. I just couldn't believe my own eyes and ears. By the time I had gathered my wits together I found myself on a couch, with Eamonn Andrews by my side talking to me. As I listened to Eamonn Andrews I began to get a grip of myself, but no sooner had I done so, than someone would appear, as if by magic, from behind the backcloth, and I would start up from my seat in surprise. One of the biggest shocks was when Betty appeared with Jean and Stanley. I could only think of how they had got there. They had, of course, caught the eight-o'clock from Blackpool that morning, and had been met at Euston Station by car and whisked down here and hidden from sight. They hadn't been in the theatre long before I arrived. Then my mother appeared. I had only been in Stoke to visit her a few days before, but she never gave me the slightest inkling that she knew about this programme. So they came on one after another as my life was laid before me, surprise followed surprise, and by the time the programme finished I didn't know whether I was standing on my head or my feet. In all my life I had never experienced so great a shock. The thing that had put me off, of course, was the painstaking rehearsal in the morning for a show the producer knew wasn't going on, and also the fact that this was the first "This Is Your Life" show to be tele-recorded.

The following week I was able to relax in an armchair at home and see it all on my television set. I really appreciated seeing it, because when it was tele-recorded I missed a number of things. And I got another surprise when I saw the televised programme. On the screen I looked rather calm, but I can assure you I didn't feel calm at all. Anyway, it was a wonderful experience. I know a lot of people say that these programmes are faked. I am asking you now not to believe that talk, because from my own experience I am convinced that the B.B.C. would never stoop so low as to fake anything; they are too proud of the tradition they have to live up to to even think of attempting to fake the smallest programme.

I had now reached a stage in my career when the invitations that arrived nearly every day in the post asking me to appear here and stay for a few days there as a guest grew and grew, until I knew I would have to do something about them. Although I appreciated the invitations, I had no intention of allowing myself to be shown off as a prize piece before my host's guests to give him the satisfaction of showing off before his friends. I knew it would be fatal even to accept one of them, because if I did I would have to accept others, and in time my private life would be ruined. So I drew a firm line from the start and refused them all. I know that I made a few enemies by doing this, but I always had at the back of my mind the thought of how many invitations I would receive if I suddenly dropped out of the limelight. You all know the answer to that one! However, there was another kind of invitation to which I gave very careful consideration.

For some time past I had been receiving invitations from various parts of the Commonwealth to take out my own team and play a series of matches during our close season. It was, of course, impossible for me to take my own team on tour, but there was nothing to stop me from appearing as a guest player with any team in the countries that had invited me. I gave this matter a great deal of thought from time to time. I couldn't, however, make up my mind what to do. It was the number of fan letters that I received from these countries that finally made up my mind for me. If these people were kind enough to write to a man they had never seen, but only read about, surely they were entitled, if it was possible, to see him play football in the flesh. I suddenly made up my mind to accept one of the invitations and the summer of 1956 saw me for the first time "guesting" away from home. I started my tour in Kenya and by the end of the short tour I was so overwhelmed by the reception I received by the natives that there and then I made up my mind to do another tour in 1957.

I returned home from my guest tour in the summer of 1956 a much wiser man. It had amazed me to watch the natives play football in their bare feet, and to see how well some of them could kick a ball. The interest they showed in the game and their wide knowledge of the players and teams in this country opened my eyes, and if I had let them they would have done anything for me. Nothing but the best was good enough and it was a wonderful experience. I hadn't been back to this country long before I fixed up to tour Ghana and South Africa as a guest player the following summer. This first tour as a guest player put me right in the news all over the world, and many of the newspapers said that this was the way to bring better relations and understanding between the Commonwealth countries and the mother country. They suggested that I had done more good than any visit from politicians would. I don't know if they were right or wrong, but I certainly enjoyed myself and so did the natives.

Another football season started and I found myself in the 1955-56 season. It was during this winter that I received and accepted an invitation that gave me the greatest of pleasure; it was to appear as guest of the evening at the National Sporting Club, London. They were holding a dinner in my honour at that most famous of all clubs. A presentation was going to be made to me on behalf of all the members, and the B.B.C. Television Service were going to televise this presentation and the speeches that came before it.

I arrived in London in good time on the day of the dinner and spent some time in the quiet of my hotel room rehearsing my speech. I am no after-dinner speaker, but I knew I would have to say something, so I faced up to it and tried to memorize the short speech I had prepared. I must confess that I felt nervous, but as I went over my speech again and again I began to feel better.

When I found myself in the guest-of-honour's seat that evening, and the hands on my wrist-watch told me that the time for the presentation was drawing near, I felt a peculiar restlessness. I glanced around me, and as I looked at the faces of some of the most famous men in England I thought, *What am I doing in the middle of these brilliant minds?* The speeches began and the television cameras were focused on the speakers. As I listened to the compliments they paid me I still couldn't believe that this scene was going into millions of homes in the country. Betty and the children would be watching all this in Blackpool. My mother would be watching it in Stoke.

Tommy Trinder, the chairman of Fulham F.C., was one of the speakers. When he got up to speak he fascinated me with the ease he got laughs and the way the words came out of his mouth with such effortless ease. I remember thinking at the time how happy it would have made me if I could have borrowed his easy-speaking talent for the next half-hour.

I was duly presented with a magnificent cocktail cabinet, and when I opened it to show the members present and the viewers at home, I was amazed to see that it was packed solid with drinks of every description. It also contained cigars and a set of cocktail glasses.

After the presentation I got up to tell them of my deep appreciation of the honour they had paid me, and I thanked them for the wonderful present. Then I should have gone on to my prepared speech, but it had gone right out of my head. I was so moved by the reception that I said—or rather spoke aloud—the thoughts that came into my head. I didn't feel at all nervous. I told them about my father and how he had in the past fought in this very club, and I said that if he were alive tonight he would indeed be England's proudest father as I was tonight England's proudest son. I sat down with the feeling that I hadn't done too badly; but, all the same, I felt a great relief when I felt my chair underneath me once more.

It is an evening that I shall never forget, and the cocktail cabinet which stands in my lounge at home is a present that I shall always cherish.

The following morning the newspapers made a big story out of the event and I was surprised to see that bits of my speech were quoted in most of them. It was during the evening of the same day that the local paper in Blackpool published a photograph of me training on the Bloomfield ground at nine o'clock on the morning after the presentation, and it caused the biggest story of the week. Everybody wanted to know how they could have taken my photograph at that hour of the morning when at 11 p.m. the previous night I was on television as guest of honour at the National Sporting Club in London.

The answer is simple. After the presentation I caught a sleeper back to Blackpool. I walked in my home at 7.30 a.m., had some breakfast, read the papers, then went down to Bloomfield Road, changed into a track suit, and commenced training. A local press photographer who happened to be down at the ground watching the other boys start training saw me and "click" went his camera. I never gave it another thought until I saw it in the evening paper. I can assure you, however, that it was no publicity stunt on my part to get back to Blackpool and have this picture taken.

During the following season (1956-57) two very important things happened in my life. The first was when the New Year's Honours List was published in January 1957 and my name was on it. Her Majesty Queen Elizabeth awarded me the C.B.E.— Commander of the British Empire—for my services to football. When I heard the news I was very much surprised, because the general rule is that when it has been decided to include a sportsman in the Honours List it is held until he has retired from that particular sport. When my award was made public I had no intentions of retiring from football. I was thrilled beyond words to receive such an honour, and it made me very proud to think that during my past playing days I had, in my small way, rendered services to the game of football which had gained this recognition from my country. Messages of congratulations began to pour into my home from all over the world and I was kept very busy for quite a few days reading these and seeing people who called to offer their congratulations in person.

One day in March in 1957 I arrived at Buckingham Palace along with Betty, Jean and Stanley to receive my award from the hands of the Queen. That indeed was a proud day for the Matthews family. When we left Buckingham Palace after the ceremony we slipped quietly away from the crowds outside and celebrated in the West End. Then we returned to Blackpool and resumed our normal life. It was a day we shall all remember, and for a long time afterwards both Jean and Stanley talked about their wonderful trip to Buckingham Palace.

The second important event happened in May 1957. The England team was due to appear in Copenhagen that month to play Denmark in the World Cup series. I had been out of the international picture for a long time, and I thought the main reason for this was the fact that I was now forty-two. As the policy of selectors at that time seemed to be to keep the average age of the England team at a low level, I can be excused for thinking that I had played my last international. The war had been over for nearly twelve years, and during those post-war years quite a number of young professional footballers had made the grade, and it was only natural that they should expect to be given every chance to play for their country.

My selection caused quite a stir among the sports writers, and many stories were written about it. Some favoured it, others didn't; but, as usual, it was something to write about, and a story that could get their readers arguing among themselves.

I went to Copenhagen with the England team, and we won the match. I wasn't included in any of the other matches, and indeed that match against Denmark is the last one to date that I have played for my country. Should it prove to be the very last time I play for England I can't grumble, because from September 1934 to May 1957 is a very long time—twenty-two years and eight months.

Almost as soon as the 1956–57 season ended I was packing my bags for my guest tour in Ghana and South Africa. It was only possible for me to do this tour by flying everywhere, and I felt like an aeroplane by the time the tour came to an end. The promoters enjoyed good "gates" at all the venues at which I appeared and were more than pleased from the money angle. For myself it was my football that counted most. I never spared myself, and in every match I played I tried to give the spectators value for their money and live up to the reputation it was evident I had in those parts.

I enjoyed myself most of all when I got among the real natives who still live with the same outlook on life and in the same housing conditions as their ancestors did hundreds of years ago. In Kenya they played football in their bare feet. It used to make me wince when I saw them take hefty kicks at the ball with their bare feet. But it couldn't have done them any harm, because they would turn to me with a broad grin on their faces to see if they had impressed me. Yes, being amongst and playing football with these simple people taught me a lot. They were football mad. They all knew me and shouted my name when they saw me. Yet they could only have heard of me by word of mouth. To them I was the king of football. Indeed one tribe crowned me, and after throwing a huge skin over my shoulder they placed me on a throne, which was lifted off the ground by four tribesmen who put the poles on their shoulders and proceeded to parade me up and down the camp. A picture of this ceremony was printed in one of the English papers in England at the time. It was almost unbelievable, and even now I still think at times I must have dreamt it.

If you think that I had it all my own way on the football field you can think again. I ran up against some very good players, and once more it didn't take me long to find out that these were natural footballers. If they had had the luck to have been born in England some of them would today be very big names indeed in the football world.

I returned to England a very contented man. I had talked with, played football with and dined with a huge number of people who a few years ago I never thought existed. My whole outlook on life was broadened by this wonderful tour, and I am pleased to say that I left behind me a lot of goodwill and many friends who still write to me.

I had not been at home very long before several people got in touch with me with regard to a similar tour for the following summer. At the time I turned down all the offers because I wanted to relax and enjoy life at home with my family until the 1957-58 season started. That was the only snag of my late tour: I missed my family.

The 1957-58 season was about three months old when I received an offer to do a world tour in the next close season. The offer came from an Australian promoter. The proposed tour would take me to Australia, the United States and finish in Singapore. It sounded very attractive to me, and I thought that if I could take the family with me I would go. I couldn't, however, see any promoter saddling himself with all that extra expense. When I wrote back I said I was interested, but only if my family could

come with me; and I remember thinking as the letter was posted—
That's that!

However, some time later I received a letter from the promoter
saying he was coming to England to meet me and requested me
to visit him at his hotel in London so that we could discuss the
matter in every detail. Within a week or so we met in London
and discussed the matter very thoroughly. The promoter had
with him, of course, the figures of the monies he might take if
the tour was a success and he also had the limit figure he could
go to with regard to salaries and all overhead expenses. He
agreed that my family could go with me, and he requested me to
approach the F.A. to see if I could get their permission to ask
one of the First Division League clubs to accompany me on the
tour so that I could play on the right wing for them in all the
matches. It was left at that for the time being.

When I returned to Blackpool I gave the whole matter some
very careful thought. I decided that I would like my own team
Blackpool to go with me, but if for any reason at all they found
it impossible to do so I would then look round for another club.
However, the F.A. fell in with the idea, and it was arranged that
I should go on the world tour with Blackpool, who also accepted
the offer. Some little time was spent getting in touch with the
promoter in Australia to finalise the whole matter, but well
before the season finished the tour was all fixed up.

There was great excitement in the Matthews household as the
time drew near for us to leave England. There were visits to the
doctor to be injected against tropical diseases, there were suitable
clothes to be bought for the tour, and a score of other things. I
was delighted to be mixed up in all this hurrying here and dashing
off there and I really felt one of a family preparing for a big
adventure.

From an early hour it had been pandemonium in our house.
Betty and Jean were dashing about as only women can do on
occasions like this, and I was busy getting some tennis equipment
sorted out that Stanley was taking with him. Finally, after the
last few checks had been made we left the house and joined the
rest of the party at Squires Gate Airport, Blackpool. At the airport we found that a great number of people had turned up to

see us off, so it was a very happy party that boarded the aircraft which was to take us on the first part of our long journey.

It turned out to be a wonderful tour; we received ovations that had to be seen to be believed. All our spare time—or at least most of it—was taken up sightseeing and attending all manner of functions given in our honour. Betty, Jean and Stanley had the time of their lives, and it pleased me to see how much they were enjoying themselves. The time passed very quickly and in next to no time we had to return to our native land. When we arrived back in Blackpool we all brought with us memories of a wonderful world tour that I am sure we shall all treasure for ever. From the footballing angle, we brought back with us a first-class record. We never suffered defeat in all the matches we played, which in itself is remarkable, because no matter how good a team is you expect to have off days, or days when the ball doesn't run too kindly.

When we reached home it took us quite a time to get settled down again. We had many visitors calling to hear all about our various experiences, and in the evenings we would gather in the lounge and talk about them. The tour had certainly put some new colour into all our lives and we felt better for it.

It didn't seem long before the 1958–59 season came along, and we nearly reached Wembley during that season. Considering that we finished in a nice healthy position in the final League table at the end of the season, there is no reason why Blackpool should not have another good season in the coming one. I would like to mention that in the season 1958–59 I did not have the best of luck. Quite early in the season, in a home match against Portsmouth, I received a kick near my right knee which kept me out of the team for a few weeks. This injury troubled me for the rest of the season, but I was able to give it the rest it needed and put it right for the winter.

So there you are—it is getting near the time for me to close my book. I have taken you, the reader, through many years of my professional football career and also the days of my boyhood. Before I finish there are one or two things I would like to express my views about. My first is on wealth.

Wealth to most people is the criterion by which they judge

success. By that I mean not only their own success in life but that of other people as well. To them money is a god to be worshipped. Without this wealth their lives would be empty and they condemn themselves as failures—just as they condemn other people who haven't enough money to make life easy. I am not a wealthy man, nor am I a poor one. As a professional footballer I have never had the chance to earn the big money that can be earned in other sports. I have never felt the wish to be wealthy from the money angle, to make it an obsession to become rich. I am, however, one of the richest men in the world, and by that I mean in the riches of happiness and contentment, which, in my opinion, are the only things that makes life worth living. I have had a full life and experienced my share of setbacks and successes. My wants are very simple—just plain home-cooked meals and a comfortable home to live in with my wife and family. I have the wealth of memories that money can't buy, and real friends in all parts of the world. I am convinced that if more people in this world spent more of their time searching for happiness and contentment it would kill all the jealousy and avarice that is prevalent in the world today.

I would also like to say a word or two to the youth of this country. Despite all the talk that goes on in the papers about conditions never being better for the working classes, there are still many people who, through no fault of their own, live in and under conditions in most of our big cities and towns that would make those people who write about these splendid conditions blush with shame. The trouble is, of course, that they have never taken the trouble to go and look at these places. It is in these homes that a wealth of talent is wasted. Some of the boys brought up in this environment have great natural ability in all classes of jobs and sport. The trouble is that very few of them ever get the slightest chance to develop these talents. In order to supplement the small income that comes into the house every week the parents both work and have to push the children into the first job that comes along. With not having any interest in their job, and with no one ɔ find out what they really like and then help them to get a job hat field, the young people get frustrated and before long they apt to be led into all kinds of trouble in order to let off steam.

I think that the Government should tackle this problem by setting up centres in every large town and in all our cities. These boys should be allowed to come and pour their hearts out to the people staffing these centres, and then be groomed to take a place for further instruction in a class dealing with the particular job that they have a natural ability for. I am sure that in the years to come it would pay big dividends. If I hadn't had the luck to have been blessed by parents who took great pains to ensure that my natural talent got a chance I might have finished up in a dead-end job, and in doing so have missed the chance of doing the job I still love so much. When the time comes when I have played my last match, and I walk off the field for the last time, something will die inside me. But I somehow know that something else will come along to replace it.